Modern Critical Views

Chinua Achebe
Henry Adams
Aeschylus
S. Y. Agnon
Edward Albee
Raphael Alberti
Louisa May Alcott
A. R. Ammons
Sherwood Anderson
Aristophanes
Matthew Arnold
Antonin Artaud
John Ashbery
Margaret Atwood
W. H. Auden
Jane Austen
Isaac Babel
Sir Francis Bacon
James Baldwin
Honoré de Balzac
John Barth
Donald Barthelme
Charles Baudelaire
Simone de Beauvoir
Samuel Beckett
Saul Bellow
Thomas Berger
John Berryman
The Bible
Elizabeth Bishop
William Blake
Giovanni Boccaccio
Heinrich Böll
Jorge Luis Borges
Elizabeth Bowen
Bertolt Brecht
The Brontës
Charles Brockden Brown
Sterling Brown
Robert Browning
Martin Buber
John Bunyan
Anthony Burgess
Kenneth Burke
Robert Burns
William Burroughs
George Gordon, Lord
    Byron
Pedro Calderón de la Barca
Italo Calvino
Albert Camus
Canadian Poetry: Modern
    and Contemporary
Canadian Poetry through
    E. J. Pratt
Thomas Carlyle
Alejo Carpentier
Lewis Carroll
Willa Cather
Louis-Ferdinand Céline
Miguel de Cervantes

Geoffrey Chaucer
John Cheever
Anton Chekhov
Kate Chopin
Chrétien de Troyes
Agatha Christie
Samuel Taylor Coleridge
Colette
William Congreve & the
    Restoration Dramatists
Joseph Conrad
Contemporary Poets
James Fenimore Cooper
Pierre Corneille
Julio Cortázar
Hart Crane
Stephen Crane
e. e. cummings
Dante
Robertson Davies
Daniel Defoe
Philip K. Dick
Charles Dickens
James Dickey
Emily Dickinson
Denis Diderot
Isak Dinesen
E. L. Doctorow
John Donne & the
    Seventeenth-Century
    Metaphysical Poets
John Dos Passos
Fyodor Dostoevsky
Frederick Douglass
Theodore Dreiser
John Dryden
W. E. B. Du Bois
Lawrence Durrell
George Eliot
T. S. Eliot
Elizabethan Dramatists
Ralph Ellison
Ralph Waldo Emerson
Euripides
William Faulkner
Henry Fielding
F. Scott Fitzgerald
Gustave Flaubert
E. M. Forster
John Fowles
Sigmund Freud
Robert Frost
Northrop Frye
Carlos Fuentes
William Gaddis
Federico García Lorca
Gabriel García Márquez
André Gide
W. S. Gilbert
Allen Ginsberg
J. W. von Goethe

Nikolai Gogol
William Golding
Oliver Goldsmith
Mary Gordon
Günther Grass
Robert Graves
Graham Greene
Thomas Hardy
Nathaniel Hawthorne
William Hazlitt
H. D.
Seamus Heaney
Lillian Hellman
Ernest Hemingway
Hermann Hesse
Geoffrey Hill
Friedrich Hölderlin
Homer
A. D. Hope
Gerard Manley Hopkins
Horace
A. E. Housman
William Dean Howells
Langston Hughes
Ted Hughes
Victor Hugo
Zora Neale Hurston
Aldous Huxley
Henrik Ibsen
Eugene Ionesco
Washington Irving
Henry James
Dr. Samuel Johnson and
    James Boswell
Ben Jonson
James Joyce
Carl Gustav Jung
Franz Kafka
Yasonari Kawabata
John Keats
Søren Kierkegaard
Rudyard Kipling
Melanie Klein
Heinrich von Kleist
Philip Larkin
D. H. Lawrence
John le Carré
Ursula K. Le Guin
Giacomo Leopardi
Doris Lessing
Sinclair Lewis
Jack London
Robert Lowell
Malcolm Lowry
Carson McCullers
Norman Mailer
Bernard Malamud
Stéphane Mallarmé
Sir Thomas Malory
André Malraux
Thomas Mann

Modern Critical Views

Katherine Mansfield
Christopher Marlowe
Andrew Marvell
Herman Melville
George Meredith
James Merrill
John Stuart Mill
Arthur Miller
Henry Miller
John Milton
Yukio Mishima
Molière
Michel de Montaigne
Eugenio Montale
Marianne Moore
Alberto Moravia
Toni Morrison
Alice Munro
Iris Murdoch
Robert Musil
Vladimir Nabokov
V. S. Naipaul
R. K. Narayan
Pablo Neruda
John Henry Newman
Friedrich Nietzsche
Frank Norris
Joyce Carol Oates
Sean O'Casey
Flannery O'Connor
Christopher Okigbo
Charles Olson
Eugene O'Neill
José Ortega y Gasset
Joe Orton
George Orwell
Ovid
Wilfred Owen
Amos Oz
Cynthia Ozick
Grace Paley
Blaise Pascal
Walter Pater
Octavio Paz
Walker Percy
Petrarch
Pindar
Harold Pinter
Luigi Pirandello
Sylvia Plath
Plato

Plautus
Edgar Allan Poe
Poets of Sensibility & the
    Sublime
Poets of the Nineties
Alexander Pope
Katherine Anne Porter
Ezra Pound
Anthony Powell
Pre-Raphaelite Poets
Marcel Proust
Manuel Puig
Alexander Pushkin
Thomas Pynchon
Francisco de Quevedo
François Rabelais
Jean Racine
Ishmael Reed
Adrienne Rich
Samuel Richardson
Mordecai Richler
Rainer Maria Rilke
Arthur Rimbaud
Edwin Arlington Robinson
Theodore Roethke
Philip Roth
Jean-Jacques Rousseau
John Ruskin
J. D. Salinger
Jean-Paul Sartre
Gershom Scholem
Sir Walter Scott
William Shakespeare
    Histories & Poems
    Comedies & Romances
    Tragedies
George Bernard Shaw
Mary Wollstonecraft
    Shelley
Percy Bysshe Shelley
Sam Shepard
Richard Brinsley Sheridan
Sir Philip Sidney
Isaac Bashevis Singer
Tobias Smollett
Alexander Solzhenitsyn
Sophocles
Wole Soyinka
Edmund Spenser
Gertrude Stein
John Steinbeck

Stendhal
Laurence Sterne
Wallace Stevens
Robert Louis Stevenson
Tom Stoppard
August Strindberg
Jonathan Swift
John Millington Synge
Alfred, Lord Tennyson
William Makepeace Thackeray
Dylan Thomas
Henry David Thoreau
James Thurber and S. J.
    Perelman
J. R. R. Tolkien
Leo Tolstoy
Jean Toomer
Lionel Trilling
Anthony Trollope
Ivan Turgenev
Mark Twain
Miguel de Unamuno
John Updike
Paul Valéry
Cesar Vallejo
Lope de Vega
Gore Vidal
Virgil
Voltaire
Kurt Vonnegut
Derek Walcott
Alice Walker
Robert Penn Warren
Evelyn Waugh
H. G. Wells
Eudora Welty
Nathanael West
Edith Wharton
Patrick White
Walt Whitman
Oscar Wilde
Tennessee Williams
William Carlos Williams
Thomas Wolfe
Virginia Woolf
William Wordsworth
Jay Wright
Richard Wright
William Butler Yeats
A. B. Yehoshua
Emile Zola

Modern Critical Views

TONI MORRISON

Edited and with an introduction by
Harold Bloom

CHELSEA HOUSE PUBLISHERS
New York ◇ Philadelphia

Cover illustration: The novelist Toni Morrison is shown against the background of the poignant scene in *Sula* where Sula observes the terror of Hannah suffering the outburst of fire, which will lead to her tragic death.—H. B.

Chelsea House Publishers

Editor-in-Chief Nancy Toff
Executive Editor Remmel T. Nunn
Managing Editor Karyn Gullen Browne
Picture Editor Adrian G. Allen
Art Director Maria Epes
Manufacturing Manager Gerald Levine

Modern Critical Views

Managing Editor S. T. Joshi
Copy Chief Richard Fumosa

Staff for TONI MORRISON

Researcher Mary Lawlor
Editorial Assistant Katherine Theodore
Assistant Art Director Loraine Machlin
Production Manager Joseph Romano
Production Assistant Leslie D'Acri
Jacket Illustration Vilma Ortiz

Printed and bound in the United States of America.

10 9 8 7 6 5 4 3 2

Library of Congress Cataloging-in-Publication Data

Toni Morrison / edited and with an introduction by Harold Bloom.
       p.   cm.—(Modern critical views)
    ISBN 1-55546-439-4
    1. Morrison, Toni—Criticism and interpretation.
2. Afro-Americans in literature. I. Bloom, Harold.
II. Series.
PS3563.O8749Z89   1990
813'.54-dc20   89-39861
                                      CIP

Contents

Editor's Note   vii

Introduction   1
   Harold Bloom

Self, Society, and Myth in Toni Morrison's Fiction   7
   Cynthia A. Davis

A Hateful Passion, a Lost Love   27
   Hortense J. Spillers

Beyond Realism: The Fictions of Toni Morrison   55
   Keith E. Byerman

Lady No Longer Sings the Blues: Rape, Madness, and
Silence in *The Bluest Eye*   85
   Madonne M. Miner

The Crime of Innocence in Toni Morrison's
Tar Baby   101
   Terry Otten

Like an Eagle in the Air: Toni Morrison   115
   Melvin Dixon

Haunted by Their Nightmares   143
   Margaret Atwood

"The Self and the Other": Reading Toni Morrison's *Sula*
and the Black Female Text   149
    Deborah E. McDowell

Toni Morrison's *Beloved*   165
    Roger Sale

The Novelist as Conservator: Stories and Comprehension
in Toni Morrison's *Song of Solomon*   171
    Theodore O. Mason, Jr.

A Different Remembering: Memory, History and
Meaning in Toni Morrison's *Beloved*   189
    Marilyn Sanders Mobley

Unspeakable Things Unspoken: The Afro-American
Presence in American Literature   201
    Toni Morrison

Chronology   231

Contributors   233

Bibliography   235

Acknowledgments   239

Index   241

Editor's Note

This book brings together a representative selection of the best literary criticism so far devoted to the novels of Toni Morrison. The critical essays are reprinted here in the chronological order of their original publication. I am indebted to Mary Lawlor for her devotion and skill as a researcher for this volume.

My introduction attempts a tentative estimation of Morrison's achievement, in the daunting context of her prime precursor figures, Faulkner and Woolf. The chronological sequence of criticism begins with Cynthia A. Davis's investigation of some of the mythic patterns of African-American communitarian freedom that Morrison sets against white America's psychic violence. Hortense J. Spillers, comparing Morrison's *Sula* to Zora Neale Hurston's *Their Eyes Were Watching God* and Margaret Walker's *Jubilee*, gives us a historical sense of changes in black female characterization.

In Keith E. Byerman's judgment, Morrison's fiction quests for a black selfhood that might negate the destructive control of white symbolic systems, and finds instances of an uncontaminated selfhood in irrational and fantastic elements of African-American experience. Madonne M. Miner, writing on *The Bluest Eye*, finds in Pecula's fate not the sign of tragedy, but of hope, the hope necessarily involved in African-American female testimony.

Morrison's *Tar Baby* is seen by Terry Otten as an instance of the novelist's incessant exposure of the victim's crime of innocence, when the victim is a black female in a white male cosmos of concepts and values. In Melvin Dixon's essay, symbolic geography becomes another of Morrison's fictive devices for subverting the value systems that alienate African-Americans from their own culture. The Canadian poet-novelist Margaret Atwood salutes Morrison's *Beloved* as a major vision of slavery, and as a realistic novel audacious enough to evoke supernatural dimensions.

   Sula is the focus of Deborah E. McDowell's argument that Morrison's achievement also includes an undermining of any heroic myth of back male identity, while *Beloved* receives an unreserved appreciation from Roger Sale. Theodore O. Mason, Jr., analyzing *Song of Solomon,* finds in it a more traditional Toni Morrison than critics generally acclaim. His Morrison is a tale teller and reteller who uses her stories to bind communities together.

   In an essay published for the first time in this book, Marilyn Sanders Mobley considers *Beloved* as Morrison's ironic revision of the genre of the slave narrative, a revision that attempts to compel African-American readers to confront a repressed element in their own past. Toni Morrison herself concludes this volume with her powerful polemic on how white American authors and critics have repressed the African-American presence in American literature.

Introduction

Toni Morrison, in a speculative essay on literary canon-making (included in this volume), proposes the difficult critical quest of uncovering the hidden obsession with African-Americans that has haunted the American novel throughout its history. Her principal example is to sketch a reading of *Moby-Dick* in which Ahab's manic obsessiveness with the whiteness of the whale becomes a synecdoche for white America's compulsive relation to the African-American aspects of its culture, past and present. Morrison's reading is in the mode of D. H. Lawrence's *Studies in Classic American Literature,* where what Lawrence saw as the doom of the white race is prefigured in Ahab's compulsiveness. I am of many minds about Morrison's critical project, if only because it would give yet another dimension to the unhappy procedure of uncovering just how much of white America cannot be exorcised from African-American fiction. Morrison's five novels, culminating so far in *Beloved,* are possible candidates for entering an American canon founded upon what I insist would be aesthetic criteria alone, if we still retain any such criteria after our current age of politicized response to narrative, dramas, and poems has passed.

Morrison, like any potentially strong novelist, battles against being subsumed by the traditions of narrative fiction. As a leader of African-American literary culture, Morrison is particularly intense in resisting critical characterizations that she believes misrepresent her own loyalties, her social and political fealties to the complex cause of her people. If one is a student of literary influence as such, and I am, then one's own allegiances as a critic are aesthetic, as I insist mine are. One is aware that the aesthetic has been a mask for those who would deny vital differences in gender, race, social class, and yet it need not be an instrument for the prolongation of exploiting

1

forces. The aesthetic stance, as taught by Ruskin, Pater, and Wilde, enhances a reader's apprehension of perception and sensation. Such a mode of knowing literature seems to me inescapable, despite times like our own, in which societal and historical resentments, all with their own validity, tend to crowd out aesthetic considerations. Yet, as an artist, Morrison has few affinities with Zora Neale Hurston or Ralph Ellison, or with other masters of African-American fiction. Her curious resemblance to certain aspects of D. H. Lawrence does not ensue from the actual influence of Lawrence, but comes out of the two dominant precursors who have shaped her narrative sensibility, William Faulkner and Virginia Woolf. Faulkner and Woolf have little in common, but if you mixed them potently enough you might get Lawrence, or Toni Morrison.

Lest this seem a remote matter to a passionate reader of Morrison, I would observe mildly that one function of literary study is to help us make choices, because choice is inescapable, this late in Western cultural history. I do not believe that Morrison writes fiction of a kind I am not yet competent to read and judge, because I attend to her work with pleasure and enlightenment, amply rewarded by the perception and sensation that her art generates. Reading Alice Walker or Ishmael Reed, I cannot trust my own aesthetic reactions, and decide that their mode of writing must be left to critics more responsive than myself. But then I reflect that every reader must choose for herself or himself. Does one read and reread the novels of Alice Walker, or of Toni Morrison? I reread Morrison because her imagination, whatever her social purposes, transcends ideology and polemics, and enters again into the literary space occupied only by fantasy and romance of authentic aesthetic dignity. Extraliterary purposes, however valid or momentous they may be for a time, ebb away, and we are left with story, characters, and style, that is to say, with literature or the lack of literature. Morrison's five novels to date leave us with literature, and not with a manifesto for social change, however necessary and admirable such change would be in our America of Chairman Atwater, Senator Helms, President Bush, and the other luminaries of what we ought to go on calling the Willie Horton election of 1988.

Morrison herself has made very clear that she prefers to be contextualized in African-American literature, or in an American literature that ceases to repress the African-American presence. I am neither a feminist nor an African-American critic, nor am I a Marxist, a deconstructor, a Lacanian, a New Historicist, a semiotician. And yet I scarcely would agree with several of the contributors to this volume, who would maintain that my theories of literary influence simply reduce to yet another logocentric, capitalistic,

white male symbolic system that has no validity or relevance for reading
and understanding the work of an African-American feminist and Marxist
novelist. Literary texts emerge from other literary texts, and they do not
choose their forerunners. They are as overdetermined aesthetically as their
human makers are overdetermined erotically. It is a great sorrow that we
cannot choose whom we are free to love, and it is almost an equal sorrow
that the gifted cannot choose their gift, or even the bestowers of their gift.
We are free to choose our ideologies, but eros and art, however intertwined
they are with cultural politics, cannot be reduced to cultural politics alone.
As an African-American woman, Toni Morrison has developed a powerful
stance that intervenes forcefully in the cultural politics of her time and place,
the United States as it stumbles towards the year 2000 of the Common Era.
As a novelist, a rhetorical tale-teller, Toni Morrison was found by Virginia
Woolf and William Faulkner, two quite incompatible artists, except perhaps
for the effect that James Joyce had upon both of them. Morrison's marvelous
sense of female character and its fate in male contexts is an extraordinary
modification of Woolfian sensibility, and yet the aura of Woolf always lingers
on in Morrison's prose, even as Joyce's presence can be felt so strongly in
Woolf's *Mrs. Dalloway* and in Faulkner's *The Sound and the Fury.* Faulkner's
mode of narration is exquisitely modulated by Morrison, but the accent of
Faulkner always can be heard in Morrison's narrators, even as Joseph Conrad's
authorial stance never quite left Faulkner. Consider the plangent closing
passages of *The Bluest Eye, Sula,* and *Song of Solomon:*

> And now when I see her searching the garbage—for what?
> The thing we assassinated? I talk about how I did *not* plant the
> seeds too deeply, how it was the fault of the earth, the land, of
> our town. I even think now that the land of the entire country
> was hostile to marigolds that year. This soil is bad for certain
> kinds of flowers. Certain seeds it will not nurture, certain fruit
> it will not bear, and when the land kills of its own volition, we
> acquiesce and say the victim had no right to live. We are wrong,
> of course, but it doesn't matter. It's too late. At least on the
> edge of my town, it's much, much, much too late.
>
> —*The Bluest Eye*

> Shadrack and Nel moved in opposite directions, each think-
> ing separate thoughts about the past. The distance between them
> increased as they both remembered gone things.
> Suddenly Nel stopped. Her eye twitched and burned a little.
> "Sula?" she whispered, gazing at the tops of trees. "Sula?"

Leaves stirred; mud shifted; there was the smell of overripe green things. A soft ball of fur broke and scattered like dandelion spores in the breeze.

"All that time, all that time, I thought I was missing Jude." And the loss pressed down on her chest and came up into her throat. "We was girls together," she said as though explaining something. "O Lord, Sula," she cried, "girl, girl, girlgirlgirl."

It was a fine cry—loud and long—but it had no bottom and it had no top, just circles and circles of sorrow.

—*Sula*

Milkman stopped waving and narrowed his eyes. He could just make out Guitar's head and shoulders in the dark. "You want my life?" Milkman was not shouting now. "You need it? Here." Without wiping away the tears, taking a deep breath, or even bending his knees—he leaped. As fleet and bright as a lodestar he wheeled toward Guitar and it did not matter which one of them would give up his ghost in the killing arms of his brother. For now he knew what Shalimar knew: If you surrendered to the air, you could *ride* it.

—*Song of Solomon*

Even decontextualized, without the narratives that they culminate, these conclusions retain considerable lyrical and dramatic vitality. If I stumbled upon them anywhere, I would know them for Morrison's fictional prose, and I do not hear any voices in them except for Morrison's passionate and caring cry of the human, her own particular eloquence. And yet part of appreciating Morrison's command here of sensation and perception involves attending to the genealogy of her art. It is not a question of allusion or of echoing but of style, stance, tone, prose rhythm, and mimetic mode, and these do stem from an amalgam of Faulkner and Woolf, the father and mother of Morrison's art, as it were. Woolf and Faulkner are poets of loss, who search past and present for the negative epiphanies of vanished moments, possibilities, radiances, hopes. The narrative voice in Morrison turns always upon the negative magic of the romancer. Her perfect sentence is: "If you surrendered to the air, you could *ride* it." That is her epitome, but it would serve also for the most Morrisonian beings in Faulkner: Darl Bundren in *As I Lay Dying* and Lena Grove in *Light in August*. And it would illuminate also the perfect heroine of Woolf, Clarissa Dalloway, whose sensibility hovers at making that surrender in the air that Septimus Smith made, only to discover that he could not ride it. The pure madness of integrities of being that cannot sustain or bear dreadful social structures is as much Morrison's center (and not just in *The Bluest Eye*) as it is Woolf's and, with a difference, Faulkner's. The most authentic power in Morrison's work is the romance writer's sense that "it's much, much, much too late," that one's cry of grief and loss "had no bottom and it had no top, just circles and circles of sorrow." In some sense, all of Morrison's protagonists leap wheeling towards the death struggle, with the fine abandon of Faulkner's doom-eager men and women. Toni Morrison, in her time and place, answering to the travail of her people, speaks to the needs of an era, but her art comes out of a literary tradition not altogether at one with her cultural politics.

CYNTHIA A. DAVIS

Self, Society, and Myth
in Toni Morrison's Fiction

Toni Morrison's novels have attracted both popular and critical attention for their inventive blend of realism and fantasy, unsparing social analysis, and passionate philosophical concerns. The combination of social observation with broadening and allusive commentary gives her fictions the symbolic quality of myth, and in fact the search for a myth adequate to experience is one of Morrison's central themes. Because her world and characters are inescapably involved with problems of perception, definition, and meaning, they direct attention to Morrison's own ordering view and its implications.

All of Morrison's characters exist in a world defined by its blackness and by the surrounding white society that both violates and denies it. The destructive effect of the white society can take the form of outright physical violence, but oppression in Morrison's world is more often psychic violence. She rarely depicts white characters, for the brutality here is less a single act than the systematic denial of the reality of black lives. The theme of "invisibility" is, of course, a common one in black American literature, but Morrison avoids the picture of the black person "invisible" in white life (Ellison's Invisible Man trying to confront passersby). Instead, she immerses the reader in the black community; the white society's ignorance of that concrete, vivid, and diverse world is thus even more striking.

The constant censorship of and intrusion on black life from the surrounding society is emphasized not by specific events so much as by a consistent pattern of misnaming. Power for Morrison is largely the power to name, to define reality and perception. The world of all three novels[1] is

From *Contemporary Literature* 23, No. 3 (Summer 1982): 323–42.

distinguished by the discrepancy between name and reality. *The Bluest Eye* (1970), for example, opens with a primer description of a "typical" American family: "Here is the house. It is green and white. It has a red door. It is very pretty. Here is the family. Mother, Father, Dick, and Jane live in the green-and-white house." And so on (*Eye*, p. 1). Portions of that description reappear as chapter headings for the story of black lives, all removed in various degrees from the textbook "reality."[2] *Sula* (1973) begins with a description of the black neighborhood "called the Bottom in spite of the fact that it was up in the hills" (*Sula*, p. 4): another misnamed, even reversed situation, in this case the result of a white man's greedy joke. The same pattern is extended in *Song of Solomon* (1977): for example, the first pages describe "Not Doctor Street, a name the post office did not recognize," and "No Mercy Hospital" (*Song*, pp. 3, 4). Both names are unofficial; the black experience they represent is denied by the city fathers who named Mains Avenue and Mercy Hospital. And *Song of Solomon* is full of characters with ludicrous, multiple, or lost names, like the first Macon Dead, who received "this heavy name scrawled in perfect thoughtlessness by a drunken Yankee in the Union Army" (*Song*, p. 18). In all these cases, the misnaming does not eliminate the reality of the black world; invisibility is not non-existence. But it does reflect a distortion. Blacks are visible to white culture only insofar as they fit its frame of reference and serve its needs. Thus they are consistently reduced and reified, losing their independent reality. Mrs. Breedlove in *The Bluest Eye* has a nickname, "Polly," that only whites use; it reduces her dignity and identifies her as "the ideal servant" (*Eye*, p. 99). When the elegant Helene Wright becomes just "gal" to a white conductor, she and her daughter Nel feel that she is "flawed," "really custard" under the elegant exterior (*Sula*, pp. 17–19).

To some extent this problem is an inescapable ontological experience. As Sartre has pointed out, human relations revolve around the experience of "the Look," for being "seen" by another both confirms one's reality and threatens one's sense of freedom: "I grasp the Other's look at the very center of my act as the solidification and alienation of my own possibilities." Alone, I can see myself as pure consciousness in a world of possible projects; the Other's look makes me see myself as an object in another perception. "The Other as a look is only that—my transcendence transcended."[3] If I can make the other into an object in my world, I can "transcend" him: "Thus my project of recovering myself is fundamentally a project of absorbing the Other" (*BN*, p. 340). The result is a cycle of conflicting and shifting subject-object relationships in which both sides try simultaneously to remain in control of the relationship and to use the Other's look to confirm identity.

The difficulty of such an attempt tempts human beings to Bad Faith, "a vacillation between transcendence and facticity which refuses to recognize either one for what it really is or to synthesize them" (*BN,* p. 547). What that means can be seen in the many Morrison characters who try to define themselves through the eyes of others. Jude Greene, for example, marries Nel so that he can "see himself taking shape in her eyes" (*Sula,* p. 71); and Milkman Dead finds that only when Guitar Bains shares his dream can he feel "a self inside himself emerge, a clean-lined definite self" (*Song,* p. 184). Such characters are in Bad Faith not because they recognize other viewers, but because they use others to escape their own responsibility to define themselves. The woman who, like Mrs. Breedlove, feels most powerful when most submerged in flesh, most like a *thing,* similarly falls into Bad Faith: ". . . I know that my flesh is all that be on his mind. That he couldn't stop if he had to. . . . I feel a power. I be strong, I be pretty, I be young" (*Eye,* p. 101). Milkman complains that he feels "used. Somehow everybody was using him for something or as something" (*Song,* p. 165). Many of Morrison's characters learn to like being used and using in return. They collaborate in their own reification so that they can feel that it is "chosen."

Such characters can fall into Bad Faith not only by dependence on one other, but also by internalizing the "Look" of the majority culture. The novels are full of characters who try to live up to an external image—Dick and Jane's family, or cosmopolitan society, or big business. This conformity is not just a disguise, but an attempt to gain power and control. There is always the hope that if one fits the prescribed pattern, one will be seen as human. Helene Wright puts on her velvet dress in hopes that it, with "her manner and her bearing," will be "protection" against the reductive gaze of the white other (*Sula,* p. 17). Light-skinned women, already closer to white models, aspire to a genteel ideal: green-eyed Frieda "enchanted the entire school," and "sugar-brown Mobile girls" like Geraldine "go to land-grant colleges, normal schools, and learn how to do the white man's work with refinement." The problem with such internalization is not that it is ambitious, but that it is life-denying, eliminating "the dreadful funkiness of passion, the funkiness of nature, the funkiness of the wide range of human emotions" (*Eye,* pp. 48, 64). One who really accepts the external definition of the self gives up spontaneous feeling and choice.

Morrison makes it clear that this ontological problem is vastly complicated in the context of a society based on coercive power relations. The individual contest for "transcendence" allows, in theory, for mutually satisfying resolutions, as Beauvoir points out: "It is possible to rise above this conflict if each individual freely recognizes the other, each regarding himself

and the other simultaneously as object and as subject in a reciprocal manner."[4] But that relation is unbalanced by social divisions of power. Helene
cannot defy the white conductor; on at least the level of overt speech and
action, his Look is unchallengeable. Thus she tries to accept the Look, and
his power to give it, by becoming a more perfect object for his gaze: she
gives him a "dazzling smile" (Sula, p. 19). The temptation to Bad Faith is
immensely greater in a society that forcibly assigns subject-power, the power
to look and define, to one person over another. In such a context, even
willed or spontaneous choices can be distorted to serve the powerful. Mrs.
Breedlove's channeling of her own need for order into the duties of "the
ideal servant" is a milder version of what happens to Cholly Breedlove, forced
to turn his spontaneous copulation into performance before the flashlights
of white hunters (Eye, pp. 114–17). Most perversely, even the attempt at
rebellion can be shaped by the surrounding culture. The change from "Doctor
Street" (as blacks originally called Mains Avenue) to "Not Doctor Street,"
for example, shows a lingering reluctance to accept white naming, but also
a recognition of the loss of the original power to name. More profoundly,
"the Days," who take revenge for white violence, are also reactive, still
achieving secondhand identity and initiative:

> . . . when a Negro child, Negro woman, or Negro man is killed
> by whites and nothing is done about it by *their* law and *their*
> courts, this society selects a similar victim at random, and they
> execute him or her in a similar manner if they can. If the Negro
> was hanged, they hang; if a Negro was burnt, they burn; raped
> and murdered, they rape and murder. (Song, p. 155)

The adoption of a rigid role, the withdrawal from life, is for Morrison as
for Sartre a failure; but her condemnation is tempered by the recognition of
the unnatural position of blacks in a racist society.

Power relations can have a similar effect on the community as a whole.
The Look of white society, supported by all kinds of material domination,
not only freezes the black individual but also classifies all blacks as alike,
freezing the group. They become a "we-object" before the gaze of a "Third":

> It is only when I feel myself become an object along with someone
> else under the look of such a "third" that I experience my being
> as a "we-object"; for then, in our mutual interdependency, in
> our shame and rage, our beings are somehow mingled in the eyes
> of the onlooker, for whom we are both somehow "the same": two
> representatives of a class or a species, two anonymous types of
> something . . .[5]

Again, the basic problem may be ontological, but the institutionalization of the relation, the coercive power of the Third, exacerbates it. This is the reason for all the misnaming: a whole group of people have been denied the right to create a recognizable public self—as individuals or as community. Given that combination of personal and communal vulnerability, it is hardly surprising that many characters choose the way of the least agony and the fewest surprises: *they "choose" their status as objects, even fiercely defend it.* Helene and Geraldine increasingly become perfect images rather than free selves. In this retreat from life they are abetted by a community so dominated by white society as the Third that order and stability are its primary values. In *The Bluest Eye,* narrator Claudia comments that the worst fear is of being "outdoors": "Being a minority in both caste and class, we moved about anyway on the hem of life, struggling to consolidate our weaknesses and hang on, or to creep singly up into the major folds of the garment" (*Eye,* p. 11). Any "excess" that might challenge the powerful Look and increase their isolation is terrifying. And so the images that caused the alienation, excluded them from the real world, are paradoxically received and imitated as confirmations of life.

Claudia is very conscious of the perversity of this position and of its roots in racist society. As a child, she says, she hated Shirley Temple, "Not because she was cute, but because she danced with Bojangles, who was *my* friend, *my* uncle, *my* daddy, and who ought to have been soft-shoeing it and chuckling with me" (*Eye,* p. 13). She recognized the diversion of feeling from her self and world into white values, emphasized by repeated references to white dolls, babies, and movie stars. She was fascinated by those images because they were "lovable" to everyone but her. She tried to "dissect" them, to discover or possess the "magic they weaved on others," but finally learned "shame" at her lack of feeling. Claudia knew, even as a child, the force of alien cultural images. She knew that white "ideals" denied her reality by forcing it into strange forms of appearance and experience. Her first reaction was appropriate: she could feel only "disinterested violence" for what, without relevance to her life, still regulated it (*Eye,* pp. 15–16).

The child Claudia learns false "love" rather than cut herself off from the only model of lovableness she is offered. But Claudia the adult narrator sees that Shirley Temple cannot really be loved or imitated because she is just a doll, an image without a self behind it. The crime of the racist society is not only the theft of black reality; it is the substitution of dead, external classifications for free self-definition. A society based entirely on the Look, on the absolute reification of the Other, reifies itself. If blacks are defined as slaves, whites are defined as masters; the Third is not a person at all, only an abstraction. There is finally a Look with no one behind it, because the freedom to define the self is denied. The movie stars and pinup girls of the white culture are not models of selfhood. The message they carry is that human life is being and appearance, not choice. To model oneself on them is to lose one's responsibility to create oneself in a world of others; to "love" them is to deny the equal freedom of others.

Life in this depthless world of images is constantly threatened; the problem of Bad Faith is that one must evade the knowledge of what one has done, to keep the illusion of freedom without the risk. This means that one must somehow justify, even collaborate with, the Look of the Other or the Third. Sartre says that one way to handle the gaze of the Third is to "ally myself to the Third so as to look at the Other who is then transformed into *our* object" (*BN*, p. 392). The internalization of white values is one such act. The choice of a scapegoat goes further, displacing onto the Other all that is feared in the self, and so remaining "free." So the genteel ladies escape "funkiness" in others, as in themselves, of disorder or aberration. Geraldine rejects in Pecola the "waste" that will "settle" in her house (*Eye,* p. 72). Helene Wright tries to reshape her daughter's nose; Milkman Dead casts off the clinging Hagar.

That displacement is parallel to the white attribution of rejected qualities to blacks. But the position of the black woman is doubly difficult. Black women in Morrison's fictions discover "that they [are] neither white nor male, and that all freedom and triumph [are] forbidden to them" (*Sula*, p. 44). Womanhood, like blackness, is Other in this society, and the dilemma of woman in a patriarchal society is parallel to that of blacks in a racist one: they are made to feel most real when *seen*. Thus the adolescent Sula and Nel, parading before young males who label them "pig meat," are "thrilled" by the association of voyeurism with sexuality. But their role as image is complicated by their blackness. They are not just women in a society that reduces women to such cold and infantile images that Corinthians Dead can think that "She didn't know any grown-up women. Every woman she knew was a doll baby" (*Song*, p. 197). They are also *black* women in a society whose female ideal is a *white* "doll baby," blonde and blue-eyed Shirley Temple. Even if they accept their reification they will always be inadequate; the black woman is "the antithesis of American beauty."[6] No efforts at disguise will make them into the images they learn to admire. Defined as the Other, made to be looked at, they can never satisfy the gaze of society.

Because they are doubly defined as failures and outsiders, they are natural scapegoats for those seeking symbols of displaced emotions. Morrison shows the Look taking on monstrous proportions as the humiliated black male allies himself with the Third by making the black woman the object of his displaced fury. So Cholly Breedlove, in his sexual humiliation, looks not at his tormentors, but at his partner, with hatred:

> Never did he once consider directing his hatred toward the hunt-
> ers. Such an emotion would have destroyed him. . . . For now,
> he hated the one who had created the situation, the one who
> bore witness to his failure, his impotence. The one whom he had
> not been able to protect, to spare, to cover from the round moon
> glow of the flashlight. (*Eye,* p. 118)

Prevented from looking outward at the oppressor, he displaces blame onto the Other who "saw." That she too is image in the white man's eye is so much worse, for he had counted (as Jude did with Nel) on her existing only for him, seeing him as he wanted her to, being *his* object and *his* subject. The desire to "protect" her was the desire to create himself as her protector. All he can do to restore his selfhood is to deny hers further. In the recurring scene of black male resentment at black women's submission to oppression (the soldiers' stony stares at Helene and the conductor, Guitar's hatred of his mother's smile and of Pilate's "Aunt Jemima act"), Morrison shows the displacement of male humiliation onto the only person left that a black man can "own"—the black woman. Beauvoir remarks that woman in a patriarchal society is "the inessential who never goes back to being the essential, . . . the absolute Other, without reciprocity."[7] The black woman—doubly Other—is the perfect scapegoat.

It is not only men who look for scapegoats. Barbara Smith points out that not only "the politics of sex" but also "the politics of race and class are crucially interlocking factors in the works of Black women writers."[8] Morrison shows the subject-object pair and the triad created by the Third operating within a society so dependent on exclusion and reification that it creates "interlocking" systems to define individuals in multiple ways. So even black women can find scapegoats. The prime example is Pecola, black and young and ugly. Claudia says,

> All of us—all who knew her—felt so wholesome after we cleaned
> ourselves on her. We were so beautiful when we stood astride
> her ugliness. . . . And she let us, and thereby deserved our
> contempt. We honed our egos on her, padded our characters with
> her frailty, and yawned in the fantasy of our strength. (*Eye,*
> p. 163)

Pecola is the epitome of the victim in a world that reduces persons to objects and then makes them feel inferior as objects. In this world, light-skinned women can feel superior to dark ones, married women to whores, and on and on. The temptations to Bad Faith are enormously increased, since one's own reification can be "escaped" in the interlocking hierarchies that allow most to feel superior to someone. Only the very unlucky, or the truly free, are outside this system.

Pecola is so far "outside" the center of the system—excluded from "reality" by race, gender, class, age, and personal history—that she goes mad, fantasizing that her eyes have turned blue and so fitted her for the world. But not all outsiders go mad or otherwise surrender. There are Morrison characters who refuse to become images, to submerge themselves in a role. These characters are clearly existential heroes, "free" in the Sartrean sense of being their own creators. But Morrison's treatment and development of this type in the social context she has staked out raise important questions about the nature of heroism and the place of external "definitions" in it.

The characters who are "outdoors," cut off from reassuring connection and definition, are profoundly frightening to the community, especially to a community dispossessed and "peripheral"; it responds by treating the free person as another kind of scapegoat, using that "excess" to define its own life. For example, Sula's neighbors fear and condemn her refusal to fit a conventional role, but her shapelessness gives them shape:

> Their conviction of Sula's evil changed them in accountable yet mysterious ways. Once the source of their personal misfortune was identified, they had leave to protect and love one another. They began to cherish their husbands and wives, protect their children, repair their homes and in general band together against the devil in their midst. (*Sula,* p. 102)

Displacing their fear and anger onto Sula, as onto Pecola, they can define themselves as "better." Sula, unlike Pecola, can bear that role, having chosen to be "outside"; it is then tempting to argue that this kind of hero is "a catalyst for good in the society."[9] But Morrison has clear reservations about this situation. In a sick and power-obsessed society, even freedom can become distorted. For one thing, these characters are "freed" by traumatic experiences. Cholly goes through abandonment, sexual humiliation, desertion and rejection: "Abandoned in a junk heap by his mother, rejected for a crap game by his father, there was nothing more to lose. He was alone with his own perceptions and appetites, and they alone interested him" (*Eye,* p. 126). Similarly, Sula is "freed" by her mother's expressed dislike of her and her

own part in Chicken Little's drowning: ". . . hers was an experimental life—
ever since her mother's remarks sent her flying up those stairs, ever since
her one major feeling of responsibility had been exorcised on the bank of a
river with a closed place in the middle" (*Sula*, p. 102). The whores in *The
Bluest Eye* are also freed by exclusion from society; Morrison's suggestion
that such freedom is more deprivation than fulfillment helps to explain their
link with Pecola.[10]

Further, their isolation makes such free characters so unable to connect
with others that they often act cruelly, out of cold detachment or fleeting
impulse. Sula humiliates others "because she want[s] to see the person's face
change rapidly" or watches her mother burn because she is "thrilled" (*Sula*,
pp. 103, 127). Cholly rapes his daughter because he feels no "stable connection between himself and [his] children. . . . he reacted to them, and
his reactions were based on what he felt at the moment" (*Eye*, p. 127).
Claudia says of Cholly's act, "the love of a free man is never safe. There is
no gift for the beloved. The lover alone possesses his gift of love. The loved
one is shorn, neutralized, frozen in the glare of the lover's inward eye" (*Eye*,
p. 163). That is, "total" freedom is another version of the Look; the hero
"transcends" others. This conception of freedom bears some resemblance to
Sartre's heroes, who commit outrageous acts in rejection of social prescrip-
tions; but the cruelty of these heroes forces remembrance of the other side
of freedom, which they neglect, the recognition of their own "facticity,"
their existence in the world of consequences. Morrison says that Sula has
"no ego" (*Sula*, p. 103); that is, she is not able to imagine herself as created
by her choices. She simply defines herself as transcendence. Similarly, Milkman wrenches free from those "using" him, and sees this as self-assertion:
"Either I am to live in this world on my terms or I will die out of it" (*Song*,
p. 129). But to achieve heroism in these terms is to accept the white-male
model of heroism as conquest, to make oneself a subject by freezing the
Other, to perfect one's image by forcing others to see it. Transcendence on
those terms is related to—the other side of—the flight into facticity that
Sula sees all around her. The interdependence of the two kinds of Bad Faith,
the relation between the transcendent hero and the reified victim, is suggested by the fact that both Sula and Mrs. Breedlove love the "power" of
the "position of surrender" in sex (*Sula*, p. 106). It also explains the collapse
of the order Sula makes possible in her town; the community falls into a
self-destructive orgy on Suicide Day after she dies. A hero defined solely by
exclusion from the community reinforces Bad Faith by showing not a clear
choosing self, but a lack of self. That is why Sula finally says, "I never meant
anything" (*Sula*, p. 127).

When Sula meets another free person, Ajax, she is unable to sustain the relation; she lapses into the possessiveness she scorned in Nel. But when she recognizes her failure, she sees it as rooted not in Nel's conformism but in her own isolation: "I didn't even know his name," she thinks: "It's just as well he left. Soon I would have torn the flesh from his face just to see if I was right . . . and nobody would have understood that kind of curiosity" (*Sula*, p. 117). The subject as detached self that can only dissect is what Claudia as a child feared to become: "When I learned how repulsive this disinterested violence was, that it was repulsive because it was disinterested, my shame floundered about for refuge. The best hiding place was love" (*Eye*, pp. 15–16). Claudia first thought the only alternative was to become the object, to "love" and emulate received images. But she learns another way. She is not fully heroic: her attempts to act on her feeling (flowers to bless Pecola's pregnancy) are thwarted by an "unyielding" world; and as an adult, she can only tell Pecola's story, "too late" to change it (*Eye*, p. 164). But she does meet her responsibility to see (not just look), to grasp the existence of herself and others without the evasions of Bad Faith, and she acts on what she sees. Freedom defined as total transcendence lacks the intention and significance that can come from commitment; "freedom," as Sartre comments, "is meaningful only as engaged by its free choice of ends" (*BN*, p. 549).

Milkman Dead, in Morrison's third novel, finally completes the heroic mission. Morrison makes his status clear by depicting him in clearly mythic terms. Milkman's life follows the pattern of the classic hero, from miraculous birth (he is the first black baby born in Mercy Hospital, on a day marked by song, rose petals in the snow, and human "flight") through quest-journey to final reunion with his double. And Milkman largely resolves the conflict between freedom and connection. At first the familiar cold hero, he comes to ask the cost of the heroic quest—"Who'd he leave behind?" (*Song*, p. 336). He learns not only that the hero serves a function for society, the exploration of limits it cannot reach, but also that it serves him: his great-grandfather Shalimar left his children, but "it was the children who sang about it and kept the story of his leaving alive" (*Song*, p. 336). More, he finds that his quest is his culture's; he can only discover what he is by discovering what his family is. By undertaking the quest, he combines subjective freedom with objective fact and defines himself in both spheres. Sartre says that one may respond to the gaze of the Third not by scapegoating and identifying with the Third, but by "solidarity" with the Other, which can allow for common transcendence of the outside definition (*BN*, p. 394). By conceiving himself as both free individual and member of the social group, the hero unites his free and factitious natures and becomes part of the historical process by which the struggle for self-definition is both complicated and fulfilled. Thus at the end of *Song of Solomon,* Milkman has restored the names of his family, recovered their song; and he can "fly." But he does not fly away; he flies toward Guitar, his wounded "brother": "For now he knew what Shalimar knew: If you surrendered to the air, you could *ride* it" (*Song,* p. 341). Only in the recognition of his condition can he act in it, only in commitment is he free.

Roger Rosenblatt has remarked that much Afro-American fiction tends toward myth because of its "acknowledgment of external limitation and the anticipation of it."[11] Morrison has always offered mythic possibilities in her emphasis on natural cycle, bizarre events, and narrative echoes. The mythic sensibility does seem to fit her view of the difficulties of freedom. But there are dangers in the use of myth that are especially acute for writers trying to combine the mythic sense of meaning with the concrete situation of the oppressed. Susan L. Blake has pointed out some of those problems in Ralph Ellison's combination of myth with black folklore. She suggests that the myth and the social situation described in the folklore "do not have compatible meanings," that in fact the correlation to "universal" Western myth "transforms acceptance of blackness as identity into acceptance of blackness as limitation. It substitutes the white culture's definition of blackness for the self-definition of folklore."[12] This question is obviously crucial for Morrison, whose fictions try to combine existential concerns compatible with a mythic presentation with an analysis of American society. But her work resolves some of the problems Blake sees in Ellison's use of myth.

First, Morrison's almost total exclusion of white characters from the books allows her to treat white culture as "necessity" without either mythicizing specific acts of oppression or positing present necessity as eternal. Blake suggests that Ellison's "ritualization" of white brutality—e.g., in the adolescent Battle Royal—suggests a reading—adolescent rites of passage—that contradicts the social reality and almost justifies the event.[13] Morrison avoids such a situation by exclusion of whites. White brutality and insensitivity are part of the environment the black characters must struggle with, but they are most often conditions, institutionalized and often anonymous, rather than events with ritualistic overtones. This allows Morrison to focus attention not on the white characters' forcing of mythic rites—as if they were gods—but on the black characters' choices within the context of oppression. In fact, when coercion is exercised by whites in these works, it is depicted as *anti*-mythic. It does not force boys into manhood (the hunters, for example, discovered Cholly in the act of copulation), or cause a tragic hero's cathartic recognition (the first Macon Dead was blown off the fence in a sudden anonymous act). It destroys the myth and denies characters entrance into it: it forces Cholly to dissociate himself from his own acts; it prevents Jude from growing into manhood and denies Nel the identity with her mother essential to a female myth;[14] it destroys the links between generations that are the foundation of a mythos. The finding of a myth in these novels is a choice that is made in spite of a dominating culture that would deny it. Morrison's allusions to traditional Western myth, then, correct it by showing how far the dominant culture has come from its roots, and emphasize the denial of responsibility in the faceless anti-myth.

But showing the myth coming from inside the black culture is not enough to correct it. Its very form must be adapted to reflect the new sense of reality, the new definition of heroism. Morrison's version of the Icarus story shows her approach. The Icarus tale offers a tempting pattern for a black writer interested in myth and folklore, since it ties in with folk tales of blacks flying back to the homeland; but its limitation, as Blake points out, is that it seems to carry a "moral" incompatible with the concrete situation of blacks, suggesting the failure of the son to be the result of *hubris* rather than oppression.[15] Morrison plays variations on the story that correct that perspective. One version of it has Shalimar flying away and trying to take his son, as did Daedalus. But Shalimar's son is a baby, and Shalimar drops him, unable to soar with him. That version emphasizes, first, that the son's "fall" is the result of a situation beyond his control; second, that the father's desire for freedom and his family ties are in conflict. That second aspect is central to Morrison's analysis and reconstruction of the myth. In the Icarus tale, freedom is available to the characters—they can fly. If they fail, it is because they want an impossible kind of freedom. To transfer that pattern to the black situation would be to suggest that blacks must accept an inferior social position. Morrison's version of the tale shifts the emphasis to divided loyalties. Shalimar is free to return to Africa—totally free. But that kind of freedom is problematic, not because in itself it is wrong, but because in the particular context he is in—family and children—it involves denial of social and personal bonds. He does not destroy himself by soaring, but he wounds others because not everyone can take that way. The conflict is not between *hubris* and common sense, but between "absolute" freedom and social responsibility. Milkman resolves the conflict when he leaps, flying *toward* his "brother," finding freedom in "surrender" to the air—not in acceptance of his situation as right or as eternal, but acceptance of it as real. Morrison rewrites myth so that it carries the power of natural ties and psychic meaning but also speaks to a "necessity" in the social order.

She is therefore very concerned with the sources of myth, with mythos and personal myth. All the novels try to show the machinery of myth, the ways that meaning can modify experience. Morrison distinguishes between false "myths" that simply reduce, misinterpret, and distort reality—from Shirley Temple to the view of Sula as "evil," from Smith's failed attempt at flight to Macon Dead's obsession with Pilate's hoard—and true myths that spring from and illuminate reality. She insistently raises questions about mythic or symbolic readings of life, often showing even the best-intentioned attempts at meaning going astray. She shifts point of view so often in her fictions that the limitation of the individual view is obvious, and the attempt to make one view into the myth, one person into the hero, is seen for the reductive act that it is.[16] For example, Milkman's early view of himself as the hero besieged by "users" is partly confirmed by the possessiveness of others; his mother realizes that "Her son had never been a person to her, a separate real person. He had always been a passion" (Song, p. 131). But her need is explained by her personal history, and closely parallels Milkman's own selfishness. Thus the multiple perspectives not only qualify the myth by showing that any specific situation may be a different myth for each of the characters involved, since each sees himself at the center of it; they also make the myth's relevance clear by showing the same problems manifested in many cases, so that Milkman's solution is for all. As the myth emerges from the multiplicity of daily lives, finally the mythic hero's estimate of his own significance is confirmed both by his centrality in other views and by his parallels to other lives. Morrison sees quite clearly the danger of myth as existentialist tract abstracted from real situations, and she adapts the myth to the black historical context, reconciling freedom with facticity on both individual and collective levels. But there is another area in which she does not adapt the myth so completely—the area of gender. She is quite able to show black women as victims, as understanding narrators, or even as "free" in the sense of disconnection. But when the time comes to fulfill the myth, to show a hero who goes beyond the independence to engagement, she creates a male hero. Her own emphasis on the effect of particulars on meaning raises questions about that choice.

The use of a male hero does not, of course, necessarily imply the subjugation of women, and Morrison has the tools to correct the male slant. Her use of multiple perspectives has always allowed her to show a number of subjects as comments and variations on the central character. And her early alternation between male and female versions of the "free" character shows that she does not exclude women from subjective life or choice. She even offers explicit commentaries on Milkman's sexism—from his sister Lena, for example (*Song,* pp. 213–18)—and parallels to women characters that make his quest a surrogate for theirs. That might seem sufficient: this is Milkman's story, so the other characters, male and female, are secondary. He is everyone's surrogate. To some extent, women are displaced because of the problem Morrison has studied all along—central versus peripheral perceptions—and she makes it clear that concentration on his life is not a denial of others'. But, as with the racial question, mere admission of multiple perspectives does not correct the mythic bias: the structure of the male-centered myth carries certain implications about gender that Morrison could disarm only by changing the story. Because she does not, her version of the hero-tale seems to allow only men as potential heroes. Thus Milkman is a surrogate for women in a very different way than for men.

The epigraph to *Song of Solomon* is, "The fathers may soar / And the children may know their names," and the heroic quest is as male as those words imply. Milkman seeks his forefathers; other than his mother, his female ancestors are nearly irrelevant. Even his grandmother Sing is barely defined, and her role in self-definition is questionable: she convinced the first Macon Dead to keep his grotesquely mistaken name, and her family changed their Indian names to "white" ones (*Song,* pp. 246, 326). Milkman "proves" himself in struggle with other men, from his father and Guitar to the male community at Shalimar. They reward him by telling him about the heroes who are his ancestors and models, by taking him on an all-male hunting trip, by giving him the name of a compliant woman. And he ends in the heroic leap toward his male alter ego, Guitar. From first to last, women exist for Milkman, and in the plot development, as functions: mother, wife, lover, sister. That narrative concentration in itself weakens Morrison's careful multiple perspectives: we understand Hagar, for example, as a subject in the sense that we see her point of view, but ultimately her story is subsumed in Milkman's search for male models.

Indeed, all the models available to Milkman are male—all the characters, however flawed, who assert independence and become inspirations to the community. Milkman learns what both Macon Deads "say" to observers with their lives:

> See what you can do? Never mind you can't tell one letter from another, never mind you born a slave, never mind you lose your name, never mind your daddy dead, never mind nothing. Here, this here, is what a man can do if he puts his mind to it and his back in it. (*Song,* p. 237)

There are no women who so focus individual and social awareness in Morrison. Most of the women are the "doll babies" of a dead culture. Those who learn to be free are led to the decision by a man, as Corinthians Dead is by Porter. The myth of heroism traced through the male line allows women to benefit but not to originate.

Milkman does have a female guide figure, his aunt Pilate, and she might further disarm the androcentric myth. She balances in her character the freedom and connection that Milkman must learn:

> . . . when she realized what her situation in the world was and would probably always be she threw away every assumption she had learned and began at zero. . . . Then she tackled the problem of trying to decide how she wanted to live and what was valuable to her. . . . she knew there was nothing to fear. That plus her alien's compassion for troubled people ripened her and . . . kept her just barely within the boundaries of the elaborately socialized world of black people. (*Song,* pp. 149–50)

Further, Pilate performs a social function by recognizing the same balance in others. At Hagar's funeral, Pilate sings and speaks to each mourner, "identifying Hagar, selecting her away from everybody else in the world who had died" (*Song,* p. 322). She pulls the individual into the group and recognizes individuality at the same time. Later, she forces Milkman to face his responsibility for Hagar's death. Her own dying words are, "I wish I'd a knowed more people. I would of loved 'em all. If I'd a knowed more, I would a loved more." That free commitment to others is just what Milkman learns; it is no wonder that he answers by wishing for a mate like Pilate, saying, "There's got to be at least one more woman like you" (*Song,* p. 340).

In these ways, Pilate too is like the hero, and the importance of her role should not be underestimated. But the terms of her life keep her from really fitting the heroic mold. It is important to the mythic conception that the hero understand what he is, and Pilate does not quite reach that point. She does have the independence and compassion of the hero, but her sense of mission is oddly garbled. She misinterprets her dead father's messages, mistakes his bones for someone else's, cannot complete her "quest" without Milkman's explanation. She does the right thing, but from intuitive rather than conscious knowledge. Thus, while she embodies Morrison's values, she is not the complete hero that Milkman is, for she lacks his recognition of meaning. By contrast to his final state, she seems intuitive, personal, and rather passive.

This distinction is bothersome because it comes so close to the old active-man/passive-woman stereotype. It is quite clearly rooted in the myth structure. It seems fitting that Pilate dies and Milkman is left only with his *imagination* of a woman like her, for in the myth, woman gets meaning from or gives meaning to man; she does not both live and know the meaning as he does. Toni Morrison commented that *Song of Solomon* is about "dominion," and about "the way in which men do things or see things and relate to one another."[17] What the novel shows is that the "universal" myth of Western culture is just such a male story; and the parallels and discrepancies between Milkman and Pilate further show the difficulty of the heroic mode for a woman. By living out the myth, Milkman both finds his own identity—chooses and corrects the myth by free participation in it—and finds a connection to society, an "image" he can be to others that leads and inspires them, that is rooted both symbolically and historically in his community. Former heroes aid that combination of social role and selfhood by becoming suggestive but not confining models. Thus Milkman attains a "definition" of the self that explodes the flat alienating images of the anti-mythic white society. But the woman seems to lack the possibilities available to the man. As a woman, Pilate cannot model herself totally on the male line, though all her meaning derives from it; and she has no true female line, only vague references to women defined by their mates. She acts out her duty to her father but she will never *become* him, as Milkman can, and so understand him from within. Beauvoir says that women "still dream through the dreams of men";[18] that problem is illustrated perfectly in Pilate, the strong and independent woman who still waits in dreams for messages from her dead father, messages she misreads until corrected by his male descendant.

Morrison often shows women denying their mothers, in the "matrophobia" Adrienne Rich has described as a rebellion against the imposed female image, an attempt to be "individuated and free." The problem with such a rejection is that it is a "splitting of the self,"[19] a denial of facticity that can produce a centerless hero like Sula. Milkman's break from his father is a parallel rebellion; but Milkman is finally reconciled with his forefathers, understanding their intent as well as their actions, grasping the mythic experience from inside and out, and he can do so because of the historical reconstruction that puts their acts in context. That sense of history is not available to women, and without it they have neither the models nor the contextual information to make themselves whole. Until women like Pilate recover their heroic female line, they cannot replace false images with true ones, and they will be left in a world, as Morrison shows, where mothers and daughters reject one another, female friendships are difficult to sustain, the dominating models of female selfhood are baby dolls and pinups, and even heroic women like Pilate cannot pass on their values to their children and grandchildren. Morrison's women can free themselves, like Sula, and be self-defined and disconnected; they can come close to a heroic life. But to serve the heroic integrative function, they need a new myth, in which women too are central, in which it is as important to know why Sing lived her life as why Macon did, and in which Sing's legacy to her descendants is also traced. Morrison has, quite consciously, depicted the male mode of heroism in *Song of Solomon;* it will be interesting to see whether and how she conceives of the female mode.

Morrison's use of mythic structure, more and more overtly as her work develops, is central to her existentialist analysis. The heroic quest for identity achieved by conquest in and of the outer world embodies the human need for transcendence and self-definition; at the same time, the mythic sense of fate and necessity corresponds to the experience of facticity, both as irrevocable consequence and as concrete conditions for choice. Between those two poles—free heroism and determined role—move Morrison's characters. Further, mythic patterns are especially appropriate to her social concerns, since the mythic hero by nature both embodies and transcends the values of his culture. These connections would be significant in most presentations of existential themes, but the special situations with which Morrison is concerned further complicate her use of myth. On the one hand, traditional myths claim to represent "universal" values and experiences; on the other, they clearly exclude or distort minority experiences by offering inappropriate or impossible models (e.g., Shirley Temple). This contradiction produces the special treatment of myth that Chester J. Fontenot, Jr., sees in black American fiction, turning on "the tension between the universal order and that produced by mankind for Black people." The myth of what may seem the "universal cosmos" in the majority view is so patently untrue to the black experience that from that perspective it is not mythic, but "linear," demanding denial of past and present reality in favor of "an obscure vision of some distant future"[20] (e.g., the struggle to become Shirley Temple). Meanwhile, the mythic consciousness adequate to the minority experience is in danger of becoming an imprisoning view of oppression as "fated." Morrison, then, must capture "universal" aspirations without denying concrete reality, construct a myth that affirms community identity without accepting oppressive definitions. In the process, she must take the outline of the mythic structure, already so well suited to the existentialist quest for freedom and identity, and adapt it to the historical circumstances that surround this version of the quest. She values the myth as a way to design, not confine, reality; it remains to be seen how much further she can carry that notion.[21]

NOTES

[1] Editions of Morrison's novels used here are *The Bluest Eye* (New York: Holt, Rinehart, and Winston, 1970), hereafter cited as *Eye; Sula* (New York: Bantam, 1975); *Song of Solomon* (New York: Signet, 1978), hereafter cited as *Song*. Dates given in the text are of the first hardcover editions.

[2] For a careful analysis of the relation between primer and novel, see Phyllis R. Klotman, "Dick-and-Jane and the Shirley Temple Sensibility in *The Bluest Eye*," *Black American Literature Forum*, 8, 4 (Winter 1979), 123–25.

[3] Jean-Paul Sartre, *Being and Nothingness*, trans. Hazel E. Barnes (New York: Citadel Press, 1966), p. 239. Subsequent references to this work (identified as *BN*) will be in the text.

[4] Simone de Beauvoir, *The Second Sex*, trans. H. M. Parshley (New York: Vintage Books, 1974), p. 158.

[5] Fredric Jameson, *Marxism and Form: Twentieth-Century Dialectical Theories of Literature* (Princeton: Princeton Univ. Press, 1971), p. 249. Most of Chapter 4, "Sartre and History," is relevant to this discussion.

[6] William H. Grier and Price M. Cobbs, *Black Rage* (New York: Bantam, 1968), p. 33. Despite their overvaluation of female "narcissism," Grier and Cobbs offer a useful analysis of the image problem, and also of the difficulties in mother-daughter relations that Morrison shows.

[7] Beauvoir, p. 159.

[8] Barbara Smith, "Toward a Black Feminist Criticism," *Women's Studies International Quarterly*, 2, 2 (1979), 185.

[9] Chikwenye Okonjo Ogunyemi, "*Sula:* 'A Nigger Joke,' " *Black American Literature Forum*, 8, 4 (Winter 1979), 130.

[10] Chikwenye Okonjo Ogunyemi, "Order and Disorder in Toni Morrison's *The Bluest Eye*," *Critique*, 19, 1 (1977), 119.

[11] Roger Rosenblatt, *Black Fiction* (Cambridge: Harvard Univ. Press, 1974), p. 9.

[12] Susan L. Blake, "Ritual and Rationalization: Black Folklore in the Works of Ralph Ellison," *PMLA*, 94 (1979), 123, 126.

[13] Blake, pp. 122–23.

[14] For discussion of the importance of mother-daughter identification, see Elizabeth Schultz, " 'Free in Fact and at Last': The Image of the Black Woman in Black American Fiction," in *What Manner of Woman: Essays on English and American Life and Literature*, ed. Marlene Springer (New York: New York Univ. Press, 1977), p. 335. On the mother-daughter "antimyth" in *Eye*, see Susan Gubar, "Mother, Maiden, and the Marriage of Death: Women Writers and an Ancient Myth," *Women's Studies*, 6 (1979), 307–8.

[15] Blake, pp. 124–26.

[16] Barbara Lounsberry and Grace Ann Hovet, "Principles of Perception in Toni Morrison's *Sula*," *Black American Literature Forum*, 8, 4 (Winter 1979), 129.

[17] Jane Bakerman, "The Seams Can't Show: An Interview with Toni Morrison," *Black American Literature Forum*, 7, 2 (Summer 1978), 60.

[18] Beauvoir, p. 161.

[19] Adrienne Rich, *Of Woman Born: Motherhood as Experience and as Institution* (New York: Bantam, 1977), p. 238.

[20] Chester J. Fontenot, Jr., "Black Fiction: Apollo or Dionysus?," *Twentieth Century Literature*, 25, 1 (Spring 1979), 75–76.

[21] This essay was written before the publication of *Tar Baby* (1981). The new novel deserves detailed treatment, but here it may suffice to remark that the patterns observed in the earlier novels do recur in *Tar Baby*. Problems of identity are raised in similar terms of self/other, seer/seen, public/private; and they are clearly depicted as complicated by social divisions and pressures—even more so, since for the first time Morrison shows intersections between black and white worlds more closely. However, some of the unresolved issues also still linger. In particular, the nostalgic, isolating, and—again—male terms in which heroism and myth are finally presented seem even more troublesome.

HORTENSE J. SPILLERS

A Hateful Passion, a Lost Love

When I think of how essentially alone black women have been—alone because of our bodies, over which we have had so little control; alone because the damage done to our men has prevented their closeness and protection; and alone because we have had no one to tell us stories about ourselves; I realize that black women writers are an important and comforting presence in my life. Only they know my story. It is absolutely necessary that they be permitted to discover and interpret the entire range and spectrum of the experience of black women and not be stymied by preconceived conclusions. Because of these writers, there are more models of how it is possible for us to live, there are more choices for black women to make, and there is a larger space in the universe for us. [1]

Toni Morrison's *Sula* is a rebel idea, both for her creator[2] and for Morrison's audience. To read *Sula* is to encounter a sentimental education so sharply discontinuous from the dominant traditions of Afro-American literature in the way that it compels and/or deadlocks the responses that the novel, for all its brevity and quiet intrusion on the landscape of American fiction, is, to my mind, the single most important irruption of black women's writing in our era. I am not claiming for this novel any more than its due; *Sula* (1973) is not a stylistic innovation. But in bringing to light dark impulses no longer contraband in the black American female's cultural address, the

From *Feminist Studies* 9, No. 2 (Summer 1983): 293–323.

novel inscribes a new dimension of being, moving at last in contradistinction to the tide of virtue and pathos which tends to overwhelm black female characterization in a monolith of terms and possibilities. I regard Sula the character as a literal and figurative *breakthrough* toward the assertion of what we may call, in relation to her literary "relatives," new female being.

Without predecessors in the recent past of Afro-American literature, Sula is anticipated by a figure four decades removed from Morrison's symbol smasher: Janie Starks in Zora Neale Hurston's *Their Eyes Were Watching God* (1937). By intruding still a third figure—Vyry Ware of Margaret Walker's *Jubilee* (1966)—we lay hold of a pattern of contrast among three African-American female writers, who pose not only differences of character in their perception of female possibilities, but also a widely divergent vocabulary of feeling. This article traces the changes in black female characterization from *Sula* back toward the literary past, beginning with Margaret Walker's Vyry and Zora Neale Hurston's Janie, forward again to *Sula* and Morrison. It argues that the agents which these novels project are strikingly different, and that the differences take shape primarily around questions of moral and social value. And it explores the mediations through which all three writers translate sociomoral constructs into literary modes of discourse.

Margaret Walker's Vyry Ware belongs to, embodies, a corporate ideal. The black woman in her characterization exists for the race, in its behalf, and in maternal relationship to its profoundest needs and wishes. Sula, on the other hand, lives for Sula and has no wish to "mother" anyone, let alone the black race in some symbolic concession to a collective need. If Vyry is woman-for-the-other, then Sula is woman-for-self. Janie Starks represents a dialectical point between the antitheses, and the primary puzzle of *Their Eyes Were Watching God* is the contradiction of motives through which Janie Starks has her being; in other words, Janie might have been Sula, but the latter only through a resolution of negative impulses. These three characters, then, describe peak points in a cultural and historical configuration of literary issues. In Sula's case, the old love of the collective, for the collective, is lost, and passions are turned antagonistic, since, as the myth of the black woman goes, the latter is loving only insofar as she protects her children and forgives her man. The title of this article is a kind of shorthand for these longhanded notations.

The scheme of these observations, as I have already implied, is not strictly chronological. Hurston's affinities are much closer to Morrison's than Walker's, even though Hurston's *Their Eyes Were Watching God* was written nearly fifty years ago. The critical scheme I offer here is not precisely linear, because the literary movement I perceive, which theoretically might take in more women writers than my representative selections, does not progress neatly from year to year in an orderly advance of literary issues and strategies. My method aims at a dialectics of process, with these affinities and emphases tending to move in cycles rather than straight lines. I see no myth of descent operating here as in Harold Bloom's "anxiety of influence," exerted, in an oedipal-like formation, by great writers on their successors.[3] The idea-form which I trace here, articulated in three individual writers' metaphors and patterns of theme and structure, does not emerge within this community of writers in strict sequential order. Ironically, it is exactly the right *not* to accede to the simplifications and mystifications of a strictly historiographical time line that now promises the greatest freedom of discourse to black people, to black women, as critics, teachers, writers, and thinkers.

As the opening exercise in the cultural and literary perspective that this article wishes to consider, then, we turn immediately to Morrison's *Sula*, the "youngest" of three heroines. Few of the time-honored motifs of female behavioral description will suit her: not "seduction and betrayal," applied to a network of English and American fictions; not the category of "holy fool," as exemplified in various Baldwinian configurations of female character; not the patient long-suffering female, nor the female authenticated by male imagination. Compared with past heroines of black American fiction, Sula exists foremost in her own consciousness. To that extent, *Sula* and *Their Eyes Were Watching God* are studies in contrast to Walker and share the same fabric of values. The problem that Morrison poses in *Sula* is the degree to which her heroine (or antiheroine, depending on one's reading of the character) is self-betrayed. The audience does not have an easy time in responding to the agent, because the usual sentiments about black women have been excised, and what we confront instead is the entanglement of our own conflicting desires, our own contradictory motivations concerning issues of individual woman-freedom. Sula is both loved and hated by the reader, embraced and rejected simultaneously because her audience is forced to accept the corruption of absolutes and what has been left in their place—the complex, alienated, transitory gestures of a personality who has no framework of moral reference beyond or other than herself.

Insofar as Sula is not a loving human being, extending few of the traditional loyalties to those around her, she reverses the customary trend of "moral growth" and embodies, contrarily, a figure of genuine moral ambiguity about whom few comforting conclusions may be drawn. Through Sula's unalterable "badness," black and female are now made to appear as a *single* subject in its own right, fully aware of a plenitude of predicative possibilities, for good and ill.

In Sula's case, virtue is not the sole alternative to powerlessness, or even the primary one, or perhaps even an alternative at all. In the interest of complexity, Sula is Morrison's deliberate hypothesis. A conditional subjunctive replaces an indicative certainty: "In a way her strangeness, her naiveté, her craving for the other half of her equation was the consequence of an idle imagination. Had she paints, or clay, or knew the discipline of the dance or strings; had she anything to engage her tremendous curiosity and her gift for metaphor, she might have exchanged the restlessness and preoccupation with whim for an activity that provided her with all she yearned for. And like any *artist with no art form* she became dangerous."[4]

In careful, exquisite terms Sula has been endowed with dimensions of other possibility. How they are frustrated occupies us for most of the novel, but what strikes me keenly about the passage is that Morrison imagines a character whose destiny is not coterminous with naturalistic or mystical boundaries. Indeed the possibility of art, of intellectual vocation for black female character, has been offered as style of defense against the naked brutality of conditions. The efficacy of art cannot be isolated from its social and political means, but Sula is specifically circumscribed by the lack of an explicit tradition of imagination or aesthetic work, and not by the evil force of "white" society, or the absence of a man, or even the presence of a mean one.

Morrison, then, imagines a character whose failings are directly traceable to the absence of a discursive/imaginative project—some *thing* to do, some object-subject relationship which establishes the identity in time and space. We do not see Sula in relationship to an "oppressor," a "whitey," a male, a dominant and dominating being outside the self. No Manichean analysis demanding a polarity of interest—black/white, male/female, good/bad—will work here. Instead, Sula emerges as an embodiment of a metaphysical chaos in pursuit of an activity both proper and sufficient to herself. Whatever Sula has become, whatever she is, is a matter of her own choices, often ill-formed and ill-informed. Even her loneliness, she says to her best friend Nel is her own—"My own lonely," she claims in typical Sula-bravado, as she lies dying. Despite our misgivings at Sula's insistence and at the very degree of alienation Morrison accords her, we are prepared to accept her negative, naysaying freedom as a necessary declaration of independence by the black female writer in her pursuit of a vocabulary of gesture—both verbal and motor—that leads us as well as the author away from the limited repertoire of powerless virtue and sentimental pathos. Sula is neither tragic nor pathetic; she does not amuse or accommodate. For black audiences, she is not consciousness of the black race personified, not "tragic mulatto," nor, for white ones, is she "mammie," "Negress," "coon," or "maid." She is herself, and Morrison, quite rightly, seems little concerned if any of us, at this late date of Sula's appearance in the "house of fiction," minds her heroine or not.

We view Morrison's decision with interest because it departs dramatically from both the iconography of virtue and endurance and from the ideology of the infamous Ogre/Bitch complex, alternately poised as the dominant traits of black female personality when the black female personality exists at all in the vocabulary of public symbols.[5] Sula demands, I believe, that we not only see anew, but also *speak* anew in laying to rest the several manifestations of apartheid in its actual practice and in the formulation of the critical postulates that govern our various epistemologies.

That writers like Morrison, Toni Cade Bambara, and Paule Marshall among them, participate in a tradition of black women writing in their own behalf, close to its moment of inception, lends their work thorough complexity. With the exception of a handful of autobiographical narratives from the nineteenth century, the black woman's realities are virtually suppressed until the period of the Harlem Renaissance and later. Essentially, the black woman as artist, as intellectual spokesperson for her own cultural apprenticeship, has not existed before, for anyone. At the source of her own symbol-making task, this community of writers confronts, therefore, a tradition of work that is quite recent, its continuities broken and sporadic.

It is not at all an exaggeration to say that the black woman's presence as character and movement in the American world has been *ascribed* a status of impoverishment or pathology, or, at best, an essence that droops down in the midst of things, as de Beauvoir describes female mystery in *The Second Sex*. Against this social knowledge, black women writers likely agree on a single point: whatever the portrayal of female character yields, it will be rendered from the point of view of one whose eyes are not alien to the humanity in front of them. What we can safely assume, then, is that black women write as partisans to a particular historical order—their own, the black and female one, with its hideous strictures against literacy and its subtle activities of censorship even now against words and deeds that would deny or defy the black woman myth. What we can assume with less confidence is that their partisanship, as in the rebellion of Sula, will yield a synonymity of conclusions.

The contrast between Sula and Margaret Walker's Vyry Ware is the difference between captive woman and free woman, but the distinction between them has as much to do with aspects of agency and characterization as it does with the kind of sensibility or sympathy that a writer requires in building one kind of character and not another. In other words, *what* we think of Sula and Vyry, for instance, has something to do with *how* we are taught *to see* and *value* them. In the terms of fiction which they each propose, *Jubilee, Their Eyes Were Watching God,* and *Sula* all represent varying degrees of plausibility, but the critical question is not whether the events they portray are plausible, or whether they confirm what we already believe, or think we do, but, rather, how each writer deploys a concept of character. Of the three, Toni Morrison looks forward to an era of dissensions: Sula's passions are hateful, as we have observed, and though we are not certain that the loss of conventional love brings her down, we are sure that she overthrows received moralities in a heedless quest for her own irreducible self. This radical intrusion of waywardness lends a different thematic emphasis to the woman's tale of generation, receding in Sula's awareness, and the result is a novel whose formal strategies are ambiguous and even discomforting in their uncertainties. Once we have examined an analogy of the archetype from which Sula deviates by turning to Margaret Walker's *Jubilee* and have explored Hurston's novel as a structural advance of the literary issues, we will return to *Sula* in a consideration of myth/countermyth as a discourse ordained by history.

In radical opposition to notions of discontinuity, confronting us as a fictional world of consecrated time and space, *Jubilee* worries one of the traditional notions of realism—the stirring to life of the common people[6]—to a modified definition. Walker completed her big novel in the mid sixties at the University of Iowa Creative Writers' Workshop. She tells the story of the novel, twenty years in the making, in *How I Wrote* Jubilee.[7] This novel of historical content has no immediate precedent in Afro-American literary tradition. To that extent, it bears little structural resemblance to Hurston's work before it, although both Hurston and Walker implement a search for roots, or to Morrison's work after it. *Jubilee,* therefore, assumes a special place in the canon.

From Walker's own point of view, the novel is historical, taking its models from the Russian writers of historical fiction, particularly Tolstoy. In its panoramic display, its massive configurations of characters and implied presences, its movement from a dense point of American history—the era of the Civil War—toward an inevitable, irreversible outcome—the emancipation of 10 million African Americans—*Jubilee* is certainly historical. Even though it is a tale whose end is written on the brain, in the heart, so that there is not even a chance that we will be mistaken about closure, the novel unfolds as if the issues were new. We are sufficiently excited to keep turning the page of a twice-told tale accurately reiterating what we have come to believe is the truth about the "Peculiar Institution." But the high credibility of the text in this case leads us to wonder, eventually, what else is embedded in it that compels us to read our fate by its lights. My own interpretation of the novel is that it is not only historical, but also, and primarily, Historical. In other words, "Historical," in this sense, is a metaphor for the unfolding of the Divine Will. This angle on reality is defined by Paul Tillich as a theonomy. Human history is shot through with Divine Presence so that its being and time are consistent with a plan that elaborates and completes the will of God.[8] In this view of things, human doings are only illusions of a counterfeit autonomy; in Walker's novel agents (or characters) are moving and are moved under the aegis of a Higher and Hidden Authority.

For Vyry Ware, the heroine of *Jubilee* and her family, honor, courage, endurance—in short, the heroic as transparent prophetic utterance—become the privileged center of human response. If Walker's characters are ultimately seen as one-dimensional, either good or bad, speaking in a public rhetoric that assumes the heroic or its opposite, then such portrayal is apt to a fiction whose value is subsumed in a theonomous frame of moral reference. From this angle of advocacy and preservation the writer does not penetrate the core of experience, but encircles it. The heroic intention has no interest in fluctuations or transformations or palpitations of conscience—these will pass away—but monumentality, or fixedness, becomes its striving. Destiny is disclosed to the hero or the heroine as an already-fixed and named event, and this steady reference point is the secret of permanence.

Set on a Georgia plantation before the Civil War, the novel is divided into three parts. The first recalls the infancy and youth of Vyry Ware, the central figure of the novel, and rehearses various modes of the domestic South in slavery. The second part recapitulates the war and its impact on the intimate life of families and individuals. One of the significant threads of the Peculiar Institution in objective time is closely imitated here—how the exigencies of war lead to the destruction of plantation hierarchy. In this vacuum of order a landscape of deracinated women and men dominates the countryside, and Walker's intensity of detail involves the reader in a scene of universal mobility—everything is moving, animate and inanimate, away from the centers of war toward peace, always imminent, in the shadows of Sherman's torch. Vyry and her first love Randall Ware are numbered among the casualties. They are separated as the years of war unhinge all former reality.

The third and final segment of the novel marks Vyry's maturity and the rebirth of a semblance of order in the South. The future is promising

for the emancipated, and Vyry takes a new lover, Innis Brown, before the
return of Randall Ware. This tying up the various threads of the narrative
is undercut by a bitterly ironical perspective. The former enslaved will
struggle as she or he has before now, with this difference: free by law, each
remains a victim of arbitrary force, but such recognition is the reader's alone.
This edge of perception reads into the novel an element of pathos so keenly
defined the Vyry's fate verges on the tragic.

Variously encoded by signs associated with a magical/superstitious
world order, echoes of maxims and common speech, *Jubilee* is immersed in
the material. We are made to feel, in other words, the brutal pull of
necessity—the captive's harsh relationship to this earth and its unrelenting
requirements of labor—as they impel the captive consciousness toward a
terrible knowledge of the tenuousness between life and death. The novel
conjoins natural setting and social necessity in a dance of temporal unfolding;
in fact, the institution of slavery described here is an elaboration of im-
manence so decisive in its hold on the human scene imposed upon it that
Walker's humanity is actually "ventriloquized" through the medium of a
third-person narrator. The narrative technique (with its overlay of mystical
piety) is negotiated between omniscient and concealed narrators. Whatever
the characters think, however they move and feel about their being, all is
rendered through the eyes of another consciousness, not their own. We
might say that the characters embody, then, historical symbols—a captive
class and their captors—which have been encoded or transliterated as actors
in a fiction. Walker's agents are types or valences, and the masks through
which they speak might be assumed as well by any other name.

In attributing to Walker a theonomous view of human reality, I am
also saying that her characters are larger than life; that they are overdrawn,
that, in fact, their compelling agency and motivation are ahistorical, despite
the novel's solid historical grounding. Walker's *lexis* operates under quite
complicated laws, complicated because such vocabulary is no longer accessible, or even acceptable, to various mythoi of contemporary fiction. Walker
is posing a subterranean structure of God terms, articulated in the novel
through what we can identify as the *peripeteia*—that point of radical change
in the direction that the forces of the novel are moving; in historical and
secular terms this change is called emancipation. Historiographic method
in accounting for the "long-range" and "immediate" causes of the Civil War
and its aftermath does not name "God" as a factor in the liberation of black
Americans,[9] and neither does Walker in any explicit way. But it seems clear
to me that "God" is precisely what she means in all the grandeur and
challenge of the Nominative, clear that the agency of Omnipresence—even

more reverberative in its imprecise and ubiquitous *thereness*—is for Walker the source of one of the most decisive abruptions in our history.

Walker adopts a syntax and semantics whose meanings are recognizable in an explanation of affairs in human time. But these delegated efficacies register at a deeper level of import so that "nature," for instance, is nature and something more, and character itself acts in accordance with the same kind of mystical or "unrealistic" tendencies.

Walker's backdrop of natural representation has such forcefulness in the work that dialogue itself is undercut by its dominance, but her still life is counterposed by human doings which elaborate the malignancies of nature, that is, torture, beatings, mental cruelty, the ugly effects of nature embodied in the formal and institutional. The slaveholder and his class, in the abrogation of sympathy, lose their human form. The captors' descent into nature is seen as pernicious self-indulgence, ratified by institutional sanction, but it also violates a deeper structural motive which Walker manipulates in the development of character. Though natural and social events run parallel, they are conjoined by special arrangement, and then there is a name for it— the act of magic or invocation that the enslaved opposes to the arbitrary willfulness of authority.

The evocation of a magical program defines the preeminent formalistic features of the opening segments of the novel. Prayers for the sick and dying and the special atmosphere that surrounds the deathwatch are treated from the outset with particular thematic prominence. In several instances mood is conveyed more by conventional notation—the number thirteen, boiling black pot, full moon, squinch owl, black crone—than any decisive nuance of thought or detail; or more precisely, fear is disembodied from internal agitations of feeling and becomes an attribute of things. "Midnight came and thirteen people waited for death. The black pot boiled, and the full moon rode the clouds high in the heavens and straight up over their heads. . . . It was not a night for people to sleep easy. Every now and then the squinch owl hollered and the crackling fire would glare and the black pot boil. . . ."[10]

The suspense that gathers about this scene is brought on by the active interaction of forces that move beyond and above the characters. An outburst would surprise. Sis. Hetta's death is expected here, and nothing more. The odd and insistent contiguity that Walker establishes among a variety of natural and cultural-material signs—"black pot boiled"; "full moon rode"— identifies the kind of magical/mystical grammar of terms to which I have referred.

"Black pot" and "full moon" may be recognized as elements that properly belong to the terrain of witchcraft, but we must understand that magic and witchcraft—two semiological "stops" usually associated with African-American rebellion and revolutionary fervor throughout the New World under the whip of slavery—are ritual terms of a shorthand which authors adopt to describe a system of beliefs and practices not entirely accessible to us now. In other words, Walker is pointing toward a larger spiritual and religious context through these notations, so that ordinary diurnal events in the novel are invested with extraordinary meaning. My own terms—theonomous meaning—would relate this extraordinary attribution to the Unseen, for which Protestant theology offers other clusters of anomalous phenomena, including "enthusiasm," "ecstasy," or the equivalent of Emile Durkheim's demon of oratorical power.[11] In specific instances of the novel, we see only pointers toward, or markers of, an entirely compelling structure of feelings and beliefs, of which "black pot," for instance, is a single sign. The risk I am taking here is to urge a synonymity between "God" and, for want of a better term, "magic." At least I am suggesting that Walker's vocabulary of God terms includes magic and the magical and the enslaved person's special relationship to natural forces.

Walker achieves this "extra" reading by creating a parallelism between natural and social/domestic issues that dominates the form of the novel. In its reinforcements, there is an absence of differentiation, or of the interplay between dominant and subdominant motifs. A nocturnal order pervades *Jubilee*—life under the confines of the slave community, where movement is constantly under surveillance; secret meetings; flights from the overseer's awful authority; illegal and informal pacts and alliances between slaves; and above all, the slave's terrible vulnerability to fluctuations of fate.

The scene of Vyry's capture after an attempted escape on the eve of the Civil War will provide a final example. After their union Vyry and Randall Ware, the free black man, have two children, Jim and Minna, and Ware makes plans for their liberation. His idea is that he or Vyry will return for the children later, but Vyry refuses to desert them. Her negotiation of a painful passage across the countryside toward the point of rendezvous groans with material burden. It has rained the day of their attempted escape, and mud is dense around the slave quarters by nightfall. Vyry travels with the two children—Jim toddling and the younger child Minna in her arms. The notion of struggle, both against the elements and the powerful other, is so forceful an aspect of tone that the passage itself painfully anticipates the fatefulness of Vyry's move; here are the nodal points:

> Every step Vyry and Jim took, they could feel the mud sucking
> their feet down and fighting them as they withdrew their feet

from its elastic hold. . . . The baby still slept fitfully while Vyry pressed her way doggedly to the swamps. . . . At last they were in sight of the swamps. Feeling sorry for little Jim she decided to rest a few minutes before trying to wade the creek. . . . She sat down on an old log, meaning to rest only a few minutes. . . . A bad spasm clutched her stomach instinctively. She tensed her body with the sure intuition that she was not only being watched but that the watchful figures would soon surround her. Impassively she saw the patteroller and guards, together with Grimes [the overseer] emerge from the shadows and walk toward her. . . . (Pp. 169–70)

This grim detail concludes with Vyry's capture and brutal punishment—"seventy-five lashes on her naked back." That Vyry has been robbed of selfhood on its most fundamental level is clear enough, but the passage further suggests that her movements replicate the paralysis of nightmare. One would move, but cannot, and awakens in spasms of terror. This direct articulation of nightmare content—puzzles and haltings, impediments and frights—dictates the crucial psychological boundaries of *Jubilee* and decides, accordingly, the aesthetic rule.

The idea that emerges here is that Vyry's condition is the equivalent of nightmare, a nocturnal order of things that works its way into the resonances of the novel's structure. Her paralysis is symptomatic of a complex of fear and repression in the service of death. We could argue that the culture of slavery projected in the novel—its modalities of work and celebration, its civic functions and legal codes, its elaborate orders of brutality and mutilation—presents a spectacle of a *culture* in the service of death. Given this reality, the slave subject has no life, but only the stirrings of it. Vyry, trapped in a bad dream, cannot shake loose, and this terrible imposed impotence foreshadows the theme of liberation and a higher liberation as well in which case the stalled movement is overcome in a gesture of revolutionary consciousness. For Vyry the freeing act is sparked by war whose intricate, formal causes are remote to her, though its mandates will require the reorganization of her human resources along new lines of stress. Above all, Vyry must move now without hesitation as the old order collapses around her.

For Vyry's class the postwar years stand as the revelation of the emotional stirrings they have felt all along. "Mine Eyes Have Seen the Glory of the Coming of the Lord" (the title of one of Walker's chapters) is as much a promise as it is an exercise in common meter, but the terms of the promise that Walker imitates are neither modern nor secular. They are eternal and self-generating, authored elsewhere, beyond the reach of human inquiry. Along this axis of time, with its accent on the eternal order of things, women and men in destiny move consistent with the stars of heaven.

This blending of a material culture located in the nineteenth century with a theme which appears timeless and is decisively embedded in a Christian metaphysic reveals the biographical inspiration behind Walker's work. *Jubilee* is, in effect, the tale translated of the author's female ancestors. This is a story of the foremothers, a celebration of their stunning faith and intractable powers of endurance. In that sense, it is not so much a study of characters as it is an interrogation into the African-American character in its poignant national destiny and through its female line of spiritual descent. A long and protracted praise piece, a transformed and elaborated prayer, *Jubilee* is Walker's invocation to the guiding spirit and genius of her people. Such a novel is not "experimental." In short, it does not introduce ambiguity or irony or uncertainty or perhaps even "individualism" as potentially thematic material because it is a detailed sketch of a *collective* survival. The waywardness of a Sula Peace, or even a Janie Stark's movement toward an individualistic liberation—a separate peace—is a trait of character development engendered by a radically different Weltanschauung.

Their Eyes Were Watching God enforces a similar notion of eternal order in the organic metaphorical structure through which Hurston manipulates her characters, but the complexities of motivation in the novel move the reader some distance from the limited range of responses evoked by *Jubilee*. Janie Starks, the heroine of the novel, defines a conglomerate of human and social interests so contradictory in its emphasis that a study of structural ambiguity in fiction might well include Janie Starks *and* her author. Perhaps "uncertainty" is a more useful word in this case than "ambiguity," since Hurston avoids the full elaboration or display of tensions that Janie herself appears to anticipate. In short, Janie Starks is a bundle of contradictions: raised by women, chiefly her grandmother, to seek security in a male and his properties, Janie quite early in her career rejects Nanny's wisdom. In love with adventure, in love with the very idea of adventure, Janie is determined to know exactly what independence for the female means for her. This includes the critical quest of sexual self-determination. Janie's quite moving sense of integrity, however, is undercut in puzzling and peculiar ways.

Janie marries her first husband Logan Killicks because her grandmother wants her to do so, but Janie has little interest in a man who is not only not "glamorous" (as Joe Starks and Virgible "Teacake" Woods will be), but also not enlightened in his outlook on the world and the specifically amorous requirements of female/male relationship. Killicks gets the brunt of a kind of social criticism in *Their Eyes Were Watching God* which mocks the rural person—hardworking, unsophisticated, "straight-arrow," earnest—and Hurston makes her point by having Killicks violate essentially Janie's "dream of the horizon." Janie will shortly desert Killicks for a man far more in keeping with her ideas concerning the romantic, concerning male gracefulness. Jody Starks, up from Georgia and headed for an adventure in real estate and town government, takes the place of Logan Killicks with an immediacy, which in "real" life, would be somewhat disturbing, a bit indecent; but here the "interruption" is altogether lyrical, appropriate, and unmourned. Starks's appearance and intention are even "cinematic" in their decidedly cryptic and romantic tenor—Janie literally goes off "down the road" with the man.

Their destination is Eatonville, Florida, a town which Joe Starks will bring to life with his own lovely ego, shortly to turn arrogant and insulting as he attempts to impose on Janie his old-fashioned ideas about woman's place and possibilities. The closure on this marriage is not a happy one either, troubled by Starks's chauvinistic recriminations and Janie's own disenchantment. Starks dies of a kidney ailment, leaving Janie "Mrs. Mayor" of Eatonville and not particularly concerned, we are led to believe, to be attached again.

Janies's new love affair with Teacake is untrammeled by incompatibility between the pair, though her friends express great concern that Teacake's social and financial status is not what it ought to be, let alone comparable to Jody Starks's. Janie is, however, at once traditionally romantic in her apparently male-centered yearnings and independent in her own imagination and the readiness to make her own choices. The convergence of these two emotional components is, in fact, not the diametrical opposition which contemporary feminists sometimes suppose; heterosexual love is neither inherently perverse nor necessarily dependence-engendering, except that the power equation between female and male tends to corrupt intimacies.[12] The trouble, then, with the relationship between Janie and Teacake is not its heterosexual ambience, but a curiously exaggerated submissiveness on Janie's part that certain other elements of the heroine's character contradict.

When, for instance, Janie follows Teacake to the Florida Everglades to become a migrant farm worker for several seasons, their love is solid and reliable, but the male in this instance is also perfectly capable, under Hurston's gaze, of exhibiting qualities of jealousy and possession so decisive that his occasional physical abuse of the female and his not-so-subtle manipulation of other females' sexual attraction to him seem condoned in the name of love. Hurston's pursuit of an alleged folk philosophy in this case—as in, all women enjoy an occasional violent outburst from their men because they know then that they are loved—is a concession to an obscene idea. One example will suffice. "Before the week was over he had whipped Janie. Not because her behavior justified his jealousy, but it relieved that awful fear inside him. Being able to whip her reassured him in possession. No brutal beating at all. He just slapped her around a bit to show he was boss. . . . It aroused a sort of envy in both men and women. The way he petted and pampered her as if those two or three slaps had nearly killed her made the women see visions and the helpless way she hung on him made men dream dreams . . . ."[13]

One might well wonder, and with a great deal of moral, if not poetic, justification if the scene above describes a *working posture* that Hurston herself might have adopted with various lovers. This scene is paradigmatic of the very quality of ambiguity/ambivalence that I earlier identified for this novel. The piece threatens to abandon primitive modes of consciousness and response from the beginning, but Hurston seems thwarted in bringing this incipience to fruition for reasons which might have to do with the way that the author understood certain popular demands brought to bear on her art. Hurston has detailed some of her notions of what Anglo-American audiences expected of the black writer and the black female writer of her time,[14] but it is not clear to me what African-American audiences expected of their chroniclers. The more difficult question, however, is what Hurston demanded of herself in imagining what was possible for the female, and it appears that beyond a certain point she could not, or would not plunge. *Their Eyes Were Watching God,* for all its quite impressive feminist possibilities, is an instance of "double consciousness," to employ W. E. B. Du Bois's conceptualization in quite another sense and intention.[15] Looking two ways at once, it captivates Janie Starks in an entanglement of conflicting desires.

More concentrated in dramatic focus than *Jubilee,* Hurston's novel was written during the mid thirties; finished in seven weeks during the author's visit to Haiti, the novel is not simply compact. It is hurried, intense, and above all, haunted by an uneasy measure of control. One suspects that Hurston has not said everything she means, but means everything she says. Within a persistent scheme of metaphor, she seems held back from the awful scream that she has forced Janie to repress through unrelieved tides of change. We mistrust Janie's serenity, spoken to her friend Phoeby Watson in the close of the novel; complementarily, the reconciliation is barely acceptable in either structural or dramatic terms. Janie Starks, not unlike her creator, is gifted with a dimension of worldliness and ambition that puts her in touch with broader experience. This daughter of sharecroppers is not content to be heroic under submissive conditions (except with Teacake?); for her, then, nothing in the manners of small town Florida bears repeating. Its hateful, antisocial inclinations are symbolized by Janie's grandmother, whom she hates "and [has] hidden from herself all these years under the cloak of pity." "Here Nanny had taken the biggest thing God ever made, the horizon . . . and pinched it into such a little bit of a thing that she could tie it about her granddaughter's neck tight enough to choke her. She hated the old woman who had twisted her so in the name of love . . ." (pp. 76–77).

The grandmother not only represents a personal trauma for Janie (as the grandmother does in the author's autobiography),[16] but also terror and repression, intruding a vision of impoverishment within the race. Clustered around the symbolic and living grandmother are the anonymous detractors of experience who assume no discriminating feature or motivation beyond the level of the mass. Hurston's rage is directed against this faceless brood with a moral ferociousness that verges on misogyny. This profound undercurrent is relieved, however, by a drift toward caricature. Exaggerating the fat of misshapen men and calling attention to their sexual impotence in public, gaining dimensions of comic monologue, and leaving no genuine clue for those who gaze at her, Janie has elements of a secret life which sustains her through the adventures of three husbands, a flood, justifiable homicide, trial, and vindication.

This psychological bent informing Janie's character is deflected by an anthropological strategy that all but ruins this study of a female soul. The pseudodialect of Southern patois gives Janie back to the folk ultimately, but this "return" contradicts other syntactical choices which Hurston superimposes on the structure through visions of Janie's interior life and Hurston's own narrative style. Janie implies new moral persuasions, while Hurston has her looking back, even returning, to the small town she desperately wishes to be free of. This dilemma of choices haunts the book from the very beginning and may, indeed, shed light on the "ancestral imperative."[17] That Janie does not break from her Southern past, symbolized in the "old talk," but grasps how she might do so is the central problematic feature of the novel, previously alluded to as an undercurrent of doubt running through Hurston's strategies.

Written long before *Jubilee*, *Their Eyes Were Watching God* anticipates the thematic emphases prominent in *Sula* to the extent that in both the latter novels only the adventurous, deracinated personality is heroic, and that in both, the roots of experience are poisonous. One would do well to avoid the plunge down to the roots, seeking, rather, to lose oneself in a larger world of chance and danger. That woman must break loose from the hold of biography as older generations impose it, even the broader movements of tribe, constitutes a controlling theme of Hurston's work.

Images of space and time, inaugurated in the opening pages of the novel, are sounded across it with oracular intensity, defining the dream of Janie Starks as a cosmic disembodiment that renders her experience unitary with the great fantastic ages. "Ships at a distance have every man's wish on board. For some they come in with the tide" (p. 5). Consonant with this history of fantasy life, Janie is something of a solitary reaper, disillusioned, stoical, in her perception of fate and death. "So the beginning of this was a woman and she had come back from burying the dead. . . . The people all saw her because it was sundown. The sun was gone, but he had left his footprints in the sky. It was time to hear things and talk . . ." (p. 5).

The novel is essentially informed by these ahistorical, specifically rustic, image clusters, giving the whole a topological consistency. Hurston, however, attempts to counterpoise this timeless current with elements of psychic specificity—Janie's growth toward an understanding of mutability and change and other aspects of internal movement. The novel's power of revelation, nonetheless, is rather persistently sabotaged at those times when Hurston intrudes metaphorical symbolism as a substitute for the hard precision of thought. Janie actually promises more than the author delivers. As a result, the novel is facile at times when it ought to be moving, captivated in stereotype when it should be dynamic.

The flood that devastates the Florida Everglades and the homes of the migrant farm workers of which Janie and Teacake are a part provides an example. The storm sequence is the novel's high point, its chief dramatic fulcrum, on which rests the motivation that will spur both Janie's self-defense against a rabid Teacake and her return to Eatonville and the Starks house. Waiting in their cabins for the storm to recede, Janie, Teacake, and their fellow laborers are senseless with wonder at its power, "They seemed to be staring at the dark, but their eyes were watching God" (p. 131). What one wants in this sequence is a crack in the mental surface of character so acute that the flood cleaves the narrative precisely in half, pre- and post-diluvial responses so distinctly contrasting that the opening lines—"their souls asking if He meant to measure their puny might against His"—mature into the ineluctable event. The reader expects a convergence of outer scene and its inner correspondence, but Hurston appears to forego the fruition of this parallel rhythm, content on delineating the external behavior of the agents.

Nothing specific to the inner life of Janie appears again for several pages; the awe that greets the display of natural phenomena is replayed through the imagination of a third-person observer, dry feet and all, well above the action of furious winds. We miss the concentration on Janie's internal life which saves the entire first half of the narrative from the pathos of character buffeted by external circumstances. Janie never quite regains her former brilliance, and when we meet her considered judgments again, she has fled the 'Glades, after having had to shoot Teacake in self-defense [as a result of his violence, rabies-induced] and is seeking peace in the town where she has been "first lady." "Here was peace. She pulled in her horizon like a great fish-net. Pulled it from around the waist of the world and draped it over her shoulder. So much of life in its meshes! She called in her soul to come and see . . ." (p. 159).

One is not certain how these images of loss and labor should be read, nor why they strike with such finality, except that the lines make a good ending, this rolling in of fish nets and cleaning of meshes, but if we take Janie as a kind of adventurer, as a woman well familiar with the rites of burial and grief, then we read this closure as a eulogy for the living; Janie has been "buried" along with Teacake.

The fault with this scene is not that Janie has loved Teacake, but, rather, that the author has broken the potential pattern of revolt by having her resigned, as if she were ready for a geriatric retirement, to the town of frustrated love. We know that all novels do end, even if they end with "the," and so it is probably fitting for Janie to have a rest after the tragic events unleashed by the flood. But her decision to go back to Eatonville after the trial strikes me as a naive fictional pose. Or, more precisely, what she thinks about her life at that point seems inappropriate to the courageous defiance that she has often embodied all along. The logic of the novel tends to abrogate neat conclusions, and their indulgence in the end essentially mitigates the complex painful knowledge that Janie has gained about herself and the other.

The promise to seize upon the central dramatic moment of a woman's self-realization fizzles out in a litany of poetic platitudes about as opposite to Janie's dream of the horizon as the grandmother's obsessive fear of experience has been. We miss the knowledge or wisdom of revelation in the perfectly resolved ending—what is it that Janie knows now that she has come back from burying the dead of the sodden and bloated? Are the words merely decorative, or do they mobilize us toward a deeper mysterious sense? In a mode of fictive assumptions similar to Margaret Walker's, Zora Neale Hurston inherits a fabric of mystery without rethreading it. That is one kind of strategic decision. There are others.

Sula, by contrast, closes with less assurance. " 'All that time, all that time, I thought I was missing Jude.' And the loss pressed down on her chest and came up into her throat. 'We was girls together,' she said as though explaining something. 'O Lord, Sula,' she cried, 'girl, girl, girl-girlgirl' " (p. 149).

Nel's lament not only closes *Sula,* but also reinforces the crucial dramatic questions which the novel has introduced—the very mystery of a Sula Peace and the extent to which the town of Medallion, Ohio, has been compelled by her, how they yearn for her, even to the point, oddly enough, of a collective rejection. Nel and Sula are more than girls together. They sustain the loss of innocence and its subsequent responsibilities with a degree of tormented passion seldom allowed even to lovers. More than anyone else in Medallion, they have been intimate witnesses of their mutual coming of age in a sequence of gestures that anticipates an ultimate disaffection between them, but the rhythm of its disclosure, determined early on by the reader as inexorable, is sporadic and intermittent enough in the sight of the two women that its fulfillment comes to both as a trauma of recognition. Nel Wright's "girl," repeated five times and run together in an explosion not only of the syntactical integrity of the line, but also of Nel's very heartbeat, is piercing and sudden remorse—remorse so long suspended, so elaborate in its deceptions and evasions that it could very well intimate the onset of a sickness-unto-death.

When Sula comes of age, she leaves Medallion for a decade in the wake, significantly, of Nel's marriage to Jude and her resignation to staid domestic life. Sula's return to Medallion, in a plague of robins, no less, would mark the restoration of an old friendship; Sula, instead, becomes Jude's lover for a brief time before abandoning him as she does other husbands of the town. Nel and Sula's "confrontation," on the deathbed of the latter, tells the reader and the best friend very little about what it is that makes Sula run. All that she admits is that she has "lived" and that if she and Nel had been such good friends, in fact, then her momentary "theft" of Jude might not have made any difference. Nel does not forgive Sula, but experiences, instead, a sense of emptiness and despair grounded, she later discovers after it doesn't matter anymore, in her own personal loss of Sula. She has not missed Jude, she finds out that afternoon, but her alter ego passionately embodied in the other woman. It turns out that the same degree of emotional ambivalence that haunts Nel plagues the female reader of this novel. What is it about this woman Sula that triggers such attraction and repulsion at once? We have no certain answers, just as Nel does not, but, rather, resign ourselves to a complex resonance of heeling which suggests that Sula is both necessary and frightening as a character realization.

In the relationship between Nel and Sula, Morrison demonstrates the female's rites-of-passage in their peculiar richness and impoverishment; the fabric of paradoxes—betrayals and sympathies, silences and aggressions, advances and sudden retreats—transmitted from mother to daughter, female to female, by mimetic gesture. That women learn primarily from other women strategies of survival and "homicide" is not news to anyone; indeed, this vocabulary of reference constitutes the chief revisionist, albeit implicit, feature of the women's liberation effort. Because Morrison has no political axe to grind in this novel—in other words, she is not writing according to a formula which demands that her female agents demonstrate a simple, transparent love between women—she is free, therefore, to pursue the delicate tissue of intimate patterns of response between women. In doing so, she identifies those meanings of womanhood which statements of public policy are rhetorically bound to suppress.

One of the structural marvels of *Sula* is its capacity to telescope the process of generation and its consequent network of convoluted relationships. *Sula* is a woman's text par excellence, even subscribing in its behavior to Woolf's intimations that the woman's book, given the severe demands on her time, is spare.[18] The novel is less than two hundred pages of prose, but within its imaginative economy various equations of domestic power are explored. For instance, Sula's relationships to her mother Hannah and grandmother Eva Peace are portrayed in selective moments. In other words, Sula's destiny is located only in part by Nel, while the older Peace women in their indifference to decorous social behavior provide the soil in which her moral isolation is seeded and nurtured. Hannah and Eva have quite another story to tell apart from Sula's, much of it induced by Eva's abandonment by her husband BoyBoy and her awful defiance in response. The reader is not privy to various tales of transmission between Eva and Hannah, but we decide by inference that their collective wisdom leads Hannah herself to an authenticity of person not alterable by the iron-clad duties of motherhood, nor the sweet, submissive obligations of female love. In short, Hannah Peace is self-indulgent, full of disregard for the traditional repertoire of women's vanity-related gestures, and the reader tends to love her for it—the "sweet, low and guileless" flirting, no patting of the hair, or rushing to change clothes, or quickly applying makeup, but barefoot in summer, "in the winter her feet in a man's leather slippers with the backs flattened under her heels. . . . Her voice trailed, dipped and bowed; she gave a chord to the simplest words. Nobody, but nobody, could say 'hey sugar' like Hannah . . ." (p. 36).

Just as Hannah's temperament is "light and playful," Morrison's prose glides over the surface of events with a careful allegiance to the riffs of folk utterance—deliberate, inclusive, very often on the verge of laughter—but the profound deception of this kind of plain talk, allegedly "unsophisticated," is the vigil it keeps in killing silence about what it suspects, even knows, but never expresses. This hidden agenda has a malicious side which Sula inherits without moral revision and correction. Morrison's stylistic choice in this passage is a significant clue to a reading of Hannah's character, a freedom of movement, a liberty of responses, worked out in a local school of realism. Hannah Peace is certainly not a philosopher, not even in secret, but that she rationalizes her address to the other in an unfailing economy of nuances implies a potential for philosophical grace. Among the women of *Sula,* the light rhythms usually conceal a deeper problem.

One of the more perplexing characters of recent American fiction, Eva Peace embodies a figure of both insatiable generosity and insatiable demanding. Like Hannah, Eva is seldom frustrated by the trammels of self-criticism, the terrible indecisiveness and scrupulosity released by doubt. Because Eva goes ahead without halting, ever, we could call her fault nothing less than innocence, and its imponderable cruelty informs her character with a kind of Old Testament logic. Eva behaves as though she were herself the sole instrument of divine inscrutable will. We are not exactly certain what oracular fever decides that she must immolate her son Plum.[19] Perhaps even his heroin addiction does not entirely explain it, but she literally rises to the task in moments of decisiveness, orchestrated in pity and judgment. Like an avenging deity who must sacrifice its creation in order to purify it, Eva swings and swoops on her terrible crutches from her son's room, about to prepare his fire. She holds him in her arms, recalling moments from his childhood before dousing him with kerosene:

> He opened his eyes and saw what he imagined was the great wing of an eagle pouring a wet lightness over him. Some kind of baptism, some kind of blessing, he thought. Everything is going to be all right, it said. Knowing that it was so he closed his eyes and sank back into the bright hole of sleep.
>
> Eva stepped back from the bed and let the crutches rest under her arms. She rolled a bit of newspaper into a tight stick about six inches long, lit it and threw it onto the bed where the kerosene-soaked Plum lay in smug delight. Quickly, as the *whoosh* of flames engulfed him, she shut the door and made her slow and painful journey back to the top of the house . . . (pp. 40–41).

Not on any level is the reader offered easy access to this scene. Its enumerated, overworked pathos, weighed against the victim's painful ignorance not only of his imminent death, but also of the requirements of his manhood generates contradictory feelings between shock and relief. The reader resents the authorial manipulation that engenders such feelings. The act itself, so violently divergent from the normal course of maternal actions and expectations, marks a subclimax. Further, it foreshadows the network of destruction, both willful and fortuitous, that ensnares Sula and Nel in an entanglement of predecided motivations. Eva, in effect, determines her own judgment, which Sula will seal without a hint or recourse to the deceptions or allegiances of kinship. Sula, who puts Eva in old age in an asylum, does not mistake her decision as a stroke of love or duty, nor does it echo any of the ambiguities of mercy.

Like Eva's, Sula's program of action as an adult woman is spontaneous and direct, but the reader in Sula's case does not temper her or his angle on Sula's behavior with compassion or second thought, as she or he tends to do in Eva's case. It could be argued, for instance, that Eva sacrifices Plum in order to save him, and however grotesque we probably adjudge her act, inspired by a moral order excluding contingency and doubt, no such excuse can be offered in Sula's behalf. We must also remember that Sula's nubile *singleness* and refusal of the acts and rites of maternity have implicitly corrupted her in our unconscious judgment and at a level of duplicity which our present "sexual arrangements" protect and mandate.[20] We encounter the raw details of her individualism, not engaged by naturalistic piety or existential rage, as a paradigm of wanton vanity. Her moral shape, however, does not come unprecedented or autonomously derived. Merging Eva's arrogance on the one hand and Hannah's self-indulgence on the other, "with a twist that was all her own imagination, she lived out her days exploring her own thoughts and emotions, giving them full reign, feeling no obligation to please anybody unless their pleasure pleased her" (p. 102).

Just as Hannah and Eva have been Sula's principal models, they have also determined certain issues which she will live out in her own career. It is probably not accidental that the question which haunts Hannah—have I been loved?—devolves on Sula with redoubtable fury. If it is true that love does not exist until it is named, then the answer to the enigma of Sula Peace is not any more forthcoming than if it were not so. Yet, certainly the enormous consequences of being loved or not are relevant by implication to the agents of the novel. Morrison does not elaborate, but the instances of the question's appearance—halting, uncertain, embarrassed, or inappropriate words on a character's tongue—conceal the single most important missing element in the women's encounter with each other. A revealing conversation between Eva and Hannah suggests that even for the adult female the intricacies and entanglements of mother love (or perhaps woman love without distinction) is a dangerous inquiry to engage. Hannah cannot even formulate the sentences that would say the magic words, but angles in on the problem with a childlike timidity which she can neither fake nor conceal. "I know you fed us and all. I was talking 'bout something else. Like. Like. Playin' with us. Did you ever, you know, play with us?" (p. 59).

This conversation may be compared with one that Sula overhears the summer of her twelfth year, between Hannah and a couple of friends. The three women confirm for each other the agonies of childrearing, but can never quite bring themselves around to admitting that love is contingent and human and all too often connected with notions of duty. Hannah tells one of the friends that her quality of love is sufficient. "You love [your child], like I love Sula. I just don't like her. That's the difference." And that's the "difference" that sends Sula "flying up the stairs," blankly "aware of a sting in her eye," until recalled by Nel's voice.

To pin the entire revelation of the source of Sula's later character development on this single episode would be a fallacy of overdetermination, but its strategic location in the text suggests that its function is crucial to the unfolding of events to come, to the way that Sula responds to them, and to the manner in which we interpret her responses. At least two other events unmistakably hark back to it. Chicken Little joins Sula and Nel later on the same afternoon in their play by the river. In the course of things Sula picked him up and "swung" him outward and then around and around. His knickers ballooned and his shrieks of frightened joy startled the birds and the fat grasshoppers. When he slipped from her hands and sailed out over the water they could still hear his bubbly laughter . . ." (p. 52).

Frozen in a moment of terror, neither girl can do more than stare at the "closed place in the water." Morrison aptly recreates the stark helplessness of two trapped people, gaining a dimension of horror because the people are children, drawn up short in a world of chance and danger. That they do nothing in particular, except recognize that Shadrack, the town's crack-brained veteran of World War I, has seen them and will not tell, consigns them both to a territory of their own most terrible judgment and isolation. In this case the adult conscience of each springs forth in the eyes of the other, leaving childhood abruptly in its wake. The killing edge is that the act itself must remain a secret. Unlike other acts of rites-of-passage, this one must *not* be communicated. At Chicken Little's funeral, Sula "simply cried" (p. 55), and from his grave site she and Nel, fingers laced, trot up the road "on a summer day wondering what happened to butterflies in the winter" (p. 57).

The interweave of lyricism and dramatic event is consistent with Morrison's strategies. Their juxtaposition does not appear to function ironically, but to present dual motifs in a progressive revelation that allows the reader to "swallow" dramatic occurences whose rhetoric, on the face of it, is unacceptable. At the same time we get in right perspective Sula's *lack* of tension—a tension that distinguishes the character stunned by her own ignorance, or by malice in the order of things. Sula, by contrast, just goes along, "completely free of ambition, with no affection for money, property, or things, no greed, no desire to command attention or compliments—no ego. For that reason she felt no compulsion to verify herself—be consistent with herself" (p. 103). That Sula apparently wants nothing, is curiously free of mimetic desire and its consequent pull toward willfulness, keep pity in check and release unease in its absence.

Sula's lack of egoism—which appears an incorrect assessment on the narrator's part—renders her an antipassionate spectator of the human scene, even beholding her mother's death by fire in calculated coolness. Weeks after Chicken's burial Hannah is in the backyard of the Peace household, lighting a fire in which she accidentally catches herself and burns to death. Eva recalls afterward that "she had seen Sula standing on the back porch just looking." When her friends insist that she is more than likely mistaken since Sula was "probably struck dumb" by the awful spectacle, Eva remains quietly convinced "that Sula had watched Hannah burn not because she was paralyzed, but because she was interested . . ." (p. 67).

This moment of Sula's interestedness, and we tend to give Eva the benefit of the doubt in this case, must be contrasted to her response to Chicken's drowning, precluding us from remaining impartial judges of her behavior, even as we understand its sources in the earlier event. Drawn into a cycle of negation, Sula at twelve is Sula at twenty, and the instruments of perception which the reader uses to decipher her character do not alter over the whole terrain of the work. From this point on, any course of action that she takes is already presumed by negating choices. Whether she steals Nel's husband or a million dollars matters less to the reader than to the other characters, since we clearly grasp the structure of her function as that of a radical amorality and consequently of a radical freedom. We would like to love Sula, or damn her, inasmuch as the myth of the black American woman allows only Manichean responses, but it impossible to do either. We can only behold in an absolute suspension of final judgment.

Morrison induces this ambiguous reading through an economy of means, none of which relate to the classic *bête noire* of black experience—the powerful predominance of white and the endless litany of hateful responses associated with it. That Sula is not bound by the customary alliances

to naturalism or historical determinism at least tells us what imperatives
she does not pursue. Still, deciding what traditions do inspire her character
is not made easier.

I would suggest that Hurston's Janie Starks presents a clear precedent.
Though not conforming at every point, I think the two characters lend
themselves to a comparative formula. In both cases, the writer wishes to
examine the particular details and propositions of liberty under constricted
conditions in a low mimetic mode of realism, that is, an instance of realism
in which the characters are not decisively superior in moral or social condition
to the reader.[21] Both Janie and Sula are provided an arena of action within
certain limits. In the former case, the character's dreams are usually too
encompassing to be accommodated within the space that circumscribes her.
The stuff of her dreams, then, remains disembodied, ethereal, out of time,
nor are her dreams fully differentiated, inasmuch as all we know about them
is their metaphorical conformity to certain natural or romantic configurations. It is probably accurate to say that the crucial absence for Janie has
been an intellectual chance, or the absence of a syntax distinctive enough
in its analytical requirements to realign a particular order of events to its
own demands. In other words, Janie is stuck in the limitations of dialect,
while her creator is free to make use of a range of linguistic resources to
achieve her vision.

The principle of absence that remains inchoate for Janie is articulate
for Sula in terms whose intellectual implications are unmistakable—Sula
lacks the shaping vision of art, and the absence is as telling in the formation
of her character as the lack of money or an appropriately ordered space might
be for the heroines, for example, of Henry James's *Portrait of a Lady* or *Wings
of the Dove;* in both of James's works the heroines are provided with *money,*
a term that James's narrator assigns great weight in deciding what strategies
enable women to do battle with the world, though the equation between
gold and freedom is ironically burdened here. In Woolf's conception of
personal and creative freedom for the woman, *money, space,* and *time* figure
prominently.

It is notable that Janie and Sula, within the social modalities that
determine them, are actually quite well off. Their suffering, therefore, transcends the visceral and concrete, moving progressively toward the domain
of symbols. In sharp contrast to Walker's Vyry, the latter-day heroines
approach the threshold of speaking and acting *for self,* or the organization
of one's resources with preeminent reference to the highest form of self-
regard, the urge to speak one's own words urgently. Hurston and Morrison
after her are both in the process of abandoning the vision of the corporate

good as a mode of heroic suffering. Precisely what will take its place defines the dilemma of *Sula* and its protagonist. The dilemma itself highlights problems of figuration for black female characters whose future, whose terms of existence, are not entirely known at the moment.

The character of Sula impresses the reader as a problem in interpretation because, for one thing, the objective myth of the black American woman, at least from the black woman's point of view, is drawn in valorized images that intrude against the text, or compete with it like a jealous goddess. That this privileged other narrative is counterbalanced by its opposite, equally exaggerated and distorted, simply reinforces the heroics to the extent that the black woman herself imagines only one heroine—and that is herself. *Sula* attempts a correction of this uninterrupted superiority on the one hand and unrelieved pathology on the other; the reader's dilemma arises in having to choose. The duplicitous reader embraces the heroics with no intent of disproof or unbelief, while the brave one recognizes that the negating countermyth would try to establish a dialectical movement between the subperspectives, gaining a totally altered perspective in the process.[22] In other words, Sula, Vyry, and Janie need not be seen as the terms of an either/or proposition. The three characters here may be identified as sub-perspectives, or *angles onto* a larger seeing. The struggle that we bring with us to *Sula,* indeed, the implicit proposition upon which the text is based, is the imperative that requires our coming to terms with the very complexities that a juggling of perspectives demands.

Sula is not the "other" as one kind of reading would suggest, or perhaps as we might wish, but a figure of the rejected and vain part of the self—ourselves—who in its thorough corruption and selfishness cannot utter, believe in, nor prepare for, love. I am not entirely sure that Sula speaks for us on the lower frequencies—though she could very well. The importance of this text is that she speaks at all.

In a conversation with Robert Stepto, Toni Morrison confirms certain critical conjectures that are made here concerning the character of Sula. "[She] was hard, for me; very difficult to make up that kind of character. Not difficult to think it up, but difficult to describe a woman who could be used as classic type of evil force. Other people could use her that way. And at the same time, I didn't want to make her freakish or repulsive or unattractive. I was interested at that time in doing a very old, worn-out idea, which was to do something with good and evil, but putting it in different terms. . . ."[23]

As Morrison goes on to discuss the idea, Sula and Nel are to her mind an alterity of agents—"two sides of the same person, or two sides of one extraordinary character."[24] Morrison does not attribute the birth of her idea to any particular cultural or historical event and certainly not to the most recent wave of American feminism, but it does seem fairly clear that a Sula Peace if *for black American literature,* if not for the incredibly rich potential of black American female personality, a radical alternative to Vyry Ware and less so, to placid Janie Crawford Starks. "This was really part of the difficulty—I didn't know anyone like her. I never knew a woman like that at any rate. But I knew women who looked like that, who looked like they *could* be like that. And then you remember women who were a little bit different in [one's] town, you know."[25]

If we identify Sula as a kind of countermythology, we are saying that she is no longer bound by a rigid pattern of predictions, predilections, and anticipations. Even though she is a character in a novel, her strategic place as *potential being* might argue that *subversion* itself—law breaking—is an aspect of liberation that women must confront from its various angles, in its different guises. Sula's outlawry may not be the best kind, but that she has the will toward rebellion itself *is* the stunning idea. This project in liberation, paradoxically, has no particular dimension in time, yet it is for all time.

NOTES

[1] Mary Helen Washington, ed., *Black-Eyed Susans: Classic Stories by and about Black Women* (New York: Anchor Books, 1975). From the introduction, xxxii.

[2] "Intimate Things in Place: A Conversation with Toni Morrison," in *Chant of Saints: A Gathering of Afro-American Literature, Art, and Scholarship,* ed. Michael S. Harper and Robert B. Stepto (Urbana: University of Illinois Press, 1979), 213–30.

[3] Harold Bloom's by-now familiar revision on the Freudian oedipal myth in relationship to the theme of literary successions and fortunes is not applicable to the community of black American women writers, even as a necessary critical fable. Bloom speaks for a powerful and an *assumed* patriarchal tradition, posited by a dominative culture, in the transmission of a political, as well as literary, wealth; in the case of black women's writing (and women's writing without modification) the myth of wealth as an aspect of literary "inheritance" tends to be sporadic. See Bloom, *The Anxiety of Influence: A Theory of Poetry* (New York: Oxford University Press, 1973), and *A Map of Misreading* (New York: Oxford University Press, 1975).

[4] Toni Morrison, *Sula* (New York: Bantam Books, 1975), 105, emphases mine. All references are from this edition, and page numbers are supplied in parentheses in the text.

[5] Bell Hooks [Gloria Watkins], *Ain't I a Woman: Black Women and Feminism* (Boston: South End Press, 1981). The particular role of Daniel Moynihan's *Report* is put in perspective here with what Hooks calls "the continuing devaluation of black womanhood," 51–87.

It is with crucial deliberation that the editors of a recent feminist collection of scholarship call their volume *All the Women Are White, All the Blacks Are Men, but Some of Us Are Brave* (Old Westbury, N.Y.: Feminist Press, 1982). Editors Gloria T. Hull, Patricia Bell Scott, and Barbara Smith realize that public discourse—certainly its most radical critical statements included—lapses into a cul-de-sac when it approaches this community of women and their writers.

[6] Erich Auerbach, "Fontunata," in *Mimesis: The Representation of Reality in Western Literature*, trans. Willard Trask (New York: Doubleday Anchor Books, 1957). In tracing the shift in stylistic convention and emotional resonance from the literature of classical antiquity to the modern period Auerbach provides a definition of the change which I would consider crucial to any consideration of the issue of "realism," "the birth of a spiritual movement in the depths of the common people, from within the everyday occurrences of contemporary life, which thus assumes an importance it could never have assumed in antique literature" (p. 37).

[7] Margaret Walker, *How I Wrote* Jubilee (Chicago: Third World Press, 1972). *Jubilee* was submitted as Walker's Ph.D. dissertation to the University of Iowa Creative Writers' Workshop. The source material for the novel is based on the life story of the author's great-grandmother, told to her by her grandmother in the best tradition of oral his/herstory. The specificities of this transmitted tale from one generation to another was researched by Walker over nearly two decades, and it anticipates another odyssey of search in Alex Haley's *Roots*, a detailed study of an African-American genealogy. Walker later on actually brought suit against Haley for the supposed plagiarizing of a theme that Walker considers special, if not unique, to her own work.

[8] Paul Tillich, *A History of Christian Thought: From Its Judaic and Hellenistic Origins to Existentialism*, ed. Carl E. Braaten (New York: Touchstone, 1972). My own use of Tillich's "theonomy" is vastly simplified and lifted out of the context that the theologian establishes between the idea and its relationship to the Christian European eras of sacred theology. But I hope that we might summarize a complicated idea here without seriously violating the original.

[9] The student of Americana will immediately recognize that "God" is manifest cause to worldly effect within a certain configuration of cultural values; Perry Miller's classic work on early New England communities renders a detailed analysis of the view; cf. "God's Controversy with New England," in *The New England Mind: The Seventeenth Century* (Boston: Beacon Press, 1961), 463–92.

[10] Margaret Walker, *Jubilee* (Boston: Houghton Mifflin, 1966), 3–4. All references are from this edition, and page numbers are supplied in parentheses in the text.

[11] Emile Durkheim, *The Elementary Forms of Religious Life*, trans. Joseph Ward Swain (New York: Free Press, 1965).

[12] Robert Hemenway, *Zora Neale Hurston: A Literary Biography* (Urbana: University of Illinois Press, 1977). This important work on Hurston's life provides an exhaustive account of the writer's various relationships. Hurston herself was a lover of males, but never sustained the liaisons quite long enough for us to see any pattern in this chapter of her biography except as short-lived serial monogamies.

[13] Zora Neale Hurston, *Their Eyes Were Watching God* (New York: Fawcett Premier Books, 1969), 121. All references are to his edition and page numbers are supplied in parentheses in the text.

[14] Zora Neale Hurston, "What White Publishers Won't Print," in *I Love Myself When I Am Laughing . . . and Then Again When I Am Looking Mean and Impressive*, ed. Alice Walker (Old Westbury, N.Y.: Feminist Press, 1979), 169–73. In discussing why white American publishers of her time would only publish the "morbid" about the lives of black Americans, Hurston suggests what is both frightening and familiar to contemplate. "It is assumed that all non-Anglo-Saxons are uncomplicated stereotypes. Everybody knows all about them. They are lay figures mounted in the museum where all may take them in at a glance. They are made of bent wires without insides at all. So how could anybody write a book about the non-existent?" (p. 170). But we might also consider whether or not the obscene didn't happen—if black people themselves did not come to see their lives as a very fixed, monolithic, immobile quality of human experience? Alice Walker in the dedication to this volume (p. 2)

points out that if Hurston were a "colorist," as some of her critics have claimed, then she "was not blind and . . . saw that black men (and black women) have been, and are, colorist to an embarrassing degree."

[15] W. E. B. Du Bois, *The Souls of Black Folk: Essays and Sketches* (New York: Fawcett Publications, 1967). Du Bois's classic reading of the African-American predicament is posed in the opening chapter of this germinal piece. He writes, "one ever feels his twoness,—an American, a Negro; two souls, two thoughts, two unreconciled strivings; two warring ideals in one dark body, whose dogged strength alone keeps it from being torn asunder" (p. 17).

[16] Zora Neale Hurston, "My Folks," *Dust Tracks on a Road,* introduction by Larry Neal (Philadelphia: J. B. Lippincott, 1971), 12–32.

[17] The term "ancestral imperative" does not originate in Albert Murray, but his use of it is dialectical and expansive. The best demonstration of Murray's argument is his *South to a Very Old Place* (New York: McGraw-Hill, 1971).

[18] Virginia Woolf, *A Room of One's Own* (New York: Harcourt, Brace and World, 1957), 61–81.

[19] Professor Nellie McKay recently reminded me that African-American women during the era of slavery often killed their offspring in order to forestall their enslavement. Read against McKay's interpretation, Eva Peace's "intervention" is historically grounded at the same time that it does not lose its awful aspects. The convergence of historical motivation, individual willfulness, and the mother's violation of blood rites would create one of the profounder bases of tension across the work.

[20] See, for example, the description of these arrangements in Dorothy Dinnerstein, *The Mermaid and the Minotaur: Sexual Arrangements and Human Malaise* (New York: Harper Colophon Books, 1976).

[21] The terms are taken from Northrop Frye, "Historical Criticism: Theory of Modes," in *Anatomy of Criticism: Four Essays* (Princeton: Princeton University Press, 1957), 36–67.

[22] Kenneth Burke, "The Four Master Tropes," in *A Grammar of Motives,* appendix D (New York: Prentice-Hall, 1945), 503–17. Burke's refinement of a notion of dialectics in art is significant both as an image and concept of radical revision. His "perspective of perspectives"—the principle of the "modified noun"—locates an ideal against which we might try to imagine the future of Afro-American letters and our meditation concerning them.

[23] Harper and Stepto, 215.

[24] Ibid., 216.

[25] Ibid., 217.

KEITH E. BYERMAN

Beyond Realism:
The Fictions of Toni Morrison

In contrast to the anguished narrative consciousnesses of Gayl Jones's fiction, Toni Morrison creates conventionally stable central characters. Moreover, she adds even greater reliability by using primarily omniscient narrations; even when there is a first-person narrator, as in *The Bluest Eye,* that voice is complemented by an omniscient perspective. ⟨. . .⟩ But in fact, she uses the narrative to present disordered, violent, perverse worlds less overt but no less troubling than those of Jones. These novels present us with murder, incest, necrophilia, child abuse, insanity, terrifying family secrets, and a general sense of life teetering on the edge of dissolution. Such material presented through reliable narration creates a tension that intensifies the emotional impact of the fiction.

The rational telling of extreme events forces a radical reconsideration of commonly held assumptions about black life and black-white relationships. Through its extremism, it defamiliarizes the reader by pointing to the violent effects of such ordinary phenomena as popular culture, bourgeois ideas about property, love, sexual initiation and sex roles, family, and the past. Perhaps more than any other writer under consideration in this study, Morrison shows the exploitative nature of logocentric orders.[1] She dramatizes the destructive power implicit in the control of various symbolic systems. In her fiction that power creates grotesque victims, often including those who seem to be in positions of domination. Her novels are quest tales in which key characters search for the hidden sign capable of giving them

From *Fingering the Jagged Grain: Tradition and Form in Recent Black Fiction* (Athens: University of Georgia Press, 1985), pp. 184–216.

strength and/or identity. In a significant twist, those who find what they seek become the most thoroughly victimized, while those who are turned in their searches toward some other goal (which is usually an absence rather than the originally desired presence) are most often triumphant. The changed pursuit is in the direction of some black folk value, such as true community, true family name, or authentic black history. The revision of goals makes possible a loosening of the control of logocentrism so as to achieve a black selfhood that negates that control.

In *The Bluest Eye* (1970) the destructiveness of control rather than the creativity of negation predominates. Pecola Breedlove, a black girl thought by everyone to be ugly, finds herself enthralled by the blue eyes of Shirley Temple. Everywhere in her world, white skin and blue eyes are taken as signs of beauty. The image manifests itself in movies, billboards, children's drinking cups, Mary Jane candies, other characters, and in the excerpts from a primary-school reader that constitute both epigraph and chapter titles in the novel. Conversely, the lack of such traits in Pecola leads her and virtually everyone else in the book to consider her worthless. Black children deflect their self-hatred by verbally assaulting her; lighter-skinned blacks, children and adults, proclaim their superiority by alternately patronizing and attacking her; and her own mother makes clear her preferences when she slaps Pecola aside in order to comfort a white child.[2]

In response to this psychological violence, Pecola takes up a quest for blue eyes. Initially, she limits herself to drinking white milk from a cup with a Shirley Temple decal and to buying and eating Mary Jane candies. Through this popular-culture Eucharist, she hopes to be transubstantiated from common black clay into spiritual whiteness. At this stage, she achieves only the momentary happiness of seeing the white faces and wishing to have one. Later on, after the trauma of being raped by her father, she loses all sense of reality, visits a self-styled conjure man, and believes that she has actually undergone the change in eye color that she so strongly and pathetically desired. Claudia, part-time narrator and childhood companion, points out the moral of Pecola's story:

> All of us—all who knew her—felt so wholesome after we cleaned ourselves on her. We were so beautiful when we stood astride her ugliness. Her simplicity decorated us, her guilt sanctified us, her pain made us glow with health, her awkwardness made us think we had a sense of humor. Her inarticulateness made us believe we were eloquent. Her poverty kept us generous. Even her waking dreams we used—to silence our own nightmares.

And she let us, and thereby deserved our contempt. We honed our egos on her, padded our characters with her frailty, and yawned in the fantasy of our strength.[3]

Perhaps more significant than the catalogue of forms of victimization in the above quotation is the "we" that makes Pecola the victim. More than the melancholy story of a little girl driven mad by the world's hostility, *The Bluest Eye* tells the story of the community and society that persecutes her. Pecola may be the central character, but she is far from the only victim of the blue eyes. "We" individually and collectively are both victimizer and victim; and, while the roles vary with each character, it is also the case that the role of victimizer results from that character's own victimization by a larger society. Each person fantasizes that he has real self-determining power. But Claudia, at the end, knows better: "We substituted good grammar for intellect; we switched habits to simulate maturity; we rearranged lies and called it truth, seeing in the new pattern of an old idea the Revelation and the Word" (*The Bluest Eye*, 159).

This pursuit of the Word entraps the characters. Pauline Breedlove differs from her daughter Pecola only in the sense that the image she believes in comes from the movie screen rather than the milk cup. Whiteness is goodness, and she feels more at home in the white kitchen where she works than in the rundown house she shares with her family. In the chapter giving her history, we learn that she has compensated for her lameness and putative ugliness by creating order wherever possible. In most cases the order is a trivial arrangement of objects, but she learns from the movies that a white home is the paragon of order. Her work in such homes makes possible a control in her life that is impossible in her own existence as a poor black woman with a family suffering under the manipulations of that very white world she loves.

She only overcomes the self-hatred implied by such values through the self-righteousness of her religion. To reinforce this goodness she needs the evil of her husband Cholly: "She was an active church woman, did not drink, smoke, or carouse, defended herself mightily against Cholly, rose above him in every way, and felt she was fulfilling a mother's role conscientiously when she pointed out their father's faults to keep them away from having them, or punished them when they showed any slovenliness, no matter how slight, when she worked twelve to sixteen hours a day to support them. And the world itself agreed with her" (*The Bluest Eye*, 102).

Cholly inverts Pauline's values. He deals with self-hatred and oppression by becoming as evil as possible, even to the point of raping his daughter and burning his own house. Behind this "bad-nigger" persona lies a history of distortions of the principal relationships and rituals of life. He is abandoned in a junkyard by his mother, who was never certain of the identity of the father. His first sexual encounter is interrupted by white men whose derisive comments render him impotent. His search for the man he believes to be his father ends at a dark alley dice game when the man chases him away, believing he has come only for money. Such events make him both anti- and asocial. He hates the girl of his sexual humiliation rather than the white men because she was a witness to his powerlessness; he has no sense of socially acceptable behavior because he has been denied primary socialization; and he is incapable of appropriate fatherly behavior because he has had no parents.

The most perverse act of his life, the rape of Pecola, is a product of his confusion of violence and love.

> She was washing dishes. Her small back hunched over the sink. Cholly saw her dimly and could not tell what he saw or what he felt. Then he became aware that he was uncomfortable; next he felt the discomfort dissolve into pleasure. The sequence of his emotions was revulsion, guilt, pity, then love. His revulsion was a reaction to her young, helpless, hopeless presence. Her back hunched that way; her head to one side as though crouching from a permanent and unrelieved blow. Why did she have to look so whipped? She was a child—unburdened—why wasn't she happy? The clear statement of her misery was an accusation. He wanted to break her neck—but tenderly. Guilt and impotence rose in a bilious duet. What could he do for her—ever? What give her? What say to her? What could a burned-out black man say to the hunched back of his eleven-year-old daughter? If he looked into her face, he would see those haunted, loving eyes. The haunt- edness would irritate him—the love would move him to fury. How dare she love him? Hadn't she any sense at all? What was he supposed to do about that? Return it? How? What could his calloused hands produce to make her smile? What of his knowl- edge of the world and of life could be useful to her? What could his heavy arms and befuddled brain accomplish that would earn him his own respect, that would in turn allow him to accept her love? His hatred of her slimed in his stomach and threatened to become vomit. But just before the puke moved from anticipation to sensation, she shifted her weight and stood on one foot scratch- ing the back of her calf with her toe. . . . The timid, tucked-

in look of the scratching toe—that was what Pauline was doing
the first time he saw her in Kentucky. Leaning over a fence staring
at nothing in particular. The creamy toe of her bare foot scratching a velvet leg. It was such a small and simple gesture, but it
filled him then with a wondering softness. Not the usual lust to
part tight legs with his own, but a tenderness, a protectiveness.
A desire to cover her foot with his hand and gently nibble away
the itch from the calf with his teeth. He did it then. . . . He
did it now. . . . The Confused mixture of his memories of Pauline
and the doing of a wild and forbidden thing excited him. . . .
Surrounding all of this lust was a border of politeness. He wanted
to fuck her—tenderly. But the tenderness would not hold. (*The
Bluest Eye,* 127–28)

The various ways in which society has conditioned Cholly so as to
control him have had the effect of denying him a socially acceptable means
of expressing an authentic human emotion. Having learned that he is nothing
but an object of disgust, he, like Pauline, can do nothing other than objectify
Pecola. Each of them exploits her because his own exploitation makes it
impossible to do otherwise.

In the larger community, objectification is also common. White store-
keepers, light-skinned children, and black middle-class adults all see this
black child as a piece of filth repugnant yet necessary to their own senses of
cleanliness.

Alternatives to this pattern of victimization can be found in two sets
of characters, the whores and the McTeer family. Though diametrically
opposed in both values and ambitions, both groups offer ways of coping
with the pain of experience. The whores accomplish this by being what they
are:

Three merry gargoyles. Three merry harridans. Amused by a
long-ago time of ignorance. They did not belong to those generation of prostitutes created in novels, with great and generous
hearts, dedicated, because of the horror of circumstance, to ame-
liorating the luckless, barren life of men, taking money incidentally and humbly for their "understanding." Nor were they from
that sensitive breed of young girl, gone wrong at the hands of
fate, forced to cultivate an outward brittleness in order to protect
her springtime from further shock, but knowing full well she
was cut out for better things, and could make the right man
happy. Neither were they the sloppy, inadequate whores who,

> unable to make a living at it alone, turn to drug consumption
> and traffic or pimps to help complete their scheme of self-
> destruction, avoiding suicide only to punish the memory of some
> absent father or to sustain the misery of some silent mother. (*The
> Bluest Eye,* 47)

They are women who do their work without illusion, self-hatred, or guilt.
They have no use for their customers or for those dishonest women who
pretend virtue but are in fact unfaithful. They respect only the innocents,
like Pecola, and truly religious women who they see as having the same
honesty and integrity as themselves.

They are also the primary folk figures in the novel. Even their names—
Poland, China, Maginot Line—suggest larger-than-life characters. Maginot
Line entertains Pecola with outlandish stories of past loves and adventures.
She keeps alive the idea of love in her recollections of Dewey Prince, the
only man she did not sell herself to. China is adept at verbal dueling,
constantly drawing Maginot Line back from the edge of sentimentality with
sarcasm. Poland is "forever ironing, forever singing" (*The Bluest Eye,* 44).
Her songs are blues, which serve less to express personal problems than to
entertain through reminders of the nature of the world in which they live.
These folk arts enable them to transcend the private obsessions of other
characters. The world may well be a place of misery and doom, but folk
wisdom dictates that one adapts to circumstances rather than resignedly
move toward evasion or self-destruction. Blues and folk tales imply that
trouble is *both* personal and communal and that life is a matter of adaptation
and survival rather than resignation and death. The whores treat themselves
and Pecola with consideration because they neither despair nor hope.

Ironically, the McTeer family, although hostile to the behavior and
attitude of the whores, make a decent life for themselves by working from
the same principles. One of the functions of the family in the novel is to
serve as a counterpoint for the Breedloves. Pauline slaps Pecola and protects
a little white girl, whereas Mrs. McTeer takes in the black girl, even though
it is a strain on her family's resources. Cholly rapes his own daughter, whereas
Mr. McTeer nearly kills a boarder who fondles his daughter. The Breedloves
are so absorbed in variations of self-hatred that they see each other only as
objects, whereas the McTeers make themselves into a family despite all the
economic, psychological, and social forces opposing them.

This is not to suggest that the McTeers are sentimentalized into the
Dick-and-Jane family of the school reader. Morrison insists that it is in fact
those who refuse such sentimentality who are the most heroic. The McTeers

live without illusion as much as possible. The parents whip their children, complain about the burdens of life, and struggle only semisuccessfully to acquire the necessities for survival. The children must face embarrassment because of their cheap clothing and lack of money and must deal with the same assaults on their race as Pecola. But unlike the Breedloves and the light-skinned Geraldine and Maureen, they do not measure their human worth by the symbols of the dominant white culture. Although the Shirley Temple cup belongs to the McTeers and although Frieda, Claudia's sister, loves the child actress's movies, no one in the family defines himself or herself by a lack of whiteness. They accept their difference from whites as a given of their existence, not as a deprivation to be evaded or mourned.

Claudia, the narrator, is the most emphatic in asserting this difference. She serves for a while as a rebel figure, similar to the young Jane Pittman in Ernest Gaines's novel. She plots insults and attacks on Maureen Peel, who glories in her lack of melanin. More important, she almost ritualistically destroys the white doll she receives for Christmas:

> The other dolls, which were supposed to bring me great pleasure, succeeded in doing quite the opposite. When I took it to bed, its hard unyielding limbs resisted my flesh—the tapered finger-tips on those dimpled hands scratched. If, in sleep, I turned, the bone-cold head collided with my own. It was a most uncomfortable, patently aggressive sleeping companion. To hold it was no more rewarding. The starched gauze or lace on the cotton dress irritated any embrace. I had only one desire: to dismember it. To see of what it was made, to discover the dearness, to find the beauty, the desirability that had escaped me, but apparently only me. Adults, older girls, shops, magazines, newspapers, window signs—all the world had agreed that a blue-eyed, yellow-haired, pink-skinned doll was what every girl child treasured. . . . I could not love it. But I could examine it to see what it was that all the world said was lovable. Break off the tiny fingers, bend the flat feet, loosen the hair, twist the head around, and the thing made one sound—a sound they said was the sweet and plaintive cry "Mama," but which sounded to me like the bleat of a dying lamb, or, more precisely, our icebox door opening on rusty hinges in July. Remove the cold and stupid eyeball, it would bleat still, "Ahhhhhh," take off the head, shake out the sawdust, crack the back against the brass bed rail, it would bleat still. The gauze back would split, and I could see the disk with

six holes, the secret of the sound. A mere metal roundness. (*The*
Bluest Eye, 20–21)

The doll is an emblem of a manipulative, inverted order. Adults and
children are encouraged to believe that this combination of wood, cloth,
and metal is an idealization of girlhood and that the noise it makes is a
human cry. Claudia herself confuses illusion and reality when she does violence to real white girls who seem to her imitations of the doll. Claudia's
instinct to penetrate to the secret of the doll's voice and demystify it is
appropriate, but her identification of objects and human beings is a measure
of her acceptance of the culture's dehumanization. Even if the white girls
take their identity from the doll, as its deliberate design and mechanism
implies that they should, even if, in other words, they take the object as
more real than themselves, their voices nonetheless remain human voices
and their pain human pain. Claudia ultimately fails, not because of her
confusion, which she overcomes, but because she refuses to live in her
demystified knowledge:

> When I learned how repulsive this disinterested violence [against
> white girls] was, that it was repulsive because it was disinterested,
> my shame floundered about for refuge. The best hiding place was
> love. Thus the conversion from pristine sadism to fabricated
> hatred, to fraudulent love. It was a small step to Shirley Temple.
> I learned much later to worship her, just as I learned to delight
> in cleanliness, knowing, even as I learned, that the change was
> adjustment without improvement. (*The Bluest Eye,* 22)

The state of rebellion cannot be sustained because it requires a perpetual
opposition and negation without hope of victory. *The Bluest Eye,* then, is
about the difficulty of achieving individuality and full humanity in an objectifying and manipulative society. To refuse that state of tension and
negation is to accept self-hatred, illusion, and even madness. In this novel,
the best that can be accomplished is an intimation of what a fully human
condition might be.

Sula (1974) probes even more deeply for the origins of oppression,
victimization, and social order. In the process, it also explores the possibilities for negating such control. Consistent with the dialectics of language, Morrison finds both control and its negation in naming. When a
place, person, thing, or event is labeled, the namer assumes it to be fixed,
present, and under his or her dominion. By such a practice, experience can
be organized and even reified. But in *Sula* the process of designation creates

possibilities not intended by the namer, possibilities that can be realized in human history, though frequently only with great suffering. The effort to escape this dialectic, as Sula does, is doomed, as she is. She cannot avoid being part of the social order, since even rebellion is named and used in the community.

The uses of naming are developed in the book long before the title character appears. The novel opens with a "nigger joke" associated with the origin of the black community. According to the legend, a white man promised freedom and land to his slave if a particularly difficult task were performed. When the work was done, the freedom was given without a second thought, but the land was a different matter. The white man convinced the black one that the rocky hill country was bottom land, since it was the "bottom of heaven." Thus, the black community of Bottom was created above the white town of Medallion. Here, as elsewhere, Morrison suggests the economic underpinnings of racism, as well as the function of language in establishing and maintaining social control. The white man manipulates the ambiguity of language to his advantage and thus determines the economic condition of blacks for generations.

But this control is not necessarily absolute: "Still, it was lovely up in the Bottom. After the town grew and the farm land turned into a village and the village into a town and the streets of Medallion were hot and dusty with progress, those heavy trees that sheltered the shacks up in the Bottom were wonderful to see. And the hunters who went there sometimes wondered in private if maybe the white farmer was right after all. Maybe it was the bottom of Heaven."[4] Thus the attempt to control through language is always subject to negation by the very nature of language itself. Compulsion can cause suffering and sorrow, as it does in the exploitation that creates and maintains the Bottom, but it cannot be totalitarian. Traces of meaning exist that make for other possibilities. Black refusal to be dehumanized by the "nigger joke" creates the ironic realization of the joke's language.

The second instance of control through naming comes in the form of National Suicide Day, created by Shadrack, a psychologically damaged veteran who walked through the fires of World War I. He suffered shell shock when, during battle, "he turned his head a little to the right and saw the face of a soldier near him fly off. Before he could register shock, the rest of the soldier's head disappeared under the inverted soup bowl of his helmet. But stubbornly, taking no direction from the brain, the body of the headless soldier ran on, with energy and grace ignoring altogether the drip and slide of brain tissue down its back" (*Sula*, 8). The surprise and the messiness together render Shadrack nearly insane.

The bullet dissolves not merely the soldier's head but also Shad's sense of reality and identity. The world ceases to have any inherent order, and he has no name. After he leaves the hospital, "a haven of more than a year, only eight days of which he fully recollected," he is on his own, "with no past, no language, no tribe, no source, no address book, no comb, no pencil, no clock, no pocket handkerchief, no rug, no bed, no can opener, no faded postcard, no soap, no key, no tobacco pouch, no soiled underwear and nothing nothing nothing to do" (*Sula,* 12). He is deprived of all the markers of an identity, which are also the markers of a social existence. Without such possessions and the social and economic orders implied by them, he cannot be a human being.

Only when he finds by accident someone who knows him, a town to live in, a job to do, and a language (that of obscenity) to speak can he begin to function. But this order cannot counteract the primal chaos of death. To live with this obsession, he must create an order for it, which he does in National Suicide Day: "In sorting it all out, he hit on the notion that if one day a year were devoted to it [death], everybody could get it out of the way and the rest of the year would be safe and free" (*Sula,* 14).

Significantly, this private neurosis becomes part of the social order: "As time went along, the people took less notice of these January thirds, or rather they thought they did, thought they had no attitudes or feelings one way or another about Shadrack's annual solitary parade. In fact they had simply stopped remarking on the holiday because they had absorbed it into their thoughts, into their language, into their lives" (*Sula,* 15). Though the designation lacks for the community the traumatic significance that it holds for Shad, nonetheless its incorporation into the group's language holds *in potentia* meaning that will later be catastrophically realized. The mad rituals of a madman seem to be naturalized and thus neutralized by the community, but that very folk process makes the actualization of the name, through repetition, in fact feasible.

An entirely different kind of order, one that appears to be no order at all, is created by Eva, Sula's grandmother. Eva begins as the victim of a white- and male-dominated society. When she and her children are abandoned by her husband, she is left with little food and no money in the middle of the winter. She saves the life of her baby by using the last of her lard to remove fecal stones from his bowels. Realizing the hopelessness of the situation, she leaves her children with a neighbor and disappears for eighteen months. When she returns, she is missing a leg but has a substantial income. The mystery of her quest becomes the material of folk legend, and she becomes a symbol of the will to survive. With the money she builds a ramshackle house and takes in boarders and various kinds of stray beings.

She establishes herself as a queen, sitting on an ersatz throne constructed from a rocking chair and a children's wagon. From this position, she entertains the men of the community.

A key element in the order Eva maintains is this relationship with men. While Morrison suggests that both Eva and her daughter Hannah are enthralled by "manlove," the men themselves seem very much mere playthings. While Hannah expresses the idea by having intercourse with any willing man, Eva is more derogatory. Her former husband is nicknamed Boyboy, while her son is called Plum, and an apparently white tenant Tarbaby. In the most bizarre naming, three boys she adopts are designated "the deweys," though they have neither appearance nor background in common. As a manifestation of Eva's power of naming, the boys become identical in mentality and sensibility; in fact, they become virtually a separate species.

In some sense, Eva sees herself as a god figure. She held the power of life and death over her children, she created the race of deweys, she names and manipulates men as she sees fit. When Plum returns from the war addicted to heroin, she chooses to destroy the remnants of his being by setting fire to him. Later on, she is punished for this hubris by having to watch helplessly as Hannah becomes accidentally engulfed in flame and then seared when neighbors throw water on her to put out the fire. Moreover, it is Eva's lack of the leg she apparently chose to sacrifice for money that makes it impossible to reach and save her daughter. Thus, the very sign of Eva's power comes to be the negation of that power.

The underlying order of which Shadrack and Eva are extreme metaphors is that of the community. It establishes the forms of male-female, parent-child, individual-society, and good-evil relationships. It creates rituals recognizing the mysteries of birth, sex, and death; it codifies acceptable attitudes toward power, whether personal, sexual, or racial. In other words, it makes the conventions that define life in the Bottom.

Morrison is at her best perhaps when showing how such rites and conventions operate in ordinary experience. At the funeral of a child, the women participate in a mourning ceremony:

> As Reverend Deal moved into his sermon, the hands of the women unfolded like pairs of raven's wings and flew high above their hats in the air. They did not hear all of what he said; they heard the one word, or phrase, or inflection that was for them the connection between the event and themselves. For some time it was the term "Sweet Jesus." And they saw the Lamb's eye and the truly innocent victim: themselves. . . . Then they left their pews. For with some emotions one has to stand. They spoke, for

they were full and needed to say. They swayed, for the rivulets
of grief or of ecstasy must be rocked. And when they thought of
all that life and death locked into that little closed coffin they
danced and screamed, not to protest God's will but to acknowledge it and confirm once more their conviction that the only way
to avoid the Hand of God is to get in it. (*Sula*, 65–66)

The need here is to express, not to explain. The funeral is not the cause but
the occasion to reaffirm a position as both victim and elect. The ritual
transforms an absence into a presence, makes a private, physical loss into a
communal, spiritual gain. The language of the passage, which modulates
into a litany, reinforces the pattern by suggesting the recurrence and thus
permanence of structures.

But the treatment and attitude toward Sula most overtly reveal the
patterns of the community. National Suicide Day could be naturalized by
the people, as could Eva's arrogance. Each in some way recapitulates the
need for an order, a name. But Sula refuses ordering and naming, so for the
community she becomes the embodiment of evil. By ignoring or deliberately
violating the conventions, she threatens the assumptions by which life in
the Bottom is organized and made meaningful. By naming her evil, they
seek to bring her within the framework of their worldview, but, as we shall
see, this effort is itself inherently ambiguous.

Morrison establishes early on the events that make Sula's identity an
essentially negative one. Sula overhears a conversation between her mother
and other women during which Hannah remarks: "You love her, like I love
Sula. I just don't like her" (*Sula*, 57). Later the same day, a little boy drowns
when he slips from her hands while they are playing. "The first experience
taught her there was no other that you could count on; the second that there
was no self to count on either. She had no center, no speck around which
to grow"(*Sula*, 118–19). For a time she has an epicenter of sorts in Nel,
her girlhood friend. Some of the best passages are devoted to the rites of
passage they go through together. Their experiences of emerging womanhood, of personal bonds, of death and guilt are very effectively rendered.

Ultimately, however, a break must come, for Nel eventually defines
herself by community conventions, while Sula exists outside such structures.
Nel's wedding, which marks the end of part 1, is the occasion of the break.
It marks the moment at which Nel actualizes her underlying desire for order
by making an identity through a man rather than through herself: "The two
of them together would make one Jude" (*Sula*, 83). From this point on,
Nel becomes one of the voices of the community; the last half of the novel
is built around her position as one who has some understanding of Sula, yet

who cannot see the world in the same way. She serves, then, as a character in the middle, between the polarities of Sula and the community.

Nel's ambivalent position becomes clear early in part 2, when Sula returns after a ten-year absence. The marriage to Jude has been frustrating in large part because of his inability to find rewarding work in a white-dominated economic system. These frustrations become self-pity which Nel is expected to nurse, in both senses of healing and feeding. Sula, however, cannot take such an attitude seriously: "I mean, I don't know what the fuss is about. I mean, everything in the world loves you. White men love you. They spend so much time worrying about your penis they forget their own. The only thing they want to do is cut off a nigger's privates. And if that ain't love and respect I don't know what is" (*Sula*, 103). She goes on to talk in the same vein about white women, black women, children of both races, and other black men. She does not permit an identity created by oppression or self-hatred. By this method she restores laughter and perspective to both Nel and Jude.

The same disregard for social convention leads to the dissolution of both the marriage and the friendship. Because she finds Jude interesting, Sula entices him into sexual play that is discovered by Nel. Having no sense of possessiveness or conventionalized identity, Sula feels no responsibility either to her friend's marriage or to Jude's need for love. Truly amoral, she can understand neither Nel's humiliation and outrage nor the husband's desire to leave.

For this crucial part of the story, Morrison shifts to Nel's perspective. This point of view makes it possible to see another character's experience of absence as an experience much different from that of Sula:

> Now her thighs were really empty. And it was then that what those women said about never looking at another man made some sense to her, for the real point, the heart of what they said, was the word *looked*. Not to promise never to make love to another man, not to refuse to marry another man, but to promise and know that she could never afford to look again, . . . never to look, for now she could not risk looking—and anyway, so what? For now her thighs were truly empty and dead too, and it was Sula who had taken the life from them and Jude who smashed her heart and the both of them who left her with no thighs and no heart just her brain raveling away. (*Sula*, 110–11)

The loss of Jude is the loss of identity and the loss of life. More specifically, it is the loss of what filled her thighs that has deprived her of identity. Jude's penis was her life, both personally and socially. Whatever the conditions of the marriage, having his name and his body gave her an acceptable place in the community. The absence of the phallus means a loss of status in the social order. She now becomes a "woman without a man" and unable to raise her eyes. For this change she blames Sula who, without a sense of ownership, cannot conceive of Jude as an object to be taken.

Nel's private experience is a metaphor for the community's treatment of alien behavior. Sula's refusal of positive identity cannot be tolerated, so she is explained as a demon. A folklore is created that includes both tales of her evil actions and interpretations of "signs" associated with her. Like her mother, she has sexual intercourse indiscriminately with the men of the Bottom. But unlike Hannah, her behavior is seen as arrogant rather than complimentary. Without evidence, she is accused of having had liaisons with white men, which is considered the essence of degradation. Her decision to put Eva into a nursing home is attacked, with everyone ignoring the old woman's previous behavior.

The "signs" are the means of objectifying the general feeling of distaste. They become the evidence necessary to fit Sula negatively into the social order. The "plague" of robins that accompanies her return is taken as an omen. Accidents are said to be caused by certain dark practices in which she engages. The most important of the signs is the birthmark over her eye. Each observer reads it in such a way as to validate his or her own interpretation of Sula's identity. When she is a child, it is seen as a rose bud. Jude, believing her both threatening and enticing, sees it as a snake. Shadrack, who fishes for a living and who thinks of her a kindred alien spirit, sees it as a tadpole. The community reads it as ashes, symbolizing both her presumed indifference to her mother's fiery death and her association with hellish forces. The assignment of meaning to an accident of pigmentation makes it possible to bring Sula within a structure set up by the interpreter. Bringing her in, even as evil, brings her under control: "There was no creature so ungodly as to make them destroy it. They could kill easily if provoked to anger, but not by design, which explained why they could not 'mob kill' anyone. To do so was not only unnatural, it was undignified. The presence of evil was something to be first recognized, then dealt with, survived, outwitted, triumphed over" (*Sula,* 118).

To make her *their* evil was to limit and explain the damage she could do. To recognize her as truly different and alien would be to accept discontinuity, disorder, and absence. She must be named so as to render her power manageable. She came to serve an important function in the community as a scapegoat. She took on for them the evil they had previously done to each other. They became righteous as a way of defining themselves as different from her. Mothers previously indifferent to their children became fearful and then protective as stories of Sula's evil power spread. Wives threatened by her promiscuity became more attentive to their husbands. The group banded together for good now that it had to evade consciousness of the true oppressors: death and white society.

Nel, though conventional enough to blame Sula for robbing her of her marriage and thereby both her happiness and her identity, does not engage so directly in the social fantasy. Instead, she creates a new identity that equates her suffering with goodness. Thus, when she learns that Sula is dying, she goes to her out of Christian charity, but not out of friendship. What she learns at the bedside again disturbs the center around which she has organized her life. Sula shows not gratitude or remorse, but a candor that is disorienting. When Nel demands an explanation for the affair with Jude, she is told that it was merely a passing fancy. And when she attempts a moral definition of friendship, the response is even more troubling:

> "What did you take him for if you didn't love him and why didn't you think about me?" And then, "I was good to you, Sula, why don't that matter?"
>
> Sula turned her head away from the boarded window. Her voice was quiet and the stemmed rose over her eye was very dark. "It matters, Nel, but only to you. Not anybody else. Being good to somebody is just like being mean to somebody. Risky. You don't get nothing for it." (*Sula,* 144–45)

Finally, Sula even asserts that perhaps she, not Nel, was the one who was good (*Sula,* 146).

For years, Nel manages to evade the implications of this confrontation. She escapes her own responsibility for self-creation and action by believing that she has been a mere victim. Like the community, she achieves a false innocence by constructing a moral hierarchy with herself at the top and Sula at the bottom. To use the language of *The Bluest Eye,* both she and the Bottom clean themselves on Sula. But such a stance cannot be maintained in the realities of the concrete historical world. The death of Sula, taken to be a sign of better times, brings trouble for the community. Unable to use the strength of the evil one, the people fall back into their selfish, antagonistic ways. The condition is exacerbated when jobs promised by the whites in power do not materialize. On Suicide Day, frustrated citizens join Shad's parade, which ends at the construction site. Here their anger is vented in destruction of the tunnel, with the attendant deaths of dozens of people.

For Nel, the impact is delayed and results in insight rather than cataclysm. As an expression of her goodness, she visits the women in the nursing homes. Twenty-five years after Sula's death and the mass death at the tunnel, she goes to see Eva. Though the old woman is senile, she still makes disturbing observations, such as identifying Nel with Sula, and accusing her of participation in Chicken Little's drowning. Though Nel denies complicity, the accusation has an effect because she was there and did nothing to prevent the death. Thus, Eva, like her namesake, forces on another the knowledge of good and evil and thereby brings Nel out of her self-created innocence into the world of history, experience, and responsibility. The mark of this fortunate fall is her embrace of the spirit of Sula:

> "All that time, all that time, I thought I was missing Jude."
> And the loss pressed down on her chest and came up into her throat. "We was girls together," she said as though explaining something. "O Lord, Sula," she cried, "girl, girl, girlgirlgirl."
> It was a fine cry—loud and long—but it had no bottom and it had no top, just circles and circles of sorrow. (*Sula*, 174)

The cry is "fine" because it is not self-protective or dehumanizing. It expresses sorrow for what had not merely been lost but thrust away through a desire to control and order one's experience. Its lack of conventional structure— no bottom and no top—makes possible the natural and human order of circles, which accepts absence as absence, irreducible yet infinitely meaningful. Nel achieves her true humanity by giving her emptiness its rightful name. This right name makes possible insight but not manipulation; as nearly pure blues expression, it offers not domination but a working through to the truth of experience.

In *Song of Solomon* (1977) the quest is explicitly rather than implicitly for a name. Milkman Dead, a central character with very conventional values, comes to a point at which he feels the need to find out his family's true name. The discovery of this name carries with it a sense of his own humanity and also certain magical qualities connected with black folklore. Naming here has associations with African cultures in which the name is the expression of the soul; because of this, the choosing and keeping of the name is a major ritual.[5] To lose the name or, in Afro-American terms, to be "called out of one's name" is an offense against the spirit.

Consistent with these folk beliefs, the Dead family, whose name was given to them accidentally after the Civil War by a drunken white soldier, act out the designation. The father, Macon Dead, has perverted his own father's efforts to acquire and work the land by becoming an exploitative landlord and real estate speculator. He defines himself and others by accumulation of alienated property. Milkman's mother, Ruth, rejects the present by literally embracing only the past and the future. Macon tells the story of seeing her lying naked on the bed with her father's corpse. And Milkman acquired his nickname by being discovered still nursing at his mother's breast when he was four years old. Ruth, as the daughter of the town's first black doctor, displays the values of the old black bourgeoisie by assuming an attitude of hauteur toward her nouveau riche husband. Their daughters, Magdalene and First Corinthians (whose names were selected by the family tradition of choosing names at random from the Bible), despite their names, are adult virgins who have never been permitted to experience love, either because all men in the community were socially beneath them or because these men lacked sufficient property. Milkman's friend Guitar becomes associated with the Seven Days, a secret society of black men dedicated to exacting retribution for the deaths of blacks killed by whites. The murder of a black child must be avenged by the similar death of a white one on the same day of the week.

Milkman, then, is born and reared in a family that is life-denying. As a sign of this, his birth is simultaneous with the suicide of a man who leaps from the roof of the hospital. As he grows up, he acquires the attitudes of his family and friends. He becomes narcissistic and selfish and treats the members of his family with disdain.

The dialectical movement necessary to move him away from this death-house begins with his discovery of the home of his Aunt Pilate, a woman his father hates for some yet-to-be-determined reason. Pilate has a history and a true name, which she literally carries with her in a small brass box fashioned into an earring. Inside is the piece of paper on which her illiterate father painstakingly copied the word Pilate, the name he insisted she have despite the objections of relatives. Her mother died while giving her birth, and she and her brother later saw their father killed by whites who wanted his land. Having given birth to herself, Pilate creates a family of women much like that of Eva Peace. She herself makes money by selling illegal liquor, and the attendant disrepute is accompanied by a certain folk status since she has no navel and thus is thought to be a child of the devil. Her daughter Reba (whose proper name is the biblical Rebekkah) is marked by her luck; she wins every contest she enters and even those she accidentally happens into. Hagar is the spoiled child of her mother and grandmother, who spend their money to satisfy all of her whims.

Milkman is initially fascinated with this matriarchal household because of its difference from his patriarchal one. Here stories are told, food is tasty and plentiful, and none of the rigidity of his own home is present. Moreover, here he has his sexual initiation with Hagar.

But fascination breeds not understanding but exploitation, which takes two forms. The first is the treatment of Hagar, whom he considers a sexual object to be used at his convenience, but never to be part of his life with his family's and his own respectable friends. Finally, he decides at Christmas to break off the affair, but he chooses to do so in a letter that is the emotional equivalent of his father's eviction notices: "He went back to his father's office, got some cash out of the safe, and wrote Hagar a nice letter which ended: 'Also, I want to thank you. Thank you for all you have meant to me. For making me happy all these years. I am signing this letter with love, of course, but more than that, with gratitude.' "[6]

This male domination through words has the effect of driving Hagar crazy. She sets out to kill him but repeatedly cannot do so. While this insane quest goes on, Morrison introduces other stories of the suppressed humanity and creativity of women. The effect is to provide a sense of a folkloric and historical tradition of oppression. In the barber shop a recent killing is said to be the work of Winnie Ruth Judd, a white woman who kills and dismembers her victims and periodically escapes from the state hospital. For these black men, she serves as a sign of the lunacy of whites who can kill for no good reason; her private torment and motivation is irrelevant to her symbolic usefulness. More pertinent to Milkman is his dream about his mother, which he is not at all certain is in fact a dream. In it, Ruth plants tulip bulbs which immediately emerge as plants and flowers; Milkman expects her to be frightened, but her response is very different: "She leaned back from them, even hit out at them, but playfully, mischievously. The flowers grew and grew, until he could see only her shoulders above them and her flailing arms high above those bobbing, snapping heads. They were smothering her, taking away her breath with their soft jagged lips. And she merely smiled and fought them off as though they were harmless butterflies" (*Song of Solomon*, 105). The chaos of creation, which the male fears, is embraced by the female. His mother, who is passive and serious, has a secret garden where she generates and plays with life.

It is in this context that Milkman receives a revisionist version of family history, one that reveals the importance of female creativity to his own life. He follows his mother one night on a long journey to the cemetery where her father was buried. Upon her exit, he confronts her with her monumentalizing tendency, including the incident of necrophilia told him by his father. She responds by expressing the feeling that the doctor was the only one who ever loved her and that she had reacted to his death by kneeling to kiss his hand, not by any perverse sexual gesture. More important, she explains to her son that she was the one who saved his own life. Her husband desired no more children, and insisted that she abort him. She appealed to

Pilate, who helped her to defeat Macon's attempts. Thus, Milkman owes his existence to the life-affirming efforts of the two women.

He responds to her story by seeking a way to escape the entire family. In this second act of exploitation, he conspires with his father to steal a green sack from Pilate, a sack which they believe contains gold. Macon tells his son about hiding out with his sister after their father's murder, in a cave where they find buried treasure. They are discovered by a white man whom Macon kills. They flee, but the brother believes that Pilate later returned and took the gold, which is now in the green sack. Milkman and Guitar, who needs money to carry out an assassination, steal the sack, only to discover that it contains human bones.

Still obsessed with the idea of getting money and thereby power, Milkman sets out to find the cave near the old family property. He is at this point also evading both the knowledge that the women have offered and the responsibility that accompanies that knowledge. Just as his father distorted the values of the first Macon Dead by emphasizing possession over creation, so Milkman distorts his father's values by taking on his greed without any sense of responsibility and seriousness. And when he arrives in the family hometown, the folk recollections reinforce this idea. His grandfather and father are remembered, but he hears in the memories a respect for material possession and manipulative energy that validates his self-image.

Only when he encounters the incredibly old woman Circe does he begin to question the object of his quest. Circe was the servant of a white family, the head of which was responsible for the murder of Milkman's grandfather. She recalls the relationship of his ancestors and the real name of his grandfather. She is also the voice of a larger history, for she tells him of the injustices committed by whites throughout the past and implicitly questions his identification with white middle-class values. She also shows him one way to act: she lives in the house of the white family with an ever-increasing pack of dogs, which she intentionally keeps inside so that they will destroy all of the objects that were purchased through the exploitation of black labor. She has willfully outlasted the whites so as to destroy everything they found precious. But she knows the price of revenge; she fully expects the dogs to eat her when she is no longer strong enough to feed them. She has reached the time envisioned by the Invisible Man's grandfather in his admonition to "agree 'em to death and destruction,"[7] but she also accepts full responsibility for her action. Her vengeance contrasts with that of Guitar in that hers is embedded in a concrete history and not an abstract, dehumanizing concept of justice.

Milkman leaves in search of the original home of his grandfather, but his quest is now ambivalent. On the one hand he wants the gold, which he still believes Pilate has hidden; on the other, he wants to know the story of his family. He has worked through concentric relational circles from himself to his parents to his grandparents. At each level the more he has probed the more he has found difference rather than the expected identity. In Shalimar he will move through one more circle, but in the process he will find a new definition of himself.

In the village he for the first time is the alien, for here his city clothes, city talk, and city values are not privileged. He is taken not as one returning to his roots, but as a threatening "white-hearted" presence. To succeed in his quest, he must undergo rituals that will strip him of his false culture and prepare him for authentic knowledge. He hears the children reciting ancient rhymes that are vaguely meaningful to him. But in order to decode them, he must become a member of the community. This happens first with a fight that demonstrates his alien status but also tests his courage, then through the opportunity to participate in a hunt. This serves as the male initiation rite that Milkman has never had and thus his possibility of moving out of his perversely extended, narcissistic childhood. He is stripped of all the symbols of the dominant culture, much as Ike McCaslin is in Faulkner's "The Bear." Though inept, he survives the test, including an unexpected murder attempt by Guitar, who feels he has been betrayed in the pursuit of the gold. Milkman discovers that he wants to live and thus is not truly Dead. He endures and thereby receives the symbols of his success: the throbbing heart of the bobcat killed in the hunt and a woman he can truly enjoy without dominating.

Most important, he begins to decipher the children's song and finds in it the narrative of his family. It is the folktale of the flying African, Solomon, who one day discovers his magical power and uses it to fly from slavery back to his African home. He left behind a wife Ryna and twenty-one children, including Jake, Milkman's grandfather. Ryna, like Hagar, goes crazy over the loss of her man, and her children are cared for by Heddy, an Indian. The random elements of the past become a coherent family story. The men (Solomon, Jake, Macon, Milkman) seek power, either magical or material; the women (Ryna, Sing, Ruth, Hagar) must suffer for this pursuit; the children are abandoned because of it, but they are saved by a surrogate mother (Heddy, Circe, Pilate) who keeps alive the history for whoever might later need it. It is also preserved as a functional part of the community, in children's songs. Thus the narrative of power and suffering and love dialectically becomes play.

He also learns the relation of the story to identity:

> Under the recorded names were other names, just as "Macon
> Dead," recorded for all time in some dusty file, hid from view
> the real names of people, places, and things. Names that had
> meaning. No wonder Pilate put hers in her ear. When you know
> your name, you should hang on to it, for unless it is noted down,
> it will die when you do. . . . He closed his eyes and thought of
> the black men in Shalimar, Roanoke, Petersburg, Newport
> News, Danville, in the Blood Bank, on Darling Street, in the
> pool halls, the barbershops. Their names. Names they got from
> yearnings, gestures, flaws, events, mistakes, weaknesses. (*Song of
> Solomon*, 329)

Names have a concrete history; they keep alive the complex, painful, disorderly, creative reality of human experience that dominant, logocentric
structures seek to suppress. They register the hidden expressions of life in
defiance of the controlling Word. They are also liberating and magical. They
free Milkman from his death-wish and thus make it possible for him to die
if necessary. And he frees Pilate, knowing as he now does that the sack of
bones belongs not to the white man Macon murdered but to her own father.
Aunt and nephew return them to the cave for proper burial. As part of the
ritual of purification, Pilate rips off the earring containing her name; it is
unnecessary in the presence of the body of the man who gave it to her and
who now himself has his right name. At this moment, she is killed by
Guitar, who, like the white man who murdered her father, values possession
over human life.

With the elimination of these two generations, Milkman can achieve
identity with Solomon/Shalimar the flying African:

> He could just make out Guitar's head and shoulders in the dark.
> "You want my life?" Milkman was not shouting now. "You need
> it? Here." Without wiping away the tears, taking a deep breath,
> or even bending his knees—he leaped. As fleet and bright as a
> lodestar he wheeled toward Guitar and it did not matter which
> one of them would give up his ghost in the killing arms of his
> brother. For now he knew what Shalimar knew: If you surrendered
> to the air, you could *ride* it. (*Song of Solomon*, 337)

This act of identification is simultaneously an act of differentiation, for
unlike Solomon, Milkman flies into history and responsibility rather than
out of it. And in the process he creates the meaning for his own name. From
being the one who sucks nourishment and life from others, he becomes the

provider, giving Jake his name and home, Pilate freedom from guilt, and Guitar the life he needs to take. His riding the air implies both play and control, or perhaps control through play, and is thus life-affirming even in the moment of death. The magic word, the true name, conquers for a moment of history, the Word.

While *The Bluest Eye* shows us the victimization that comes in a black community without a sustaining folklore and *Sula* shows us the oppressive nature of a community that uses its folk material as a means of control and evasion, *Song of Solomon* reveals the power that can be achieved through the embrace of a folk history. Claudia tells us of her own failure to overcome oppressive forces in the process of telling of Pecola's madness; Nel achieves an insight that makes true sorrow possible; and Milkman acquired the magical power that can hold joy and sorrow together. In *Tar Baby* (1981), Morrison makes use of the same dialectic of dominant culture and folk experience, but does so in a more complex fashion. Unlike her other works, this novel personifies the culture in the two characters of Valerian and Margaret Street. One purpose seems to be to dramatize the sexually differential effects of the culture on those who wield its power. Another difference is the division of the middle character into two parts: Son and Jadine. In this way it is possible to have both success and failure in achieving insight. Finally, the setting is not the American Midwest and South, but an isolated Caribbean island, Isle des Chevaliers. Though all the major characters are American, the setting is useful in clarifying the effects of the dominant order on personality. Separated from the context of American society, the Americanness of the characters, especially in regard to race, can be more directly observed. The inclusion of native black characters serves not merely as counterpoint but also to suggest a broader sense of Afro-American folk experience.

Isle des Chevaliers is a perverse Eden. Valerian Street, a wealthy American candy manufacturer, purchased it years earlier and gradually built it into a clean, sterile paradise for himself and the few white families to whom he sold some of the land. He has created a carefully controlled environment, but primeval nature constantly threatens to reassert its authority, as is suggested by repeated personifications of butterflies, trees, flowers, and the land itself. Valerian, who has retired from his inherited business, has brought with him to the island his wife, a former beauty queen; two black servants, Sydney and Ondine; and Jadine, the niece of the blacks. Also present are two native workers, known as Yardman and Mary because no one has bothered to learn their real names.

Two elements trouble this paradise. One, an absence, is Michael, the son that Margaret perpetually believes will return but who never in fact makes an appearance. Valerian, who considers her an obsessively protective mother, can rather easily handle the absence until he learns the horrifying history of the mother-child relationship.

The other disruption is an intrusive presence in the form of Son, a black seaman who has jumped ship. Though Valerian tries to naturalize this alien influence by in effect making Son a surrogate for Michael, he is ultimately devastatingly unsuccessful. Son is a traditional figure in black history and lore, the fugitive from an unfair system; but he has reversed the journey of runaway slaves by escaping south to the plantation and its white patriarchy, loyal blacks, and tragic mulatto. He has many identities, but he very quickly learns the true names and relationships of everyone else, including the natives.

The responses to his intrusion reveal the natures and insecurities of the residents. Margaret, in whose closet he is found, has the southern white woman's rape fantasy (even though she is from Maine); she believes that a strange black man would be in a white woman's room only because he intends to sexually assault her. Sydney and Ondine, being proper "Philadelphia Negroes," see in Son a threat to the racial respectability they have achieved. Though they are servants, they have taken on middle-class values, and being black, they feel contaminated by anyone of their race who does not uphold the image they have created. Valerian, considering himself in total control, experiences no fear; he invites Son into the group, confident that his patronizing liberalism will neutralize any threat.

The response of Jadine is the most complex, for she blends together elements of the others. A sensual woman, she is both terrified and fascinated with the sexual energy of Son: she both fears and invites rape. Having an even more refined aura of respectability than her relatives, she is repulsed by his unkempt appearance, uncouth behavior, and lack of education. And yet, like her benefactor, she wants to be in control of situations and people; Son provides an opportunity to test her manipulative skills.

These conditions and personalities set up the double quest that structures the book. Jadine's is epitomized by an African woman she has seen in Paris:

> Under her long canary yellow dress Jadine knew there was too much hip, too much bust. The agency would laugh her out of the lobby, so why was she and everyone else in the store transfixed? The height? The skin like tar against the canary yellow dress? The woman walked down the aisle as though her many-colored sandals were pressing gold tracks on the floor. Two upside-down

V's were scored into each of her cheeks, her hair was wrapped in
a gelee as yellow as her dress. The people in the aisles watched
her without embarrassment, with full glances instead of sly ones.[8]

Later, when the woman leaves the grocery, she pauses outside the door and
spits on the sidewalk. In this image is all that Jadine wants: racial pride,
arrogance, power in the white world yet disdain for it. In her present world,
power and race are divided into the characters of Valerian and Son, and she
seeks what each has. But the quests are as separate as the men, and her
struggle is to unite them.

On the other hand, Son wants beauty and blackness, which are characterized for him by Jadine and the native woman Thérèse. In Jade he sees
pulchritude, intelligence, and sophistication, all things not previously available to him. In Thérèse, he discovers the powerful though subterranean
forces of his race.

Jade and Son serve as tarbabies for each other. Their contact with each
other and the attachment of each to what the other represents denies them
the freedom to pursue the goal which is truest for each of them. Ultimately,
Morrison establishes a hierarchy of values that sees Son's freedom as success
and Jadine's as failure. The hierarchy is based on what is earned by each
character, in the sense that the struggle with the tarbaby either does or does
not force the character to confront and work through the truth of the self
and history. The hierarchy, which is an inversion of surface realities, can be
seen in the personifications of the opposed goals Jade and Son free themselves
for.

Valerian, the model of Jadine's pursuit of power, was named for an
emperor and had a candy bar named after him. The bar, a pink and white
confection, was successful only in black neighborhoods, while white boys
thought its name and color vaguely homosexual. The family provided Valerian with everything, including a good wife when the time came. Deciding
that he would not have the same obsession with the company that his relatives
had, he used some of his income to purchase Isle des Chevaliers as a place
of retirement and escape. When his first marriage did not work out, he
discovered Margaret, Miss Maine, whom he loved in large part because her
complexion reminded him of his candy bar. When Jadine was orphaned,
Valerian financed her education and early modelling career as a favor to
Sydney and Ondine. He created, in effect, a perfect patriarchal system, with
everyone created in his own image. Despite flaws in the order, such as
Michael's absence and Margaret's mental aberrations, Valerian considered
himself a successful deity.

But like his candy bar, his world was an insubstantial confection. One of his eccentric schemes, to have the servants join the family for Christmas dinner, backfires when Ondine, in a moment of stress, reveals Margaret's compulsion as a young mother to abuse Michael with sharp pins and lighted cigarettes. This history destroys Valerian, not because of its horror, but because it exposes his arrogant innocence and impotence. Because he refused to see Margaret and Michael as other than his creations, he could not see the depth of human frustration and suffering implied by such behavior. What he has always taken as his wife's stupidity was in fact the expression of her guilt, a guilt that makes her totally other and thus beyond his control. His power has been an unearned one, and is therefore destroyed by concrete reality. At the end of the novel, he sits in a chair mumbling, while Sydney feeds him and Margaret runs the house.

In Thérèse we find a very different blindness, one that is both literal and magical. Repeatedly, she and other characters refer to her failing eyesight, but this is compensated for by her ability to see what others cannot. For example, she knows of Son's presence days before Margaret finds him. She names him the chocolate-eater and thus predicts his ultimate commitment to his color rather than Valerian's. She sees the past as well as the present and future: she is said to be one of the blind race, for whom the Isle des Chevaliers is named:

> Son asked who were the blind race so Gideon told him a story about a race of blind people descended from some slaves who went blind the minute they saw Dominique. . . . Their ship foundered and sank with Frenchmen, horses and slaves aboard. The blinded slaves could not see how or where to swim so they were at the mercy of the current and the tide. They floated and trod water and ended up on that island along with the horses that had swum ashore. Some of them were only partially blinded and were rescued later by the French, and returned to Queen of France and indenture. The others, totally blind, hid. The ones who came back had children who, as they got on into middle age, went blind too. What they saw, they saw with the eye of the mind, and that, of course, was not to be trusted. Thérèse, he said, was one such. . . . "They ride those horses all over the hills. They learned to ride through the rain forest avoiding all sorts of trees and things. They race each other, and for sport they sleep with the swamp women in Sein de Vieilles." (*Tar Baby,* 152–53)

Thérèse believes Son to be one of the race; what she does not see is that he must be enslaved before he can become one of the blind and free.

Valerian and Thérèse are the polarities between which Jade and Son will move. And they are interacting polarities even though they have no contact with each other. Thérèse defines herself in part over against the white world, both that of the Valerian Streets who dominate Caribbean life and the white slave masters who originally brought her race to the islands. And Valerian carves his empire out of and against the world of the black natives; he judges his power in part by his ability to keep natural growth out of his palace and his intellectual superiority by his ability to dismiss such folk history as the blind horsemen.

Morrison does not arrange parallel movements between these poles for Son and Jadine. Rather, she has each move between a pole and that in the other which resembles the opposite pole. Thus Son literally and figuratively alternates between Thérèse and those sophisticated qualities in Jade that she shares with Valerian.

Jadine stands at a crossroads: she has received her advanced degree in art history and has achieved substantial success as a model in Europe. As a consequence of the latter, a wealthy European has asked to marry her. She comes to the island to make a choice without interference. Her choices, however, are all within the realm of white society, consistent with the values taught her by Ondine and Sydney and the opportunities provided her by Valerian.

The costs of such values are indicated in her childhood memory of Baltimore after her first encounter with Son. She remembers female dogs being in heat and willing to be mounted by males in the middle of the street. A neighbor tries to get rid of them:

> Every goddamn dog in town'll be over here and he went back inside to get a mop handle to run the males off and crack the bitch over the back and send her home, she who had done nothing but be "in heat" which she couldn't help but which was her fault just the same so it was she who was beaten and cracked over the head and spine with the mop handle and made to run away and I felt sorry for her and went looking for her to see if she was hurt and when I found her she was behind the gas station standing very quietly while another dog sniffed her ass embarrassing me in the sunlight.
>
> All around her it was like that: a fast crack on the head if you let the hunger show so she decided then and there at the age of twelve in Baltimore never to be broken in the hands of any

man. . . . When her mother died and she went to Philadelphia
and then away to school, she was so quick to learn, but no
touchee, teacher, and no, I do not smile, because Never. It
smoothed out a little as she grew older. The pugnacious lips
because a seductive pout—eyes more heated than scary. But
beneath the easy manners was a claw always ready to rein in the
dogs, because Never. (*Tar Baby,* 124)

She has ordered and defined her life by a firm control of sexual desire.
She has equated sexuality with animality and desire with exploitation and
has chosen to make herself into a gemstone rather than a woman. But Son
disturbs her order: "He did not know that all the time he tinkled the [piano]
keys she was holding tight to the reins of dark dogs with silver feet" (*Tar
Baby,* 158). Eventually, his sheer physical beauty, obvious desire for her,
and "savannahs in his eyes," which suggest an African nobility, compel her
to loosen the reins.

After the Christmas revelations make the Street house unbearable, the
two of them go to New York, which in its modernity and sophistication is
her natural territory. Here the influence of Valerian becomes clear as she
seeks to remake Son into her image of the African prince, which is ultimately
the only way she can accept him. Mutual affection for a time disguises this
manipulative impulse, and because he loves her, he does not resist the
education, the parties, and the pretensions. Finally, after a visit to his home,
a Florida village she finds unbearably provincial, she realizes that he will
always be a native Son, never an African prince, and she leaves him to return
to her European suitor.

She rejects not merely him but her own Afro-American heritage and
her blackness, the first represented by Florida and the latter by the Caribbean
islands. She chooses the fixed life of white values, which are repeatedly
associated with death, to the uncertainties of her race, which Morrison
consistently associates with life and nature. Moreover, she chooses in effect
to be a creation rather than a creator, an art historian rather than artist, a
model rather than designer, a wife rather than woman. Thus, the very choice
to have a clearly defined identity denies her access to origins and thus negates
the very thing she seeks.

For Son, the struggle is much harder because he works from absence
toward and finally away from presence. His values are not dominant, his
identity is not fixed, his origin is ambiguous. He lacks conventional identity:

He was dwelling on his solitude, rocking in the wind, adrift. A
man without human rites: unbaptized, uncircumcised, minus
puberty rites or the formal rites of manhood. Unmarried and

undivorced. He had attended no funeral, married in no church, raised no child. Propertyless, homeless, sought for but not after. . . . In those eight homeless years he had joined that great underclass of undocumented men. And although there were more of his kind in the world than students or soldiers, unlike students or soldiers they were not counted. They were an international legion of day laborers and musclemen, gamblers, sidewalk merchants, migrants, unlicensed crewmen on ships with volatile cargo, part-time mercenaries, full-time gigolos, or curbside musicians. What distinguished them from other men (aside from their terror of Social Security cards and *cédula de identidad*) was their refusal to equate work with life and an inability to stay anywhere for long. (*Tar Baby,* 165–66)

What marks Son and others like them is their refusal to participate in those social orders which categorize and systematize; they create identities by deliberately evading the conventional markers of identity—family, job, education, religion, politics—and they equate this evasion with life. In Son's case, the absence of positive identity literally keeps him from imprisonment since he was responsible for the death of his wife.

Jade tempts him from his world of uncertainty and anonymity by offering visible signs of success: education, money, herself as physical presence and as actual the picture of elegance: in their first encounter, Son is enthralled by photographs of her printed in a Paris fashion magazine. Just as she sees in him a primitive energy to be channeled into civilization, so he sees in her sophisticated beauty in need of passion. In New York he realizes his ambition as long as she is willing to center her existence on him. But once she moves out into her world and tries to take him with her, he begins again to feel the impingement of the documented world.

He tries to overcome this by taking her to Florida, back to his origins, where the name Son has meaning because his father is called Old Man. But the language of this world is one she refuses to understand, seeing it as an alien culture unworthy of her interest. Blackness, so appealing when mediated by Son's beauty, is unattractive in its ordinary folk form of uneducated people, sexual circumspection, and the clothes of working people rather than fashion models. Most disturbing is Son's at-homeness in this world and his ability to love it and her simultaneously. This capacity for inclusion is one she lacks precisely because she, like Sydney and Ondine and Valerian before her, has created her visible and positive identity by excluding such blackness, by making this reality an invisibility and negation. But that very act renders it an ever-present, intolerable part of her existence. Son, who loves both beauty and blackness, and in fact sees them as a totality, cannot understand her need to escape this black village.

Back in New York, the conflict reaches a climax, as each of them assumes the role of savior:

> She thought she was rescuing him from the night women who wanted him for themselves, wanted him feeling superior in a cradle, deferring to him; wanted her to settle for wifely competence when she could be almighty, to settle for fertility rather than originality, nurturing instead of building. He thought he was rescuing her from Valerian, meaning *them,* the aliens, the people who in a mere three hundred years had killed a world millions of years old. . . . Each was pulling the other away from the maw of hell—its very ridge top. Each knew the world as it was meant or ought to be. One had a past, the other a future and each one bore the culture to save the race in his hands. (*Tar Baby,* 269)

The inability to achieve resolution is fundamentally an insistence by both on an origin that can be made present. Each in effect denies history: Son by believing in the possibility of returning to a prewhite black purity and Jadine by assuming that blackness was merely an aberration from the truth of Eurocentric Progress.

But Morrison makes it clear that Jadine's is the greater flaw. She must turn Son into an abstraction; her love is totalitarian and cannot incorporate the differences that are part of his concrete being. When he will not submit, she goes to the island, then to Paris to her wealthy European. He comes, on the other hand, to realize that his love must assume difference; because of this, he leaves, returns, and then pursues her back to the Caribbean.

This very gesture makes possible his rite of passage, for it brings his experience into the realm of folk experience in the sense that he cannot have that which he most needs to live, yet must go on living nonetheless. He goes to Thérèse, thinking she will help get back Jadine, but she knows better the meaning of his return. She deceives him by letting him believe he is going to Valerian's house, but in fact lets him off on the part of the island inhabited by the blind horsemen: " 'The men. The men are waiting for you.' She was pulling the oars now, moving out. 'You can choose now. You can get free of her. They are waiting in the hills for you' " (*Tar Baby,* 306). Fearful and unable to see, he stumbles over the rocks at first. "By and by he walked steadier, now steadier. The mist lifted and the trees stepped back a bit as if to make the way easier for a certain kind of man. Then he ran. Lickety-split. Lickety-split. Looking neither to the left nor to the right. Lickety-split. Lickety-split. Lickety-lickety-lickety-split" (*Tar Baby,* 306).

   Tar Baby marks the final step of immersion into the black folk world. Son achieves his truest nature by becoming one, not with the tellers of tales, as in Ellison, Gaines, and Walker, but with the tales themselves. Like the horsemen, he has been blinded by the prospect of enslavement, but also like them, this very handicap gives him freedom and power. He does not go back to the womb, as Jadine thought, but into the domain of the true black man.

   Significantly, such a conclusion is only possible in a magical fictional world, one which in some ways mirrors the submerged Afro-American world of voodoo, conjure, and tricksters. Morrison takes as ordinary experience what more realistic black writers assume to be fantastic. She differs from Jones in taking for granted that what is considered irrational is in fact only a perversion of the natural order by a mechanistic, oppressive social system, whereas Jones is concerned to show that that system generates madness. Thus, for the author of *Tar Baby,* the sight of the blind, the magical power of the impotent, and the spiritual vitality of nonhuman nature makes greater sense than the insanities, grotesqueries, and ironies of the realm of "normality" and order. The particular dialectical structure of her work serves to develop the interrelated irrationalities of white and black culture.

NOTES

[1] Here *logocentric* is used to suggest the assumption of a fixed relationship between signifier and signified that does not allow for the ambiguity of language. See Jacques Derrida, *Of Grammatology,* translated by Gayatri Spivak (Baltimore: Johns Hopkins University Press, 1976), 3–5; and Christopher Norris, *Deconstruction: Theory and Practice* (London: Methuen, 1982), 29–31.

[2] As her own marker of such characters, Morrison consistently gives them names with the diminutive suffix *-ene:* Maureen, Geraldine, Pauline (*The Bluest Eye*); Helene (*Sula*); Magdalena (*Song of Solomon*); and Ondine and Jadine (*Tar Baby*).

[3] Toni Morrison, *The Bluest Eye* (New York: Holt, Rinehart, Winston, 1970; rpt. New York: Pocket Books, 1972), 159. All further references to this work will be cited in the text.

[4] Toni Morrison, *Sula* (New York: Knopf, 1973), 5–6. All further references to this work will be cited in the text.

[5] See Janheinz Jahn, *Muntu: An Outline of Neo-African Culture,* translated by Marjorie Grene (London: Faber and Faber, 1961), 125.

[6] Toni Morrison, *Song of Solomon* (New York: Knopf, 1977), 98–99. All further references to this work will be cited in the text.

[7] Ralph Ellison, *Invisible Man* (New York: Random House, 1952), 13.

[8] Toni Morrison, *Tar Baby* (New York: Knopf, 1981), 45. All further references to this work will be cited in the text.

MADONNE M. MINER

Lady No Longer Sings the Blues:
Rape, Madness, and Silence
in The Bluest Eye

Robert Stepto begins a recent interview with Toni Morrison by commenting on the "extraordinary sense of place" in her novels. He notes that she creates specific geographical landscapes with street addresses, dates, and other such details.[1] His observations certainly hold true for Morrison's first novel, *The Bluest Eye,* set in a black neighborhood in Lorain, Ohio, in 1941. Reading *The Bluest Eye,* I feel as if I have been in the abandoned store on the southeast corner of Broadway and Thirty-fifth Street in Lorain where Pecola Breedlove lives, as if I have been over the territory traversed by the eleven-year-old black girl as she skips among tin cans, tires, and weeds.

Morrison's skill in creating this very specific place accounts, in part, for my sense of the strangely familiar, the uncanny, when I read her novel—but only in part. While reading, I am familiar not only with Pecola's neighborhood but also, in a more generalized way, with Pecola's story. The sequence of events in this story—a sequence of rape, madness, and silence—repeats a sequence I have read before. Originally manifest in mythic accounts of Philomela and Persephone, this sequence provides Morrison with an ancient archetype from which to structure her very contemporary account of a young black woman. In the pages which follow I want to explore intersections between these age-old myths and Morrison's ageless novel.

For an account of Philomela, we must turn to Ovid, who includes her story in his *Metamorphoses* (8 A.D.). According to the chronicler, this story begins with an act of separation: Procne leaves her much-loved sister, Philo-

From *Conjuring: Black Women, Fiction, and Literary Tradition,* edited by Marjorie Pryse and Hortense J. Spillers (Bloomington: Indiana University Press, 1985), pp. 176–91.

mela, to join her husband, Tereus, in Thrace. After several years, Procne
convinces Tereus to make a trip to Athens and escort Philomela to Thrace
for a visit. In Athens, Tereus barely manages to curb the lust he feels for
Philomela. He caresses her with his eyes, watches possessively as she kisses
her father good-bye, and uses each embrace, each kiss,

> . . . to spur his rage, and feed his fire;
> He wished himself her father—and yet no less
> Would lust look hideous in a father's dress.[2]

Arriving in Thrace, Tereus drags Philomela into a dark wood and rapes her.
The virgin calls out the names of father, sister, gods, but to no avail. Having
indulged his lust, Tereus prepares to leave this "ringdove . . . with blood-
stained plumes still fluttering" when she dares cry out against his sin:

> "I'll speak your deed, and cast all shame away.
>
> . . . .
>
> My voice shall reach the highest tract of air,
> And gods shall hear, if gods indeed are there."[3]

Tereus cannot tolerate such sacrilege against his name, so he perpetrates yet
another rape: with pincers he

> . . . gripped the tongue that cried his shame,
> That stammered to the end her father's name,
> That struggled still, and strangled utterance made,
> And cut it from the root with barbarous blade.[4]

Deprived of speech and lodged in "walls of stone," Philomela weaves the
tale of her plight into a piece of fabric, which she then sends to Procne.
When Procne learns of her sister's grief and her husband's treachery, she
determines upon a most hideous revenge; she slays the son she has had with
Tereus and feeds his remains to the unsuspecting father. While Ovid's story
ends with this feast, popular mythology adds yet another chapter, transforming Philomela into a nightingale, damned forever to chirp the name of
her rapist: tereu, tereu.

Obviously, male-violating-female functions as the core action within
Philomela's story. Under different guises, this violation occurs several times:
first, when Tereus ruptures the hymen of Philomela; second, when Tereus
ruptures the connecting tissue of Philomela's tongue; and, finally, when he
enters her body yet again ("Thereafter, if the frightening tale be true, / On
her maimed form he wreaked his lust anew"[5]). With each act Tereus asserts

his presence, his sensual realm, and denies the very existence of such a realm (encompassing not only sensuality, but the senses themselves) to Philomela. As if to reinforce the initial violation, Tereus, following his act of rape, encloses Philomela in silence, in stone walls. He thereby forces her to assume externally imposed configurations instead of maintaining those natural to her.

If man-raping-woman functions as the most basic "mythemic act"[6] in Philomela's story, the most basic mythemic *inter*-act involves not only this pair, but another: father and sister of the rape victim. When, for example, Ovid notes that Tereus, lusting for Philomela, "wished himself her father," and when the chronicler describes Philomela, in the midst of the rape, calling out her father's name (for help, of course, but for what else?) he sets the act of violence within a familial matrix. Thus, we cannot limit consideration of this act's motivations and ramifications to two individuals. Interestingly enough, however, just as the basic mythemic act (man raping woman) robs the woman of identity, so too the mythemic interact; dependent upon familial roles for personal verification ("mother of," "sister of," "wife of"[7]) the female must fear a loss of identity as the family loses its boundaries—or, more accurately, as the male transgresses these boundaries.

Having noted the most important structural elements in Philomela's story, we cross an ocean, several centuries and countless historical, racial, and class lines before coming to the story of Pecola. Despite obvious contextual differences between the two stories, structural similarities abound. Individual mythemes from Philomela's story appear, without distortion, in that of Pecola. First, in various ways and at various costs, the female figure suffers violation: by Mr. Yacobowski, Junior, Bay Boy and friends, Cholly, Soaphead. Second, with this violation a man asserts his presence as "master," "man-in-control," or "god" at the expense of a young woman who exists only as someone to "impress upon." Third, following the violation/assertion, this woman suffers an enclosure or undesirable transformation; she cowers, shrinks, or resides behind walls of madness. Finally, the most characteristic example of violation/assertion/destruction occurs within the family matrix; Cholly Breedlove rapes his own daughter, violating a standard code of familial relations. We now might look more closely at individual instances of mythemes structuring the Pecola story.

An early, and paradigmatic, example of male transgression and subsequent female silence occurs in the "See the Cat" section. Junior, a tyrannical, unloving black boy, invites a rather credulous Pecola into his house, ostensibly to show her some kittens; like Philomela, Pecola has no idea of the dangers involved in trusting herself to a male guide. Once inside, engrossed in admiration of the furnishings, she forgets about Junior until he insists that she acknowledge him:

> She was deep in admiration of the flowers when Junior said, "Here!" Pecola turned. "Here is your kitten!" he screeched. And he threw a big black cat right in her face.[8]

Pecola immediately responds to this unexpected penetration by sucking in her breath; metaphorically she draws herself inward. She then attempts to flee, but just as Tereus confines Philomela behind stone walls, Junior confines Pecola behind the wall of his will:

> Junior leaped in front of her. "You can't get out. You're my prisoner," he said. His eyes were merry but hard. . . . He pushed her down, ran out the door that separated the rooms, and held it shut with his hands. (pp. 73–74)

Male realms expand as those of the female suffer an almost fatal contraction.

Junior does not actually rape Pecola. Morrison, however, duplicates the dynamics of the scene between Junior and Pecola in a scene between Cholly and Pecola, where rape *does* occur. Eleven-year-old Pecola stands at the sink, scraping away at dirty dishes, when her father, drunk, staggers into the kitchen. Unlike Tereus and Junior, Cholly does not carry his victim into foreign territories; rather, Pecola's rape occurs within her own house, and this fact increases its raw horror (Morrison denies us the cover of metaphor and confronts us directly with a father's violation of his daughter). As Morrison explains, several factors motivate Cholly, but the two thoughts floating through his besotted brain immediately prior to his penetration of Pecola point, once more, to his desire for confirmation of his presence. First, a gesture of Pecola's, a scratching of the leg, reminds him of a similar gesture of Pauline's—or, more accurately, reminds him of *his own* response to this gesture. He repeats his response, catching Pecola's foot in his hand, nibbling on the flesh of her leg, just as he had done with Pauline, so many years before. Of consequence here is not Pecola's gesture, but Cholly's belief that he can regain an earlier perception of himself as young, carefree and whimsical by using this girl/woman as medium. When Pecola, however, unlike the laughing Pauline, remains stiff and silent, Cholly shifts to a second train of thought, a second stimulus to self-assertion: "The rigidness of her shocked body, the silence of her stunned throat, was better than Pauline's easy laughter had been. The confused mixture of his memories of Pauline and the doing of a wild and forbidden thing excited him, and a bolt of desire ran down his genitals, giving it length" (p. 128). Thus, on a literal level, Cholly expands as Pecola contracts:

> The tightness of her vagina was more than he could bear. His soul seemed to slip down to his guts and fly out into her, and the gigantic thrust he made into her then provoked the only sound she made—a hollow suck of air in the back of her throat. Like the rapid loss of air from a circus balloon. (p. 128)

As in the episode with Junior, Pecola sucks inward, but without positive effect; like a deflating circus balloon, she *loses* the benefits of lifegiving oxygen and the power of speech.

To enforce this silence, Cholly need not cut off Pecola's tongue or imprison her behind stone walls. The depresencing of Pecola Breedlove takes a different form from that of Philomela. Upon regaining consciousness following the rape, Pecola *is* able to speak; she tells Mrs. Breedlove what has happened. But as Mrs. Breedlove does not want to hear and does not want to believe, Pecola must recognize the futility of attempted communication. Thus when Cholly, like Tereus, rapes a second time, Pecola keeps the story to herself; in silence this eleven-year-old girl steps across commonly accepted borders of reason and speech to enter her own personal world of silence and madness. Pecola's "self" becomes so crazed, so fragmented, that it conducts conversations with itself—and with no one else:

> How come you don't talk to anybody?
> *I talk to you.*
> Besides me.
> *I don't like anybody besides you. . . .*
> You don't talk to anybody. You don't go to school. And
> nobody talks to you. (p. 153)

Of course, when Pecola comments that her mirror image does not engage other people in conversation, she engages in self-commentary; "I" and "you" are one and the same. Tragically, even when combined, this "I" and "you" do not compose one whole being. Claudia's description of the mutilated Pecola leaves no doubt that she no longer exists as a reasonable human being; like Philomela-turned-nightingale, the "little-girl-gone-to-woman" undergoes a transformation:

> The damage done was total. . . . Elbows bent, hands on shoulders, she flailed her arms like a bird in an eternal, grotesquely futile effort to fly. Beating the air, a winged but grounded bird,

intent on the blue void it could not reach—could not even see—
but which filled the valleys of the mind. (p. 158)

Silent, isolated, insane: Pecola cannot escape.

In depicting the effects of rape on one young woman, Morrison sets
into motion a series of associations that take their cue from gender. Men,
potential rapists, assume presence, language, and reason as their particular
province. Women, potential victims, fall prey to absence, silence, and madness.[9] An understanding of the powerful dynamics behind this allotment of
presence/absence, language/silence, reason/madness along sexual lines contributes to an understanding of the painful truths contained in Philomela's
story, in Pecola's story, and in the story of yet another rape victim: Persephone. While clearly related to the Philomela myth, that of Persephone
differs in certain details which, when brought to *The Bluest Eye,* prompt an
even richer reading of the novel. Before engaging in an application of Persephone's story to that of Pecola, however, we might look at three different
renditions of the Persephone myth, each of which may advance our understanding of the way Persephone's and Pecola's stories intersect mytho-
poetically.

Homer sets a springtime mood of warmth, gaiety, youthfulness, and
beauty as he begins his rendition of Persephone's story:

> Now I will sing/of golden-haired Demeter,
> the awe-inspiring goddess,
> and of her trim-ankled daughter,
> Persephone,
> who was frolicking in a grassy meadow.[10]

When Pluto, god of the underworld, abducts the "trim-ankled" young
woman (and surely it is not mere coincidence that Morrison specifies Pecola's
ankles as a stimulant to Cholly's desire) this mood changes abruptly; in
terror, the virgin shrieks for her father, Zeus. While noting that Persephone
directs her shrieks to her father, Homer also comments on the virgin's hopes
relative to her mother:

> Still *glimpsing* the earth,
> the brilliant sky,
> the billowing, fish-filled sea
> and the rays of the sun,
> Persephone vainly hoped *to see* her mother again.[11]

Homer establishes a causal connection between rape and the loss of a particular *vision.* He further substantiates this connection in Demeter's response

to her daughter's rape, a punitive response which involves Demeter's changing the world so that its occupants will no longer see fruits and flowers:

> She made that year
> most shocking and frightening
> for mortals who lived on the nourishing earth.
> The soil did not yield a single seed.
> Demeter kept them all underground.[12]

The goddess imposes a sensual deprivation on mortals parallel to the sensual
deprivation suffered by her daughter (note that *The Bluest Eye* opens with a
statement of similar deprivation: "Quiet as it's kept, there were no marigolds
in the fall of 1941"). By the end of the hymn, Demeter and Pluto reach a
compromise; half of the year Persephone resides with her mother and the
flowers grow; during the other half, Persephone remains with Pluto and the
earth produces no fruits.

James Frazer, in *The Golden Bough,* relates another version of the Persephone story. In substance, Frazer comes very close to Homer; in detail:
however, the two diverge, and Frazer's details reverberate in *The Bluest Eye.*
First, Frazer provides more specifics about Persephone's "frolic"; the young
woman gathers "roses and lilies, crocuses and violets, hyacinths and narcissuses in a lush meadow."[13] Individual flowers in Frazer's catalog call forth
associations of importance to *The Bluest Eye:* the virginal lily, bloody hyacinth
(taking its color from the slain youth, Hyacinthus, beloved of Apollo) and
narcotic Narcissus (taking its name from the self-enclosed youth, Narcissus,
capable of seeing only himself).[14] The mythic situation itself, flower picking,
finds an analog in the novel as Pecola, on her way to the candy store, peers
into the heads of yellow dandelions. Second, Frazer's more detailed description of Persephone's abduction and underworld residence might serve as
metaphoric description of Pecola's state of mind following her rape: "the
earth gaped and Pluto, Lord of the Dead, issuing from the abyss, carried
her off . . . to be his bride and queen in the *gloomy subterranean world.*"[15]
Finally, when Frazer concludes the story, he notes that although the "grim
Lord of the Dead" obeys Zeus's command to restore Persephone to Demeter,
this Lord first gives his mistress the seed of a pomegranate to eat, which
ensures that she will return to him. Tereus and Cholly also "give seeds" to
women, thereby ensuring that the women never will be able to resume their
previously experienced wholeness.

In a very recent reworking of the Persephone story, Phyllis Chesler
focuses most intently on the fate of this myth's female characters. Because
she places women's experiences at the center of her version, Chesler begins

with a chapter of the story which does not appear in Homer and Frazer: Persephone menstruates. Further, Chesler specifies the nature of certain acts and relationships that her male counterparts choose to obscure; she identifies rape as rape, fathers as fathers:

> One morning Persephone menstruated. That afternoon, Demeter's daughters gathered flowers to celebrate the loveliness of the event. A chariot thundered, then clattered into their midst. It was Hades, the middle aged god of death, come to *rape* Persephone, come to carry her off to be his queen, to sit beside him in the realm of *non-being* below the earth, come to commit the first act of violence earth's children had ever known. Afterwards, the three sisters agreed that he was old enough to be Persephone's *father*. Perhaps he was; who else could he be? There were no known male parents . . . and thus they discovered that in shame and sorrow childhood ends, and that nothing remains the same. [16]

Morrison, like Chesler, pays attention to female rites of passage; she includes a description of Pecola's first menstruation, an experience which bonds Pecola to her adopted sisters, Claudia and Frieda. Also like Chesler, Morrison insists on the paternal identity of the rapist (Pecola need not shriek the name of father as Philomela and Persephone do; father is right there) and emphasizes that the rape act brings one entire way of life to a close ("nothing remains the same"). This rapport between Chesler's Persephone and Morrison's Pecola surfaces in conclusions to the stories as well. Chesler writes:

> Persephone still had to visit her husband once each year (in winter, when no crops could grow), but her union with him remained a barren one. Persephone was childless. Neither husband nor child—no stranger would ever claim her as his own. [17]

Pecola's fate runs along strikingly parallel lines. Despite the offerings and incantations of Claudia and Frieda, Pecola miscarries and remains childless. Grown people turn away, children laugh, and no stranger attempts to share Pecola's world.

Structurally, the stories of Philomela, Persephone, and Pecola share the same blueprint: violated by a male relative, a young virgin suffers sensual loss of such an extreme that her very identity is called into question. In one brutally explicit scene Ovid conveys the terror of Philomela's sensual loss— Tereus severs his sister-in-law's tongue and deprives her of speech. As chroniclers of this same basic female experience, Homer, Frazer, and Chesler also must convey the terror of sensual loss. In their versions, however, *sight* rather than speech assumes priority, and they convey the terror of deprivation not in one explicit scene, but by depicting the ramifications of an altered vision. Of course, this particular emphasis encourages yet further consideration of the Persephone myth and Morrison's novel, the very title of which suggests an interest in the way vision structures our world. This interest, reflected in the novel's title (what does it mean to see through "the bluest eye"?) and in sectional titles (how does one "see mother," "see father"?) springs naturally from Morrison's more fundamental interests: how does the world see a young black girl? How does a young black girl see a world? And finally, what are the correspondences between presence/absence, vision/nonvision, male/female?

As described by various psychologists and psychoanalysts,[18] the processes of identity construction and personal integration involve an extremely sensitive and constantly shifting balance between seeing and being seen—so that, for example, only after an infant sees itself reflected in the mother's eyes (that is, given a presence) can the infant, through its own eyes, bestow a presence on others. Throughout *The Bluest Eye,* Morrison provides several examples of the ways sex and race may prompt a dangerous distortion of this visual balance. An early instance of this distortion, and subsequent personal disintegration, occurs during an exchange between Pecola and Mr. Yacobowski, white male proprietor of a candy store on Garden Avenue.[19] Pecola enjoys her walk to Mr. Yacobowski's store. Many times she has seen that crack in the walk, this clump of dandelions. Having seen them, she grants them a reality, a reality which redounds to include Pecola herself:

> These and other inanimate things she saw and experienced. They
> were real to her. She knew them. . . . She owned the crack . . .
> she owned the clumps of dandelions. . . . And owning them
> made her part of the world, and the world a part of her. (p. 41)

Such a happy rapport between viewer and vision is short-lived, however. When Pecola enters the candy store and comes under Mr. Yacobowski's eyes, her existence, as well as the existence of her world, become matters of doubt. Mr. Yacobowski *does not see* her:

> Somewhere between retina and object, between vision and view,
> his eyes draw back, hesitate, and hover. At some fixed point in
> time and space he senses that he need not waste the effort of a
> glance. He does not see her, because for him there is *nothing to
> see.* (pp. 41–42, my italics)

In effect, this scene parallels previously described rape scenes in the novel: male denies presence to female. Pecola cannot defend herself against this denial: "she looks up at him and sees the vacuum where curiosity ought to

lodge. And something more. The total absence of human recognition—the
glazed separateness" (p. 42). Nor can she defend her world; walking home,
she rejects dandelions she formerly has favored. They, like Pecola herself,
certainly will not satisfy standards that the blue eyes of a Mr. Yacobowski
may impose:

> Dandelions. A dart of affection leaps out from her to them. But
> they do not look at her and do not send love back. She thinks
> "They *are* ugly. They *are* weeds." (p. 43)

Before contact with this white male, Pecola creates belief in both a world
and a self; following contact with Yacobowski, her conjuring powers im-
paired, she abandons the effort.

A second example of visual distortion finds Pecola face to face with
Geraldine, one of those "brown girls from Mobile and Aiken" able to construct inviolable worlds by imposing strict boundaries between the acceptable
and the unacceptable, the seen and the unseen. Unlike Mr. Yacobowski,
Geraldine does *look* at Pecola, but, like Yacobowski, Geraldine does not *see*
Pecola; she sees only a series of signs, a symbolic configuration. Thus, when
Geraldine returns home and discovers a shrieking son, a frying feline on the
radiator, and an unfamiliar black girl in her living room, she responds by
distancing herself from Pecola. With no qualms whatsoever she relegates
the young girl to the general category of "black female who is an embarrassment to us all", or, "black female whom we would prefer to keep out
of sight":

> She looked at Pecola. Saw the dirty torn dress, the plaits sticking
> out on her head, hair matted where the plaits had come undone,
> the muddy shoes with the wad of gum peeping out from between
> the cheap soles, the soiled socks, one of which had been walked
> down into the heel of the shoe. She saw the safety pin holding
> the hem of the dress up. . . . She had seen this little girl all of
> her life. (p. 75)

Pecola, for Geraldine, serves as symbol of everything ugly, dirty, and de-
grading. Physically as well as symbolically, Geraldine must negate Pecola,
must deny the ragged eleven-year-old access to her world. The woman who
does not sweat in her armpits or thighs, who smells of wood and vanilla
(pp. 70–71) says to Pecola, *quietly* says to Pecola: " 'Get out. . . . You nasty
little black bitch. Get out of my house!' " (p. 75). In other words, get out
of my world, out of the vision I construct before and about me. Pecola

leaves. As she leaves, she hangs her head, lowers her eyes; incapable of defending herself against visual distortion, Pecola attempts to deny vision altogether. But, even here, she fails: "she could not hold it [her head] low enough to avoid seeing the snowflakes falling and dying on the pavement" (p. 76). These snowflakes, falling and dying, suggest the visual perimeters of Pecola's world. In an earlier comment, Morrison generalizes as to the nature of these perimeters: "She would see only what there was to see: the eyes of other people" (p. 40). As these eyes do not see her, or see her only as a sign of something other, Pecola loses sight of herself.

Although Pecola's encounters with Mr. Yacobowski and Geraldine serve as the most complete and sensitively drawn examples of visual imbalance, they merely reenforce a pattern of imbalance begun much earlier in Pecola's life—for that matter, begun even before Pecola sees the light of day, while she is in Pauline's womb. During the nine months of pregnancy, Pauline spends most afternoons at the movies, picking up an education in white values of beauty and ugliness. Morrison describes this education as yet another violation of male on female, white on black. There, in a darkened theater, images come together, "all projected through the ray of light from above and behind" (p. 97). This ray of light resembles a gigantic eyeball (apologies to Emerson) which defines the boundaries of existence and which, of necessity, projects a white male vision. Having absorbed these silver-screen values, Pauline conjures up "a mind's eye view" of her soon-to-be-born child more in keeping with white fantasy than black reality. Upon birth, Pecola gives the lie to this view, and Pauline expresses her disappointment:

> So when I seed it, it was like looking at a picture of your mama when she was a girl. You know who she is, but she don't look the same. . . . Head full of pretty hair, but Lord she was ugly. (p. 99)

As various psychologists attest, the mother's gaze is of primary importance in generating a child's sense of self. Tragically, Pauline looks at her infant daughter and then looks away.

Morrison's novel contains repeated instances of Pecola's negation as other characters refuse to see her. *The Bluest Eye* also provides numerous instances of Pecola's desire to hide her own eyes, thereby refusing to acknowledge certain aspects of her world. Morrison articulates this desire for self-abnegation most explicitly in a postscript to her description of a typical fight between family members in the Breedlove home. Mrs. Breedlove hits Cholly with a dishpan, Cholly returns the blow with his fists, Sammy strikes at Cholly while shouting "you naked fuck," and Pecola covers her head with a quilt. The quilt of course cannot completely block out this scene, so Pecola

prays that God will make her disappear. Receiving no response from the
man in the sky, she does her best on her own:

> She squeezed her eyes shut. Little parts of her body faded away.
> Now slowly, now with a rush. Slowly again. Her fingers went,
> one by one; then her arms disappeared all the way to the elbow.
> Her feet now. Yes, that was good. The legs all at once. It was
> hardest above the thighs. She had to be real still and pull. Her
> stomach would not go. But finally it, too, went away. Then her
> chest, her neck. The face was hard, too. Almost done, almost.
> Only her tight, tight eyes were left. They were always left.
>
> Try as she might, she could never get her eyes to disappear.
> So what was the point? They were everything. Everything was
> there, in them. (p. 39)

These paragraphs forcefully convey Pecola's desire and her notion of how she
might realize it. If Pecola were to *see* things differently, she might *be seen*
differently; if her eyes were different, her world might be different too.[20]
As Morrison deals out one ugly jigsaw piece after another, as she fits the
pieces together to construct Pecola's world, we come to understand the
impulse behind Pecola's desire, as well as its ultimate futility. When boys
shout at her, " 'Black e mo Black e mo Ya daddy sleeps nekked' " (p. 55),
Pecola drops her head and covers her eyes; when Maureen accuses her of
having seen her father naked, Pecola maintains her innocence by disclaiming,
" 'I wouldn't even look at him, even if I did see him' " (p. 59); when
Maureen attacks her yet again Pecola tucks her head in "a funny, sad, helpless
movement. A kind of hunching of the shoulders, pulling in of the neck, as
though she wanted to cover her ears" (p. 60). By covering ears, eyes, and
nose Pecola attempts to shut out the testimony of her senses. Reminded of
her own ugliness or that of her world, she repeatedly resorts to an elemental
self-denial.

Pecola quavers when Mr. Yacobowski and Geraldine refuse to acknowledge her. She shrinks in fear when Maureen and Bay Boy insist on acknowl-
edging her ugliness. Quavering and shaking, Pecola *does* maintain a hold on
her world and herself—until Cholly smashes her illusions about the possibility of unambivalent love in this world. Throughout the novel, Pecola
ponders the nature of love, pursues it as a potentially miraculous phenomenon. On the evening of her first menstruation, for example, she asks, " 'How
do you do that? I mean, how do you get somebody to love you' " (p. 29).
And, after a visit to Marie, Poland, and China, Pecola ponders, "What did
love feel like? . . . How do grown-ups act when they love each other? Eat

fish together?" (p. 48). When Cholly rapes his daughter, he commits a sacrilege—not only against Pecola, but against her vision of love and its potential. Following the rape, Pecola, an unattractive eleven-year-old black girl, knows that for her, even love is bound to be dirty, ugly, of a piece with the fabric of her world. Desperate, determined to unwind the threads that compose this fabric, Pecola falls back on an early notion: the world changes as the eyes which see it change. To effect this recreation, Pecola seeks out the only magician she knows, Soaphead Church, and presents him with the only plan she can conceive. She asks that he make her eyes different, make them blue—blue because in Pecola's experience only those with blue eyes receive love: Shirley Temple, Geraldine's cat, the Fisher girl.

In its emotional complications, Soaphead's response to Pecola's request resembles Cholly's response to Pecola's defeated stance; both men move through misdirected feelings of love, tenderness, and anger.[21] Soaphead perceives Pecola's need and knows that he must direct the anger he feels not at her, but rather at the God who has encased her within black skin and behind brown eyes. But finally, when Soaphead decides to "look at that ugly black girl" and love her (p. 143), he violates her integrity in much the same way Cholly violates her body when he forces open her thighs. Prompted by the desire to play God and to make his performance a convincing one, Soaphead casts Pecola in the role of believer. Thus, although he *sees* Pecola more accurately than other characters do, he subordinates his vision of her to his vision of self-as-God. He later boasts in his letter "To He Who Greatly Ennobled Human Nature by Creating It":

> I did what You did not, could not, would not do: I looked at that ugly little black girl, and loved her. I played You. And it was a very good show! (p. 143)

Of course, the script for this show sends Pecola into realms of madness. Even Soaphead acknowledges that "No one else will see her blue eyes" (p. 143), but Soaphead justifies himself first on the grounds that "she will love happily ever after" and then, more honestly, on the grounds that "I, I have found it meet and right to do so" (p. 143). In other words, Soaphead's creation of false belief is not necessarily right for Pecola, but for himself. Morrison substantiates this assessment of Soaphead's creation a few pages later, when she portrays its effect on Pecola. Imprisoned now behind blue eyes, the schizophrenic little girl can talk only to herself. Obviously, this instance of male-female interaction parallels earlier scenes from the novel: "rape" occurs as Soaphead elevates himself at the expense of Pecola.

In *The Raw and the Cooked* Lévi-Strauss observes: "There exists no veritable end or term to mythical analysis, no secret unity which could be grasped at the end of the work of decomposition. The themes duplicate themselves to infinity."[22] Although the stories of Philomela, Persephone, and Pecola do not form a composite whole, each of them, with its varied and individual emphases, contributes to a much larger woman's myth, which tells of denial and disintegration, which unveils the oft-concealed connections between male reason, speech, presence and female madness, silence, absence. As a young black woman, Pecola assumes an especially poignant position in this growing complex of mythic representations; she is absent (and absenced) in relation to the norms of male culture and in relation to the norms of white culture. Ultimately, I read Pecola's story as a tragic version of the myth; this twentieth-century black woman remains behind blue eyes, an inarticulate, arm-fluttering bird. But I cannot read *The Bluest Eye* as tragedy; Claudia, our sometimes-narrator, *speaks,* as does Morrison, our full-time novelist. Thus, although the novel documents the sacrifice of one black woman, it attests to the survival of two others—a survival akin to that of Philomela or Persephone—filled with hardship, but also with hope.

NOTES

[1] Robert Stepto, " 'Intimate Things in Place': A Conversation with Toni Morrison," in *The Third Woman,* ed. Dexter Fisher (Boston: Houghton Mifflin, 1979), p. 167.

[2] A.E. Watts, trans., *The Metamorphoses of Ovid* (Berkeley: University of California Press, 1954), p. 131.

[3] Watts, p. 133.

[4] Ibid., p. 133.

[5] Ibid., p. 133.

[6] I take this term from Claude Lévi-Strauss. For an explanation of Lévi-Strauss's *modus operandi* see Robert Scholes, *Structuralism in Literature* (New Haven: Yale University Press, 1974), pp. 68–74.

[7] "From her initial family upbringing throughout her subsequent development, the social role assigned to the woman is that of serving an image, authoritative and central, of man: a woman is first and foremost a daughter/a mother/a wife." Shoshana Felman, "Women and Madness: The Critical Phallacy," *Diacritics* 5 (1975), p. 2.

[8] Toni Morrison, *The Bluest Eye* (New York: Pocket Books, 1979), p. 73. I will include all further page citations from Morrison's novel within the body of my text.

[9] An observation from Shoshana Felman about Balzac's short story "Adieu" condenses many of the associations described. Felman notes: "the dichotomy Reason/Madness, as well as Speech/Silence, exactly coincides in this text with the dichotomy Men/Women. Women as such are associated both with madness and with silence, whereas men appear not only as the possessors, but also as the dispensers, of reason, which they can at will mete out to—or take away from—others. . . . Masculine reason thus constitutes a scheme to capture and master, indeed, metaphorically RAPE the woman" (p. 7).

[10] Penelope Proddow, trans., *Demeter and Persephone, Homeric Hymn Number Two* (Garden City, N.Y.: Doubleday, 1972), n.p.

[11] Ibid., my italics.

[12] Ibid., n.p.

[13] Sir James George Frazer, *The Golden Bough* (New York: Macmillan and Company, 1950), p. 456.

[14] According to Frazer, in the original Homeric myth Persephone, drawn by the sight of narcissuses, moves beyond the reach of help. The choice of this particular plant as lure is of interest not only because of the Narcissus myth, but also because of recent psychoanalytic readings of this myth. These readings stress the importance of a child's progression through a stage of narcissistic self-love and suggest that this progression can occur only with the help of a mother-figure who assures the child of external love.

[15] Frazer, p. 456.

[16] Phyllis Chesler, *Women and Madness* (New York: Avon Books, 1973), p. xiv.

[17] Ibid., p. xv.

[18] See, for example, D.W. Winnicott, "Mirror-Role of Mother and Family in Child Development," in *The Predicament of the Family*, ed. Peter Lomas (New York: International University Press, 1967), pp. 26–33; Heinz Lichtenstein, "The Role of Narcissism in the Emergence and Maintenance of a Primary Identity," *International Journal of Psychoanalysis* 45 (1964), pp. 49–56.

[19] Why specify "Garden Avenue"? Perhaps Morrison wants to suggest that Pecola's experience is the twentieth-century urban counterpart to Persephone's experience in an actual garden?

[20] "If she looked different, beautiful, maybe Cholly would be different, and Mrs. Breedlove too. Maybe they'd say, 'Why, look at pretty-eyed Pecola. We mustn't do bad things in front of those pretty eyes' " (p. 40).

[21] Compare, for example, Cholly's response (pp. 127–28) to that of Soaphead (p. 137).

[22] Lévi-Strauss, *The Raw and the Cooked* (New York: Harper's, 1969), p. 5.

TERRY OTTEN

The Crime of Innocence
in Toni Morrison's Tar Baby

In Toni Morrison's fictional world no greater crime exists than innocence, for she understands well what the romantics learned long ago, that in a culture run by an oppressive order not to sin perpetuates an immoral justice. In such a world innocence is itself a sign of guilt because it signals a degenerate acquiescence. Not to fall becomes more destructive than to fall. Morrison's novels are peopled with conventionally evil characters, outsiders in a decadent, white-dominated culture, Cains and Liliths in the guise of Cholly Breedlove (*The Bluest Eye*) or Sula (*Sula*) or Guitar (*Song of Solomon*) or Son (*Tar Baby*). Ambiguous figures—on one hand characters of extreme violence and cruelty and, on the other hand, rebels against a morally deficient system—each of these suggests that evil can be redemptive and that goodness can be enslaving. In the language of existential theology, those who sin against the flawed order become the agents of experience and so run the risk of freedom. Those who do not are often doomed to moral entropy. Morrison herself has remarked that "evil is as useful as good" and "sometimes good looks like evil; sometimes evil looks like good."[1]

Yet Morrison's fictions are not simplistic polemics on the viciousness generated by a white society, though to be sure she unreservedly indicts the materialistic white culture and severely judges those blacks who adopt its values. Morrison's work exceeds mere invective. At their most profound level, the novels penetrate the characters themselves, exposing their own capacity for cowardice. Rather than sympathetic victims, they become responsible for their own actions and inactions. In all her major novels the

From *Studies in American Fiction* 14, No. 2 (Autumn 1986): 153–64.

fall from innocence becomes a necessary gesture of freedom and a profound act of self-awareness. It assumes the nature of a potentially tragic action, a paradoxical victory and defeat. In one way or another each work describes a fall wrought with anguish and destructive power but morally superior to a prolonged state of self-ignorance and sterile accommodation.

Of course, the theme of the Fall has been part of American literature from the Puritan age. As critics have long suggested, man's depraved spiritual condition has been an essential concern in writers from Nathaniel Hawthorne to Herman Melville to Edgar Allan Poe to Henry James, Eugene O'Neill, and James Dickey. Studies such as Robert Spiller's *The Cycle of American Literature* (1955), R. W. B. Lewis' *The American Adam* (1955), Sacvan Bercovitch's *The Puritan Origins of the American Self* (1975) and *The American Jeremiad* (1978), and, most recently, William Shurr's *Rappaccini's Daughters* (1981) have explored the persistence and variation of the Fall and related themes in recent as well as early literature. In adapting and modifying the traditional Fall pattern to fit her conception of the black experience in contemporary society, Morrison does not restrict so much as enlarge the scope of her vision, accommodating the particular features of American black culture while maintaining a universal mythic perspective. In particular, her novels mirror the realization R. W. B. Lewis attributes to Henry James, the recognition that Adam "had to fall, had to pass beyond childhood in an encounter with 'Evil,' had to mature by virtue of the destruction of his own egoism."[2] Morrison applies this "fortunate fall" idea through characters who must violate the prescribed conditions of a white society, must destroy the false identity ascribed them as blacks in a spurious "garden" to achieve wholeness and self-consciousness. Those co-opted by the system, such as Pauline Breedlove or Helene Wright or Ruth Dead, or those victimized by it, such as Pecola Breedlove, endure unredeemable defeat. Only those courageous and strong enough to deny the order can gain a measure of victory.

Morrison's most recent novel, *Tar Baby,* employs the idea of a necessary fall more explicitly than any of her other works, though all her novels examine the theme. Cynthia A. Davis has suggested that Morrison's fiction generally tries "to combine existential concerns compatible with a mythic presentation with an analysis of American society." In doing so, she continues, Morrison avoids simply grafting white myth onto the black experience by excluding whites, or at least focusing "attention not on the white characters' forcing of mythic rites . . . but on black characters' choices within the context of oppression."[3] *Tar Baby* to some degree challenges the thesis for it includes whites as central figures in the action. In developing these characters Morrison seemingly makes the mythic frame of the work more inclusive than that undergirding the earlier novels with their exclusively black characters and settings, although all the novels to some degree treat the primal theme of the Fall. To be sure *Tar Baby* is still, finally, a "black" novel in that it portrays the protagonist Jadine's quest to recover her black identity in a decadent white culture. But arguing that *Tar Baby* is "deeply expressive of the black's desire to create a mythology of his own to replace the stereotypes and myths the white man has constructed for him,"[4] John Irving overstates the case and ignores the novel's primary structure. In fact, this "black fable," as William Faulkner might have said, "grieves on universal bones." It incorporates the contemporary "black" experience in a larger, traditional myth. It gains universality in its inherited Fall pattern, the movement from a spurious garden state through confrontation with a serpent emanating from the self, to a frightening self-awareness, to expulsion and its consequences. As Valerian Street, the major white character, observes with pointed accuracy, "something in the crime of innocence" can paralyze the human spirit.[5] However devastating, only the loss of innocence can lead to selfhood and an existentially earned freedom.

Morrison employs images of a fallen paradise in all her novels. One of Pecola Breedlove's early encounters with white contempt takes place on "Garden Avenue" where she goes to Mr. Jacobowski's candy store to buy Mary Jane candies. *Sula*'s tragic events take place in Bottom, so called because "when God looks down, it's bottom. . . . It's the bottom of heaven—best land there is"[6] In *Song of Solomon* Guitar Bains alludes derisively to the "nigger heaven," Honoré Island, where wealthy blacks try to establish an island resort free from the suffering in the black community.[7]

The setting in *Tar Baby* explicitly parallels the lost Garden of Eden. It is a wealthy Caribbean estate where a retired Philadelphia candy manufacturer, Valerian Street, lives with his much younger wife, Margaret, and his two long-time black servants, Sydney and Ondine. Visiting is Jadine, Sydney and Ondine's beautiful niece, whom they have raised. A fashionable Paris model, she has been educated at the Sorbonne with Valerian's money and has spent most of her time in Paris or New York among aesthetes and the wealthy, including a rich white man who wants to marry her. The small community of expensive winter homes had been built by Haitian laborers and constructed above a swamp called Sein de Veilles, witch's tit. Valerian's house, L'Arbe de la Croix, is the most impressive of these isolated homes. The locals tell a story of one-hundred blind, black horsemen, descendants of slaves who swam from a sinking French slave ship carrying horses. Their free progeny are said to inhabit the island, and local blacks believe they still ride horses over the hills: "They learned to ride through the rain forest avoiding all sorts of trees and things. . . . They race each other, and for sport they sleep with the swamp women in Sein de Veilles" (pp. 152–53). On the edge of this mysterious realm, Valerian Street retreats to his greenhouse where he listens to classical music and reads plant catalogues, trying to evade a modern world of "disorder and meaninglessness." Yet even after three years his house has a "tentativeness." Valerian's greenhouse, with its artificially grown hydrangea, becomes a specious garden; the house itself, built above the ruins of a once idyllic land, has "a hotel feel about it" (p. 12).

Here, Morrison has remarked, characters have no "escape routes that people have in a large city. . . . No police to call. . . . No close neighbors to interfere." Here, she goes on to say, the characters are "all together in a pressure cooker . . . a kind of Eden."[8] Those living in this paradise bring with them the evidence of their own flawed humanity. And they await the serpent who somehow can force them to confront themselves, can make them see the truth that could set them free from their spiritual incapacity.

Enter Son. Like Guitar Bains or Sula, he threatens the tenuous peace and harmony of the already flawed world. The serpent in paradise is a black outlaw, a fugitive who, similar to Leggett in Joseph Conrad's "The Secret Sharer," first appears at night emerging from the waters of the unconscious self. Son hides out in a ship where Jadine and Margaret first appear in the novel. When they land and depart by jeep, he follows them to the estate. He secretly enters the house, partly from hunger, partly because it looks "cool and civilized." After several days he ventures upstairs "out of curiosity" and feels enraptured when he sees the sleeping Jadine, symbol of refinement and civilization. The house ironically becomes his "nighttime possession" (p. 138) in which he roams as a shadow figure of each character's undiscovered self. Once he is found out, he seeks acceptance like Beast in the legendary tale of Beauty and Beast: he showers, struggles to tame his wild hair, and tries to be worthy of Jadine, his Beauty. Suggestively, Valerian compares him with Michael, his own alienated son who always promises to visit but never does, for reasons that surface later. Though it is always Margaret who insists that Michael will return because he loves her so much, it is Valerian who feels most sorrowful when his son does not return. When Son is first discovered hiding in Margaret's closet, all the others express outrage at his being there, but Valerian finds himself defending Son, welcoming him, in part as Michael's surrogate and in part as just contempt for Jadine, Sydney, and Ondine's condemnation of another black.

The arrival of a criminal in the garden sends the characters scurrying to protect their innocence. Sydney, who prides himself on being "one of those Philadelphia Negroes," wants to call the police and get the "nigger" out as soon as possible. And Ondine, too, rejects him: "The man upstairs wasn't a Negro—meaning one of them. He is a stranger, a nasty and ignorant . . . nigger" (p. 102). And Jadine is indignant at Margaret's question, "you don't know him, do you?" She protests, "know him? How would I know him?" (p. 128). She had not seen a "Black like him" for some ten years when she lived on Morgan Street in Baltimore before her mother died and she went to Philadelphia at age twelve to live with her Uncle Sydney and Aunt Ondine. She considers Son's hair symbolic of criminality: "Wild, aggressive, vicious hair that needed to be put in jail. Uncivilized, reform school hair. Mau, Mau, Attica, chain-gang hair" (p. 113). Yet she finds in him that part of herself she has long denied. When he first grabs her from behind and presses against her, she has to acknowledge her own culpability: "He had jangled something in her that was so repulsive, so awful, and he had managed to make her feel that the Thing that repelled her was not in him, but in her. That was why she was ashamed" (p. 123). She had sworn at age twelve that she would "never" let herself be victimized by a man mounting her like a dog in heat, yet she could not deny that Son was drawn to her by her own animal nature, "which she couldn't help but which was her fault just the same" (p. 124). In short, Son enters paradise like the biblical serpent, articulates forbidden desires, and galvanizes Jadine into action. In his insistence that she acknowledge the "darker" side of herself, the authentic self obscured in the distorted mirror of her adopted Eden, Son forces Jadine to see the "beast" in the glass.

Until now, conditioned by her sophisticated European education, Jadine is detached from her own blackness, much like Helene Wright or Ruth Dead or Geraldine in *The Bluest Eye*. Eight years earlier when she last saw Michael while on vacation with the Streets, he had accused her of abandoning her people. Though she knew his idealistic scheme of generating social reform by having black welfare mothers "do crafts, pottery, clothing in their homes" was silly, she admitted that he "did make me want to apologize for what I was doing, what I felt. For liking 'Ave Maria' better than gospel music" (p. 74). Yet when they talk about Michael's hopeless plot, Jadine tells Valerian that "Picasso *is* better than Itumba mask" (p. 74), and she confesses her embarrassment at attending "ludicrous" art shows put on by pretentious blacks in Europe. Michael had encouraged her to return to Morgan Street with Sydney and Ondine to do handicraft. "Can you believe it?" she asks Valerian. "He might have convinced me if we'd had that talk on Morgan Street. But in Orange County on a hundred and twenty acres of green velvet?" (p. 75). She had long since moved in a white society where "the black people she knew wanted what she wanted" and where success required her "only to be stunning. . . . Say the obvious, ask stupid questions, laugh with abandon, look interested, and light up at any display of their humanity if they showed it" (pp. 126–27).

Nonetheless, Son's presence restores something of her black awareness, just as Guitar Bains awakens Milkman's black consciousness in *Song of Solomon*. He prompts her to recall the guilt she felt two months before when a beautiful African woman in a canary yellow dress spit on her in disgust in a Paris street. The embodiment of Jadine's own black heritage, the woman floated through glass like a vision out of her self, an alter ego manifesting judgment.[9] As with the woman, Jadine felt something ambivalent toward Son even from the beginning. Her "neck prickled" when she heard Margaret call him a gorilla, even though she herself "had volunteered nigger" (p. 129). And she experienced a "curious embarrassment" picturing herself watching "red-necked gendarmes zoom him away in a boat" (p. 126). Somehow Son spoke from her dream consciousness, just as the African women invaded her psyche. The very morning Son was found in the house, Jadine had stared out her window trying to visualize the one-hundred black horsemen who supposedly roamed the hills. She had run away from Paris to decide whether or not to marry a wealthy white man, Son's opposite, and felt somehow "inauthentic." On the edge of a fall, Jadine, too, awaits the tempter who can penetrate her illusory garden room, which Son himself describes as "fragile—like a dollhouse for an adult doll" (p. 131).

And Son too is ambiguous. Though he "burrowed in his plate like an animal" and sat "grunting in monosyllables," sipping from his saucer and wiping up salad dressing with his bread, he is no wild boar. Even Ondine confesses that "he's been here long enough and quiet enough to rape, kill and steal—do whatever he wanted and all he did was eat" (p. 99). Enthralled by Jadine, he had stared at her through the night with an "appetite for her so gargantuan it lost its focus and spread to his eyes, the orange of his shirt, the curtains, the moonlight" (p. 138); but he never violated her, standing before her image like Beast trembling outside Beauty's door in Jean Cocteau's brilliant surrealistic film of Beauty and the Beast. When Valerian welcomes him into the civilized circle, he willfully adapts. He puts on a Hickey Freeman suit, apologizes to Jadine and Ondine, begins using "ma'am," "Mr.," and "Sir," and talks about his own "mama" with Ondine. He even tells Valerian how to get rid of ants by using mirrors and revitalizes Valerian's cyclamens by flicking them with his fingers. Valerian accepts Son as surrogate to Michael, the legitimate "son" having turned prodigal, the outlaw "Son" having returned in the guise of a black "other." In so characterizing Son, Morrison makes him something more than "the official heroic black male"[10] some critics see when they read *Tar Baby* as a stereotypical black novel. Criminal and hero, Son embodies the ambivalence of the serpent figure: forbidden but unconsciously willed, possessing healing powers but potentially destructive. He recalls growing up with Cheyenne, a demon-like lover who always waited for him outside Mrs. Tyler's house where he took piano lessons. Toward the end of the novel, he tells Jadine how at eighteen he went to Vietnam, was busted, went back to Eloe, Florida, where he grew up, and married the promiscuous but nonetheless innocent Cheyenne. When he came home drunk after a fight and found her sleeping with a thirteen year old, he ran his car through the house and started a fire that killed her. But like Conrad's ambiguous Leggatt, Son ran away not in simple fear but because, he recalls, "I didn't want their punishment, I wanted my own" (p. 172). Without roots, "sought for but not after," he had spent eight years among Huck Finns, Nigger Jims, Calibans; a Cain "driven across the face of the earth," he also possesses the moral consciousness of a romantic rebel, the ambiguity of the satanic figure in William Blake or Melville.

No wonder Jadine is threatened by him. On one hand, like a black Jane Eyre, she wants to clean, tame, and control him; and when he begins to show his civilized nature, she finds it impossible to resist him. Yet it is his raw, powerful being that most challenges her. At one point he tells Jadine that "there is something in you to be smelled which I have discovered myself. And no seal-skin coat or million-dollar earrings can disguise it" (p. 125). Once when Jadine waits for him to return with gas for the jeep, she gets trapped accidentally in the swamp quicksand. Like Milkman caught in the Virginia woods in *Song of Solomon,* she is stripped of every vestige of civilization; and the "swamp women" who supposedly mate with the legendary black horsemen temporarily claim her. Suggestively, though, it is at the ill-fated Christmas dinner when Jadine and the other characters confront the devastating self-knowledge that drives them out of paradise.

Here, all the lies concocted to preserve innocence prove futile. For long years Margaret and Valerian Street had evaded the truth, Sydney and Ondine had settled into a passive acquiescence, Jadine had sacrificed her blackness to succeed in a white world. As they approach Christmas day their lives have been suddenly revived by Son's coming. New hope arises: Valerian and Margaret sleep together for the first time in many years, Jadine awakens from long self-repression, there is renewed hope that Michael really will come, and even Valerian's plants begin to thrive under Sons's "black magic." Symbolically, like a Christ child, Son seemingly "made something grow that was dying." Yet when Valerian fires the black servants, Gideon and Thérèse, because they were supposedly stealing apples, paradise falls. Son's illusion that Valerian is a worthy white man collapses, and he sees in the rich man's harsh gesture the suppression he had found in other white oppressors. Valerian could now see in Son's eyes "one hundred black men on one hundred unshod horses" (p. 206). The precarious balance of deceit that had sustained the garden can no longer endure: the truth gives witness to a fallen world.

All stand exposed. The community of whites and blacks, owners and servants, is torn asunder when Son, the outcast, threatens the order. His rebellion against Gideon and Thérèse's dismissal reveals the lies each character has grasped to guard against self-knowledge. His anger releases Ondine's long held secret. In her violent outcry she confesses that Margaret had abused Michael as a child. As a nineteen year old mother, Margaret, once "the Principle Beauty of Maine," had stuck pins into Michael and burned him with cigarettes. She had grown up satisfied in a "tackey" trailer in South Suzanne until, at fourteen, she became conscious of her beauty and so lost her innocence. Married by the insistent Valerian when she was only seventeen, Margaret moved into his wealthy home where she felt the intimidating presence of Valerian's ex-wife and "stiffened like Joan Fontaine in *Rebecca*" (p. 58). Driven to perversion by a profound loneliness, she had tortured her son. Still wanting desperately to believe that Michael loved her and would return for her sake at Christmas, she had tried to recreate the trailer she grew up in in her bedroom at L'Arbe de la Croix until the "nigger in the woodpile," the serpent haunting her unconscious, invaded her reconstructed paradise.

But the guilt is a composite guilt in which Valerian also shares. He, too, yearns to go to Michael, "find him, touch him, rub him, hold him in his arms" (p. 232), but he himself had caused Margaret's loneliness, had driven her to see her child as a threat to her in "its prodigious appetite for security," in its "criminal arrogance" (p. 236). Responding to her profound guilt, Margaret seeks punishment from Valerian, asking him to hit her; but he always responds "tomorrow, perhaps, tomorrow" for he is too incapacitated by his own guilt to act. While she seeks absolution by washing her red hair again and again and drying it in the sun "against every instruction ever given her about the care of her hair" (p. 285), Valerian isolates himself in his greenhouse caring for nothing. He, too, knows his culpability, "because he had lived with a woman who had made something kneel down in him the first time he saw her, but about whom he knew nothing," because he "had watched his son grow and talk but also about him he had known nothing." And there was "something in the crime of innocence so revolting it paralyzed him. He had not known because he had not taken the trouble to know" (p. 242). Though Morrison gives Valerian a measure of sympathy as he recalls the time he lost his own childhood the day a black, toothless washerwoman told him his father was dead, she speaks decidedly of his guilt in one of her most eloquent passages:

> An innocent man is a sin before God. Inhuman and therefore unworthy. No man should live without absorbing the sins of his kind, the foul air of his innocence, even if it did wilt rows of angel trumpets and cause them to fall from their vines (p. 243).

Pearl Bell's contention that Morrison's own feelings toward Valerian vacillate between "fondness and outrage"[11] may in fact be true, but the outrage is directed to more than his racism, and the "fondess" exceeds mere sentimentality. His ambiguous nature, worthy both of judgment and compassion, results from his essential, flawed humanity, not from his mere whiteness.

Even Ondine and Sydney share in the crime. Ondine had not stopped Margaret from torturing Michael even though she knew of her cruelty. When Ondine protests that she did not stop Margaret because it was not her job, Margaret responds "no, it's not your job, Ondine. But I wish it had been your duty, I wish you had liked me enough to help me" (p. 241). And even in his dreams, Sydney knew he lived in a false Eden with Valerian Street. He prided himself on being "one of those Philadelphia Negroes," but each night he dreamed his "tiny dream" of the lost Eden in Baltimore he gave up for security and position. No one, neither black nor white, can claim innocence.

After the fall, Valerian and Margaret seem to be beyond recovery, and Sydney and Ondine remain uncertain about their end. Only Son and Jadine act. They leave the irreparable garden to go to New York, where Jadine intends to assimilate Son into her world of security. The contraries cannot coexist, though, and neither character proves capable of integrating the opposite. Gideon had warned Son about Jadine: "Your first yalla? . . . Look out. It's hard for them not to be white people. Hard, I'm telling you. Most never make it" (p. 155). Jadine's acceptance of white values is reflected in her urban environment. She is pure city: Baltimore, Philadelphia, Paris, New York. And Son is all rural Florida, "Eloe." He stands outside the white system, a riotous Cain; she sells herself to the monied urban culture. Yet fleeing the debunked Edenic island, they try vainly to stay together. In contrast to Jadine's easy indifference, Son cannot help empathizing with the outcast blacks he finds in the city. Once, while working a demanding job loading boxes, he brought home a wild, tempestuous black woman who reminded him of his sister. The direct contrast to Jadine, she was cursing a man in the middle of traffic, shouting obscenities in "the voice of a sergeant," her "face . . . as tight and mean as broccoli" (p. 227), her eyes narrow and angry, a ring glittering in her nose. Embracing this seemingly unlovable primal being, Son took her to dinner with Jadine and then back to their apartment, where she stole his change and left during the night. In Jadine's world, Son cannot be of it. For her part, Jadine temporarily finds something restorative in Son's impulsiveness and powerful black pride. "He unorphaned her completely. Gave her a brand-new childhood" (p. 229). But clearly Son cannot live comfortably in Jadine's self-constructed paradise. When Son takes her to his lost garden in Eloe, it is apparent that she cannot live in his world either with its apparent poverty and ignorance and isolation. Eloe embodies all the "blackness" she had long struggled to escape.

Eloe represents the opposite to Son: self-worth, wholeness, and values. Long separated from his father because he fled after his wife's death, Son carried with him the guilt of a prodigal son. Though he had written money orders to his father, he felt ashamed that he had never written a note. His father had not cashed the money orders, in part because Son wrote his name on them, and he treasured Son's handwriting, "pretty, like your mama" (p. 250). A returned prodigal suffering remorse, Son honored his father's moral judgment that Jadine should not stay in his house if she and Son were not married. Made morally sensitive, Son insists to Jadine that she stay at his Aunt Rosa's modest house.

Jadine, too, becomes morally alive. She experiences profound self-awareness when Aunt Rosa accidentally sees her naked in bed: "No man made her feel that naked, that unclothed. Leerers, lovers, doctors, artists— none of them had made her feel exposed. More than exposed. Obscene" (p. 253). And here too she dreams of judgment. She sees all the black women in her life in the dark out the door: "The night women were not merely against her . . . not merely looking superior over their sagging breasts and folded stomachs, they seemed somehow in agreement about her, and they were all out to get her, tie her, bind her. Grab the person she had worked hard to become and choke it off with their soft loose tits" (p. 262). Even when he first saw her sleeping at Valerian's estate, Son yearned "to press his dreams" into Jadine's consciousness, to will her out of the white man's house and into a world of "fat black ladies in white dresses minding the pie tables in the basement of the church and white wet sheets flapping on the line" (p. 119). But though he devastated Valerian's white paradise, he could not reclaim her. His failure becomes apparent when Jadine tells him that while he was playing criminal driving his car into his wife's bed, hiding from the law, she was being educated with the help of a "poor old white dude." "Stop loving your ignorance," she tells him; "it isn't lovable" (p. 256). Yet he also denies *her* pride. What they taught you in college "didn't include me," he tells her, and so they kept you ignorant, "because until you know about me, you don't know nothing about yourself" (p. 264).

Coming to a frightening awareness, naked after the fall, Jadine eludes the truth, flees back to the elite society where she will never recover from her loss of innocence. Incapable of a saving sin against her security, she will never integrate her other self. According to Susan Lydon, Jadine is caught between her sex and her race. To be true to her freedom as a woman, she must resist Son's male insistence that she play the subservient role of "fat black ladies" serving pies in the church basement. To be true to her black heritage, though, she needs to sacrifice success in a white culture. Says Lydon, "she is neither female enough nor black enough to make it in her culture."[12] Viewed in this context, Jadine's "fall" leads to no recovery. Cast East of Eden, she exists in unresolved duality, knowing Good and Evil, Black and White.

And Son, too, cannot survive. When he returns to the island looking frantically for Jadine, the wise Thérèse, descendant of the blind horsemen, asks, "if you cannot find her what will you do? Live in the garden of some other white people house?" (p. 305). She tells him to forget Jadine because "she has forgotten her ancient properties" (p. 305). And finally she offers him the only escape, joining the legendary horsemen in the hills: "They are waiting in the hills for you. They are naked and they are black too. . . . Go there. Choose them" (p. 306). Elizabeth House argues that Son is "the rabbit" that escapes to the briars, "that Jadine, the tar baby, will not successfully lure Son again."[13] Perhaps so, but Morrison allows Son no victory separate from the timeless world of legend and darkness. Becoming an eternal night rider returning to the dark unconscious from which he emerged, Son retreats from a world where he can find no reconciliation, no solution to his fallen humanity.

Jadine and Son, Valerian and Margaret, Sydney and Ondine, all bear the consequences of self-knowledge. All move East of Eden. The Fall motif of *Tar Baby* does not explain away the novel's possible flaws, the sometimes obscure character motivation, the near self-indulgent style in some descriptive passages, or the rather awkward shift in tone and focus when Jadine and Son leave the island. But it makes Morrison's work considerably more substantial and meaningful than some critics have contended. To be sure, Morrison partly follows in the tradition of distinctly American literature with the depiction of the essential conflict between primitivity and civilization, rural and urban, redskin and pale face. But like her other novels,

Tar Baby describes the passage from innocence to experience with biblical
and theological elements: garden images, references to the "snake," expression of guilt and lost innocence, a yearning for the garden. In all this she
incorporates the black search for identity. Without significantly reducing
the social commentary, the Fall theme raises the novel to a more universal
level; without stereotyping characters as allegorical types, it gives them a
symbolic dimension; without imposing structure, it provides an integrating
pattern; and without sacrificing the novel's integrity, it allows for artistic
ambiguity. Their duality exposed, the characters all seek equilibrium and
struggle to exist in creative tension with their own dark sides. Cast from
Edenic existence by virtue of their self-awareness, they all live after the Fall.
Yet Morrison makes clear in all her novels that the authentic life can only
be lived after a fall, that the ultimate crime is innocence itself; the "tar
baby" that ensnares her characters is their own self-ignorance. In her fictional
realm "good" and "evil" constantly shift, and all her characters are convicted
of their humanity. In just such a world, a fall from innocence is ironically
essential to being, however frightening the risks, however ironic the end.

NOTES

[1] " 'Intimate Things in Place': A Conversation with Toni Morrison," in *Chants of Saints: A Gathering of Afro-American Literature, Art, and Scholarship,* eds. Michael S. Harper and Robert B. Stepto (Urbana: Univ. of Illinois Press, 1979), p. 216.

[2] R. W. B. Lewis, *The American Adam: Innocence, Tragedy and Tradition in the Nineteenth Century* (Chicago: Univ. of Chicago Press, 1953), p. 55. For a discussion of the fortunate fall in English romantic and modern literature, see my study *After Innocence: Visions of the Fall in Modern Literature* (Pittsburgh: Univ. of Pittsburgh Press, 1982), pp. 8–51.

[3] Cynthia A. Davis, "Self, Society, and Myth in Toni Morrison's Fiction," *Contemporary Literature,* 23 (1982), 334–35. See also Peter Bruck's full treatment of Morrison's use of Afro-American Myths in *Song of Solomon* and other works. "Returning to One's Roots: The Motif of Searching and Flying in Toni Morrison's *Song of Solomon,*" in *The Afro-American Novel since 1960,* eds. Peter Bruck and Wolfgang Karrer (Amsterdam: B. R. Gruvern, 1982), pp. 289–305.

[4] John Irving, "Morrison's Black Fable," *New York Times Book Review* (March 29, 1981), p. 31.

[5] Toni Morrison, *Tar Baby* (New York: New American Library, 1981), p. 242. Subsequent page numbers will be cited parenthetically in the text.

[6] Toni Morrison, *Sula* (New York: New American Library, 1973), p. 5.

[7] Toni Morrison, *Song of Solomon* (New York: New American Library, 1977), p. 104.

[8] Nellie McKay, "An Interview with Toni Morrison," *Contemporary Literature,* 24 (1983), 417.

[9] Morrison identifies the African woman in yellow as the "original self—the self we betray when we lie, the one that is always there. And whatever that self looks like . . . one measures one's self against it." See McKay, p. 422.

[10] Webster Schott, "Toni Morrison: Tearing the Social Fabric," *Book World, The Washington Post* (March 22, 1981), p. 1.

[11] Pearl K. Bell, "Self-Seekers," *Commentary* (August, 1981), p. 57.

[12] Susan Lydon, "What's an Intelligent Woman to Do?" *The Village Voice* (July 1–7, 1981), p. 41.

[13] Elizabeth B. House, "The 'Sweet Life' in Toni Morrison's Fiction," *American Literature*, 56 (1984), 201.

MELVIN DIXON

Like an Eagle in the Air:
Toni Morrison

In recent interviews Toni Morrison has talked about her midwestern, Ohio background and the possibilities it presents for new settings in Afro-American fiction. "It's an interesting state from the point of view of black people because it is right there by the Ohio River, in the south, and at its northern tip is Canada. And there were these fantastic abolitionists there, and also the Ku Klux Klan lived there . . . So I loved writing about that because it was so wide open" (*Chant*, 215). On another occasion she remarked, "Ohio offers an escape from stereotyped black settings. It is neither plantation nor ghetto" (Tate, 119). From a home that is neither typically North nor South, Morrison, like Ellison, who comes from Oklahoma, freely explores new physical and metaphorical landscapes in her fiction. She envisions space with fewer historically or politically fixed boundaries and endows her characters with considerable mobility. Her play of language upon and from within the land creates areas of symbolic activity for both author and protagonists: house and yard become scenes of psychological dislocation in *The Bluest Eye* (1970); land gradations and moral codes have inverted meaning in *Sula* (1973); mountain, farm, and island emerge as stages for enacting dramas of self-creation, racial visibility, and cultural performance in *Song of Solomon* (1977) and in *Tar Baby* (1981). Starting with her birthplace in Lorain, Ohio, and subsequent transformations of that place into several charged fields in fiction, Toni Morrison has imagined a complex and multitextured world.

The symbolic geography in Morrison's fiction emerges from the precise

From *Ride Out the Wilderness: Geography and Identity in Afro-American Literature* (Urbana: University of Illinois Press, 1987), pp. 141–69.

115

physical details that give her black neighborhoods so much startling character and presence. Medallion, Ohio, or Shalimar, Virginia, fixes firmly in the imagination and shapes either terrestrial or celestial images through which Morrison initiates a dialogue with earlier texts discussed in this study, most notably with Ralph Ellison's *Invisible Man*. In the three novels that have earned Morrison an indisputable prominence in contemporary American letters, the author enlarges and completes many previous attempts to show the importance of both place and person in the development of Afro-American culture. From the songs her characters sing to transform otherwise dreary households into spiritual havens, and from the journeys they undertake through history and myth as in the early slave narratives (as the author revealed, "You know, I go sometimes and, just for sustenance, I read those slave narratives—there are sometimes three or four sentences of half a page, each one of which could be developed in an art form, marvelous" [*Chant*, 229]) comes the achievement of form and art in Morrison's fiction.

Attentive to the physical and cultural geography of the small black towns that have shaped her and her characters, Morrison constructs familiar yet new dialectical oppositions between enclosed and open spaces, between the fluid horizontality of neighborhoods (shifting, migrating populations, a profusion of character types and changing morals) and the fixed verticality, hence presumed stability, of the house. Morrison calls for an end to Ellisonian inertia and a delight in the free fall. These oppositions produce various exciting results that propel characters and readers toward the principal move-ment in Morrison's fiction: the leap from land into sky. Pecola Breedlove, for one, ventures to the "cave" of Elihue's mind (the cerebral force, readers will recall, that pushed Ellison's protagonist to consider ending his under-ground hibernation, "Because, damn it, there's the mind, the *mind*. It wouldn't let me rest" [433]) and its reservoir of conjure and magic. Pecola comes away with the cherished blue eyes that she alone can see (a blindness that completes the invisibility she had suffered from others). She wears a vision of the sky but never gains its reward of flight (is the name Pecola a variant of peacock?). For Pecola's aesthetic choice sinks her evermore into the mire of self-hatred that had initially created her desire. Sula, on the other hand, longs for flight and song but gets no farther than the upper rooms of Eva's house of death. The house opposes the space of Ellison's cellar, but it is filled with the same inertia (the stunted growth of the eternally juvenile Deweys is one example). The one character who eventually learns to resist the gravitational pull of social conformity and to grasp what his newly stretched imagination can reach is Milkman Dead. He earns the authority to sing his real name, for he not only has discovered the long-sought-for ancestor Solomon, he becomes him when he tries the air. That test of the air—the risk, the ultimate surrender to it, and the strengthening *ride*—culminates Morrison's metaphorical triumph over conventional terrestrial frontiers or boundaries to identity, moving up into the celestial infinity of its achievement. Milkman's journey from No Mercy Hospital to the cave in Danville, Pennsylvania, and from a wilderness hunt to a mountaintop discovery in Shalimar, Virginia, offers a more satisfying solution to black homelessness than the reflective yet artificial hibernation Ellison had proposed.

THE BLUEST EYE. "WHEN THE LAND KILLS OF ITS OWN VOLITION"

Claudia MacTeer, the occasional and maturing narrator in Morrison's first novel, discovers one of the earth's peculiar traits that the may mitigate the guilt she feels for the failure of her marigold seeds to grow: *"For years I thought my sister was right: it was my fault. I had planted [our seeds] too far down in the earth. It never occurred to either of us that the earth itself might have been unyielding"* (3). This revelation brings only partial relief. It offers one explanation of the novel's theme: the loss of innocence. The underlying question concerns the earth's role in bringing on misfortune, in creating a climate for Pecola's suffering and insanity as well as confusing the parameters of moral responsibility. The actual telling of the story, the sharing of narration among several voices, including Pauline's interior monologues, leads Claudia to confess too late the community's and her own complicity in acquiescing to hostility by taking life's misery too much for granted. "We acquiesce and say the victim had no right to live. We are wrong, of course, but it doesn't matter. It's too late" (164). The victim here is not only Pecola's premature and dead baby, sired by Pecola's own father, but also Pecola herself. The loss of Claudia's and Frieda's innocence, as they witness and report Pecola's decline, makes them victims as well.

The Bluest Eye is Morrison's study of a community out of touch with the land and the history that might have saved them. The displacement of blacks had begun long before Claudia's retrospective narration about the failed marigolds. The distance between their lives and the ideal American home or family, depicted in the passage from the grade-school reader that opens the novel, is also measured by the increasingly distorted passage, parts of which later introduce the subject of each subsequent chapter. This technique reveals the pervasive trauma of dislocation suffered by Pecola, Claudia, Soaphead Church, and the entire community.

The grade-school text is designed primarily to teach language skills by describing supposedly familiar situations lodged in social myths of education and upward mobility. The environment evoked by Mother, Father, Dick, and Jane in their neat little house and yard with the requisite cat and dog juxtaposes starkly against the lives of the pupils who are learning to read. They do learn their position outside the text as readers, but, more important, their place outside the "home" and "neighborhood" depicted here. Pecola's distance from the text and from society increases greatly when her most intimate spaces—the home and parts of the body—are violated when she is raped by her father. Pecola's deteriorating emotional balance and the trouble witnessed by Frieda and Claudia that forces their early maturation appear first in a gradual compression of print in the passage until the words jumble together. The distortion represents the girls' actual education. The syntactical and typographical disorder reveals the increasing violation of physical, social, and personal space. The position of the words and set of type on the page as well as that of reader to the text have been altered not only by the difference between ideal and actual settings, but also by those forces in society that constantly displace individuals by offering negative refuge. Morrison returns us once again to the prototypical nameless, homeless, landless situation of black Americans in literature and in society. The myth of recovery and replacement and the false Pecola constructs—having blue eyes—are more damaging.

The concern for place and home hinted at by the grade-school text is developed further in Claudia's description of her neighborhood and the difference between her house and Pecola's storefront residence. Their respective homes indicate more than a difference in social class; they set the stage for Morrison's view of the ambivalent attraction and repulsion of the middle class for lower-class vitality. In Morrison's later novels, the prissy Nel is drawn to Sula's "woolly house" (29) and bourgeois Milkman Dead finds vibrant life in the disorder at Pilate's ramshackle cabin. Morrison is less concerned with class conflict, however, than with the spontaneous affirmation of cultural and spiritual well-being that exists outside the borders of middle-class respectability.

"Our house is old, cold, and green" (5), says Claudia, bringing to mind a variation of the "green and white" house in the grade-school text. Claudia's assessment of place and house introduces her perception of black homelessness and wilderness that motivates an almost desperate urge to own property and secure refuge. Cholly Breedlove violates the primacy of the home in an affront to middle-class aspirations by burning his storefront dwelling and putting his family out. He incurs Claudia's wrath and exposes her insecurity as well as her fear of homelessness and the uncertain outdoors (a wilderness of sorts): "If you are put out, you go somewhere else; if you are outdoors, there is no place to go" (11). Outdoors becomes the real terror of the middle class, a grim reminder of their political and economic vulnerability. To relieve this insecurity, people buy property with a vengeance. Cholly Breedlove, however, a "renting black" (12), exists apart from this class concern. His violent behavior turns his son Sammy into a perennial runaway and his daughter Pecola into a welfare "case" (11), which is how she enters the MacTeer family temporarily and begins a precarious friendship with Frieda and Claudia. Breedlove, in his disdain for property (burning his residence) and family (putting them out*doors*) is seen as part of the moral as well as physical wilderness: "having put his family outdoors, [he] had catapulted himself beyond the reaches of human consideration. He had joined the animals; was, indeed, an old dog, a snake, a ratty nigger" (12). He lands in jail. Until her family is reunited, Pecola has more than a taste of the comfortable life: she drinks three quarts of milk a day from a Shirley Temple glass.

The Breedloves' storefront residence is a "box of peeling gray" (25) on the top floor of which live several prostitutes: China, Poland, and the Maginot Line (Miss Marie), named for landscapes they would neither visit nor represent. The whores become a surrogate family to Pecola, for they are comfortable in their profession, their self-chosen place. They offer Pecola a social education her more-displaced mother refuses to give. Pauline, who "never felt at home anywhere, or that she belonged anyplace" (86), finds a world where her sense of order, arrangement, and privacy can have full reign, working, ironically, as a maid for the white Fisher family. They not only allow Pauline this private, self-defined space, but also give her a nickname so place-specific that it signifies both the "illusion" of privacy and its invasion each time she is called Polly. More devastating is Pauline's proprietary selfishness; she refuses to share the kitchen with her own children: "Pauline kept this order, this beauty, for herself, a private world, and never introduced it into her storefront, or to her children" (100). Given such maternal neglect, it is small wonder that Pecola would also seek an illusion of beauty in wanting blue eyes.

Morrison's further explorations into the relation between person and place, between identity (visible or invisible) and land center in the lives of Pecola and Cholly and inform all of her fiction. Invisibility is foisted upon Pecola not only because she is black and female, but also because she is ugly. She suffers "the total absence of human recognition—the glazed separateness" (36), alienating her from others. Cholly, when young, mired himself in ugly behavior and self-hatred when he started to see himself as negatively as whites viewed him. On the night following his Great-Aunt Jimmy's funeral, Cholly was caught in the act of making love in the woods by white hunters. The flashlight they shone on his nakedness also illuminated their view of him: "Get on wid it, nigger. . . . An' make it good" (116). Turning his rage inward and onto Darlene instead of at the whites, Cholly experiences the self-hatred he will later inspire in Pauline and Pecola. Furthermore, the physical ugliness that makes Cholly and Pecola so visible that they are invisible also makes them, in Claudia's view, willful prisoners of their shabby storefront: "They lived there because they were poor and black, and they stayed there because they believed they were ugly" (28).

What might have redeemed Cholly in his own eyes and have prevented the internalization of ugliness was his search for his estranged father. Cholly's journey when young had led him not to the "green and white" (1) house of social myth, nor to the "old, cold, and green" (5) house of the black middle class, but to the folded greenbacks poking from the fists of city gamblers. Among them he finds his father, who is more interested in scoring a hit than recognizing his son. Crushed by this rejection, Cholly loses control of himself (indeed, his very bowels) and retreats into the woods. There by the Ocmulgee River, he washes himself and his clothes in a kind of purification ritual, which is complete only when pent-up tears of grief and loneliness finally cascade down his face. Cholly had been prepared to show his grief (a form of recognition itself) by nesting in the woods ("the dark, the warmth, the quiet, enclosed Cholly like the skin and flesh of an elderberry protecting its own seed" [124]), undressing, and feeling about on his hands and knees for the cleansing edge of water. When he cries, he becomes the "new young boy" (125) who will be received back in town by three women offering him lemonade and his manhood through sex. But the freedom Cholly experiences so briefly needs connections to be fully meaningful, even to Cholly, and he longs for a song to sing to activate his new identity. Lacking the music, his transformation and self-confidence are all too brief:

> The pieces of Cholly's life could become coherent only in the head of a musician. Only those who talk their talk through the gold of curved metal, or in the touch of black-and-white rectangles and taut skins and strings echoing from wooden corridors, could give true form to his life. Only they would know how to connect the heart of a red watermelon to the asafetida bag to the muscadine to the flashlight on his behind to the fists of money to the lemonade in a Mason jar to a man called Blue and come up with what all of that meant in joy, in pain, in anger, in love,

and give it its final and pervading ache of freedom. Only a
musician would sense, know, without even knowing that he
knew, that Cholly was free. (125)

Without music, Cholly's freedom has no voice, no meaningful or cohering
performance to tie together the loose tangling strands of his life thus far.
His failure to act upon or act with the identity he has discovered renders
his freedom tenuous, his virility inadequate. Cholly's one effort to make
connections to the past and present through love results in his rape of Pecola.
Cholly had perceived Pecola's unconscious and innocent scratching of her
leg with the opposite foot as a reminder of the moment he had fallen in
love with Pauline, who was leaning against a road fence—like Hurston's
Janie—"scratching herself with a broken foot" (126). Cholly's warped confusion of time and place becomes his odd performance. His one effort to
heal displacement ends up sending Pecola and Pauline more out*doors* than
before, right to "the edge of town."
      Pecola's rape neither begins nor completes her emotional disintegration.
That deed is left to Soaphead Church, another figure alienated from the land
("Dear God: . . . . Once upon a time I lived greenly and youngish on one
of your islands" [140]), who had accepted the nickname in exchange for his
false conjure and magic. He grants Pecola's wish for blue eyes. His appearance
and act in the novel as a *deus ex machina* borrowed from drama are more
diabolical than Cholly's deed, which at least offered Pecola a kind of love
and recognition, however perverted. Soaphead offers insanity. Both men
keep Pecola grounded—if not pinned bodily—to the kitchen floor until she
loses consciousness or becomes mired in schizophrenia and delusion. Both
family and community, loved ones and landscape, have banished Pecola. A
devastating inertia prevents her from achieving the flight she thought would
come with the blue eyes. Pecola wears a vision of the sky (like Cholly's
search for transcendent, cohering music) but fails to achieve its reward of
flight: "The damage done was total. She spent her days, her tendril, sap-
green days, walking up and down, up and down, her head jerking to the
beat of a drummer so distant only she could hear. Elbows bent, hands on
shoulders, she flailed her arms like a bird in an eternal, grotesquely futile
effort to fly. Beating the air, a winged but grounded bird, intent on the
blue void it could not reach—could not even see—but which filled the
valleys of the mind" (162).
      As Pecola scavenges through garbage, her birdlike gestures diminish
"to a mere picking and plucking her way between the tire rims and the
sunflowers, between Coke bottles and milkweed, among all the waste and

beauty of the world" (162), and Claudia realizes the extent to which Pecola had absorbed the waste she and others had dumped on her. In return Pecola simply gave the only beauty she had: her innocence. Claudia, now mature, realizes that the failure of marigold seeds to grow that year was not only the fault of "the earth, the land, of our town" (164), but hers as well. Having acquiesced to the easy victimization of Pecola, Claudia had failed to acknowledge the earth's own will to kill and the readiness of humans to accomplish the deed.

SULA. "IT'S THE BOTTOM OF HEAVEN—BEST LAND THERE IS"

A more complex figuration of land and identity emerges in *Sula*. Beyond the psychological boundaries that imprison Pecola and allow the MacTeer sisters to bear witness to the loss of sexual and mental place, *Sula* tells the story of two women who renegotiate the pressures of place and person through their long friendship, which is not without moments of rupture and discord. The growing bond between Nel Wright and Sula Mae Peace as well as their complementary personalities are first revealed to us by the contrasting features of the land.

Two key terrestrial images frame the novel: the hillside signifying the creation of the black community of Medallion, Ohio, known as the Bottom (through the chicanery of a white planter unwilling to fulfill his promise of valley land to an industrious and newly emancipated slave), and a tunnel under construction at New River Road that collapses upon participants in Shadrack's last march to commemorate National Suicide Day. At first glance, the hillside and the tunnel appear dichotomous. The hillside, or the Bottom, is named ironically, and it is viewed through a passing of time: "there was once a neighborhood." The phrase introduces a narrative about an entire community, but also prophesies its destruction, the hell of mutability alluded to by Nel: "Hell ain't things lasting forever. Hell is change" (108).

One reading of these two regions suggests they have male and female characteristics: the phallic hillside and the vaginal tunnel, particularly when one recalls that the Bottom was established as a black community through a barter between two men. But Morrison gives the two regions feminine traits and infuses them with a preponderance of female properties, in the dual sense. One then suspects a different personification at work. Irene's Palace of Cosmetology, Reba's Grill, the dance of a "dark woman in a flowered dress doing a bit of cakewalk, a bit of black bottom, a bit of 'messing around' to the lively notes of a mouth organ" (4), all depict a procreative, female environment. The hillside is nurturing; it is a veritable breast of the earth. Within a feminine figuration (accompanying the narrative of a nurturing friendship between Nel and Sula) the hillside complements rather than contrasts with the womblike tunnel, which upon "breaking water" becomes a haunting, unsuspecting grave when several Bottom luminaries drown. This "abortion" of life occurs right at the time Medallion is undergoing a kind of rebirth through urban renewal. Whites and blacks are changing geographical spaces: the former moving to the cooler hills, the latter descending to the crowded valley floor. This change and death reverse the notion of economic upward mobility for Medallion blacks, who have only a promise of work on New River Road, and foreshadow the further decline, or bottoming *out,* of the community. The nurture-destruction tension in Morrison's figuration of the land this early in the novel more than prepares us for the complementary relationship, shifting moral dualism, and irony between Sula Mae Peace, who makes and unmakes peace in the community, and Nel Wright, who is never fully as right or as morally stalwart as she would like to appear.

The double figuration of the land as a framing device also foreshadows the novel's curiously double closure. One ending, effected by Shadrack's haunting, successful celebration of death, culminates his search for a "place for fear" as a way of "controlling it" (14) and brings his social marginality to a shocking conclusion. A second ending, however, forces the reader to revise this reading of the novel. Nel's visit to the elderly Eva, now in a nursing home, picks up the unfinished business between Nel and Sula (here represented by Eva) with shattering results: Nel is forced to acknowledge the guilt she shares with Sula for the accidental drowning of Chicken Little who had slipped from Sula's swinging hands and had entered the "closed place of the water" (61). The scene also foreshadows the tunnel's sudden collapse. Nel must also acknowledge the grief for Sula she had tried to suppress, only to discover in her solitary walk home that grief like guilt has no prescribed boundaries; it demands open public expression. When she realizes the extent of her accountability to Sula's friendship—"We was girls together"—Nel lets loose the emotion she had artificially held in check all these years: the cry without "bottom" or "top," but "circles and circles of sorrow" (174). The ever-spiraling geometry of Nel's grief returns readers to the scene of Chicken Little's death and forces us to rethink and replace the event. Sula's "evil" now appears innocuous and Nel's guilt more calculating and malevolent. We must also reconsider Nel's [W]rightness, for her cry admits a moral responsibility for wrongdoing that was not Sula's alone. Riding the spiral of Nel's grief back through the novel, we encounter other geometrical and geographical images that clearly establish the theme of moral dualism and double meaning in society and in nature. *Sula* then becomes as much a novel about the shifting patterns of accountability in Sula and Nel's friendship as it concerns a community's acceptance of moral relativism.

The boomerang effect of the shifting moral and physical geography of Medallion, Ohio, can be seen, for example, in the medallion Sula wears, the birthmark above her eye, the meaning of which changes according to who reads it. Morrison's novel is as much about interpretation as it is about art. How members of the community *read* Sula tells us a great deal about their relation to the land, to themselves, and to the meaning they create. The first indication of this theme is the novel's epigraph, taken from *The Rose Tattoo,* which implicates an entire community, a "they," in the speaker's nonconformist assertion of self: *"Nobody knew my rose of the world but me. . . . I had too much glory. They don't want glory like that in nobody's heart."* No one really knows Sula or why she sets about—as she tells Eva—to "make herself." But nearly everyone has an opinion about Sula's medallion: a sign they believe of her "evil," her *"too much glory"* in flaunting her disregard of social conventions. At first Sula's birthmark is described as a "stemmed rose" (52); as she matures, it becomes a "stem and rose" (74), suggesting the duality in nature as well as Sula's developing thorny yet attractive personality. With age, the mark becomes "the scary black thing over her eye" (97–98). When Jude begins to see the mark as a "copperhead" (103) and a "rattlesnake" (104), he is seduced by Sula. And as Sula becomes the evil the community fears yet abides, her mark indicates either "Hannah's ashes" (114) or, as Shadrack sees it, "a tadpole" (156). No one, not even Nel, knows Sula's heart. Indeed, Sula's closest kin, in terms of the community's social and moral landscape, is none other than Shadrack whose madness makes him at once both an outsider and insider: "Once the people understood the boundaries and nature of his madness, they could fit him, so to speak, into the scheme of things" (15). His shack in the woods or wilderness, halfway between the order of the town and the disorder of the lake where Chicken Little drowned, becomes Sula's refuge, a more useful shelter after the accident than Nel's calculated silence. When Shadrack answers "always" (62) to the distraught Sula's unvoiced question, he seals the doubling of their characters in one word of recognition.

The shifting geometry of Sula's birthmark also shapes her actions throughout the novel and identifies the forces directing her. Readers will recall that we know nothing of Sula's life away from Medallion—her time spent in college, in New York, and in other parts of the country—because Sula's real character, however enigmatic, comes from this community, this Medallion. It is her home and, as suggested above, her landmark. When

Sula returns home after an absence of ten years, she fully claims the territory as hers by dispossessing Eva of the house. Sula then occupies Eva's third floor bedroom. Her hibernation behind the boarded window seals her fate in the family and in the community. Sula's appropriation of height in the upper room does not, however, bring the desired refuge or elevation. Nor does it become the place of performance where the creation of character, the "making of oneself" can take place. Although she repossesses a space, Sula, like Cholly Breedlove, fails to find therein a voice for her identity. The self she finds in the house where she was born is still incomplete, as fragile and infantile as her uncle Plum. When Eva descended the stairs on her one leg— the only time she actually went down those stairs—she found Plum in a stupor of drug addiction, trying to return to her womb. Childlike, he clearly needed a new identity, a new birth, but one that Eva could neither provide nor accommodate. She set fire to him. Plum's vision before he burned to death may offer a clue to Sula's fate: "He opened his eyes and saw what he imagined was the great wing of an eagle pouring a wet lightness over him. Some kind of baptism, some kind of blessing, he thought" (47). Plum succumbs to the "bright hole of sleep" (47) without achieving flight on the eagle's wing. Sula, who had returned to Medallion during a plague of robins, also yearns for flight as the fulfillment of the self-creation she thought she had achieved. In the upper room, now the setting for her ardent lovemaking with Ajax, Sula discovers her human frailty (sexual possessiveness and emotional vulnerability). It is also the place where she dies.

Flight appears in Morrison's oeuvre as early as *The Bluest Eye*. Pecola, enticed into Junior's house, encounters his black cat with fascinating blue eyes, suggesting the probability that a black person can also have blue eyes. Junior ruthlessly snatches the cat from Pecola and begins to "swing it around his head in a circle." Defying Pecola's cries for him to stop, Junior lets the cat go "in midmotion" (71), throwing it against the window; it falls dead behind the radiator, its fur singeing. In a similar geometrical gesture, "Sula picked [Chicken Little] up by his hands and swung him outward then around and around," until he slips "from her hands and sailed away out over the water," still laughing in delight (60–61). When he lands in the "closed place in the water" (61), his flight, like that of the blue-eyed cat, is aborted in death. But the height and sense of the free fall he achieves brings him to the cutting edge of the kind of freedom and transcendence Sula herself seeks.

Sula's own quest for height and power through performance occurs in Eva's third floor bedroom. Mounted *on top of* Ajax in their lovemaking, Sula "rocked there, swayed there, like a Georgia pine on its knees, high above the slipping, falling smile, high above the golden eyes and the velvet helmet of hair, rocking, swaying . . . She looked down, down from what seemed an awful height at the head of the man whose lemon-yellow gabardines had been the first sexual excitement she'd known. Letting her thoughts dwell on his face in order to confine, for just a while longer, the drift of her flesh toward the high silence of orgasm" (129–30). Sula's discovery of height and freedom confirming her self-centered identity and place is only partially realized because the milk-bearing Ajax, in a gesture of sexual nurture, counters her contrived image of flight with a more realistic, attainable one of his own. When Sula experiences the human frailty of love and possessiveness that ultimately destroys her at the same time that it brings her closer to Nel, she becomes just domestic enough to make the adventuresome Ajax lose interest: "when Ajax came that evening . . . the bathroom was gleaming, the bed was made, and the table was set for two" (131–32). Ajax's compelling desire, however, is to attend an air show in Dayton. Sula has indeed met her match.

Moreover, Ajax shows how trivial, self-indulgent, and incomplete is Sula's notion of the "free fall" (120), which she felt made her different from Nel, whose imagination had been driven "underground" by her repressive mother, and from the other women of Medallion. Ajax's presence heightens Sula's self-contradictions as he effectively matches her false, showy nonconformity with his more authentic eccentricity: he is the son of a conjurer mother, and his knowledge of magic and lore surpasses Sula's allure. Here Morrison's prevailing metaphor of flight begins with a leap, or free fall, and offers a rectifying alternative to Ellison's idea of hibernation. As Sula hibernates on the upper floor at 7 Carpenter Road, not in an underground cellar, she longs for the kind of performance that would complete her discovery of self-mastery and complete control. This metaphor is hinted at in *The Bluest Eye,* sketched out and challenged by Ajax in *Sula,* and finds its fullest, if not most conclusive statement in *Song of Solomon.*

The relation between Sula and Nel ruptures when Sula interprets Nel's possessiveness of her husband, Jude, to mean that Nel is one of *them,* the conventional housewives of Medallion. Nel had earlier shared Sula's vision of "the slant of life that makes it possible to stretch [life] to its limits." Becoming the clichéd wronged wife, outraged at Jude and Sula's adultery, Nel is too quickly linked with other women in the community who had "interpreted" Sula as incarnating some kind of evil. They had measured themselves morally and socially by abiding "evil"—as Pauline Breedlove did with Cholly in *The Bluest Eye*—and garnering a false dignity, even heroism, by tolerating it: "The purpose of evil was to survive it" (90). When Nel shows her natural jealousy and hurt, she begins to belong, in Sula's view, "to the town and all of its ways" (120). Nel also begins to oppose Sula's notion of invention and free fall on which Sula had based her ascendant self-mastery and their complementary friendship: "But the free fall, oh no, that required—demanded—invention: a thing to do with the wings, a way of holding the legs and most of all a full surrender to the downward flight if they wished to taste their tongues or stay alive. But alive was what they, and now Nel, did not want to be. Too dangerous" (120).

"Dangerous" more than evil is an accurate description of Sula. As an "artist with no art form" (121) Sula is vulnerable to the shifting interpretations of the only form she carries in her very being: her birthmark. Like Hannah, Sula's art lay in lovemaking, in her enjoyment of the sheer abandon of sex. This clearly is how Sula makes the leap from sexual conventions that lead to marriage and braves the outer limits of promiscuity, the ultimate breach of which is to have sex with white men. It was through carefree sex, nonetheless, that Sula found the cutting edge and the leap of free fall, her performance:

> During the lovemaking she found and needed to find the cutting edge. When she left off cooperating with her body and began to assert herself in the act, particles of strength gathered in her like steel shavings drawn to a spacious magnetic center, forming a tight cluster that nothing, it seemed, could break. And there was utmost irony and outrage in lying *under* someone, in a position of surrender, feeling her own abiding strength and limitless power. But the cluster did break, fall apart, and in her panic to hold it together she *leaped* from the edge into soundlessness and went down howling, howling in a stinging awareness of the endings of things: an eye of sorrow in the midst of all that hurricane rage of joy. There, in the center of that silence was not eternity but the death of time and a loneliness so profound the word itself had no meaning. (122–23, emphasis mine)

In an interview published in *Nimrod,* Morrison once discussed the importance of venturing to the cutting edge and experiencing the leap. What is needed, she said, is complete self-control, divesting oneself of the vanities that weigh people down. This surrender is a triumph and results in a stark change of territory: from land to sky, from the confining boundaries of conventional morality and selfishness to the thrill of self-creation, a riding of the air. "Suppose it were literally so, what would it take to fly?" Morrison speculated. "But suppose you could just move one step up and fly? What would you have to be, and feel, and know, and do, in order to do that?" *Sula* begins to answer Morrison's own question. The author, however, asks for more: "You would have to be able to surrender, give up all of the weights, all of the vanities, all of the ignorances. And you'd have to trust and have faith in the harmony of your body. Your would also have to have perfect control" (49). Sula indeed wishes for power, control, and the reward of flight. Ajax, the aviation-dreaming lover, brings her milk in blue, sky-colored glass bottles: "Ajax looked at her through the blue glass and held the milk aloft like a trophy" (127). Perhaps it is Ajax who can lift Sula from the ground, or perhaps she will lift him up into the flight and transendence he also seeks. The only uncertainty is Sula's ability to let herself go and to release Ajax from the confining domesticity of housebound sex.

Sula fails. Her wish for total freedom, for flight, becomes as much a delusion as Pecola's blue eyes. Even the unobstructed mobility or license granted by Sula's land/birthmark is illusory because Sula is both ostracized and nourished by the same community, the same land; her mobility is limited by the interpretative needs of the community, shown by Medallion's quick regression into antagonistic behavior once the "threat" of Sula passes with her death and just prior to the parade into the tunnel. The illusory nature of Sula's desire is revealed in the contrast between her and Ajax, who, like Bigger Thomas in *Native Son* or Buster and Riley in Ellison's story "That I Had the Wings," yearns for freedom through aviation. Although Ajax's dream is realized only in his frequent trips to airports, he establishes a degree of realism against Sula's illusion of control and flight through sex. (It is he who requests that she mount him.) He thinks equally about his conjurer mother and airplanes: "when he was not sitting enchanted listening to his mother's words, he thought of airplanes, and pilots, and the deep sky that held them both" (126). The blue bottle of milk offered to Sula as a trophy connects her to the blue sky and the maternal milk. Flight and aviation as the exercise of creativity, the fulfillment of perfect control, hold both Sula and Ajax in its cobalt blue glow.

Yet the moment that Sula falls in love with Ajax and discovers possessiveness, both she and Ajax are more grounded than either desires. Ajax escapes this confinement by losing interest in Sula, but she remains trapped, totally overwhelmed by feeling human and vulnerable. When she takes Ajax through her newly cleaned house—"the spotless bathroom where dust had been swept from underneath the claw-foot tub"—she shows him her nest, a space for her hibernation, nurture, and fulfillment of sexual desire. Ajax makes love to her in the more conventional position, but he thinks less about Sula than "the date of the air show in Dayton" (134). Sula is "under" him now, and he moves "with the steadiness and the intensity of a man about to leave for Dayton" (134).

In his stunning absence, Sula tries to come to terms with her love for Ajax, for the flight of fancy he represented, for the adventuresome love, not the self-gratifying control that grounds her. Like Pecola, Sula is weighed down by the human, emotional vulnerability she succumbs to, particularly the self-willed grief she hibernates in, shut away in Eva's room. Like Cholly Breedlove, Sula reaches a momentary height of self-awareness in her admission of loneliness and possessiveness of Ajax (particularly when she realizes she never really possessed him, for she never knew his name), but she fails to give full voice to this spark of self-recognition. Hence, her freedom is never fully realized. Her flight is not only aborted, but Sula also dies. The song she wanted to sing might have saved her by providing a different kind of performance and presentation of self, as Milkman's song performance will. But the right lyrics elude her; she can only mouth repeated nonsense words. Sula, then, like Cholly, is a failed "person"-of-words, left dreaming, like Pecola, of "cobalt blue" (137) without even an air show in Dayton to claim her: "When she awoke, there was a melody in her head she could not identify or recall ever hearing before. . . . Then it came to her—the name of the song and all its lyrics just as she had heard it many times before. . . . She lay down again on the bed and sang a little wandering tune made up of the words *I have sung all the songs all the songs I have sung all the songs there are* until, touched by her own lullaby, she grew drowsy, and in the hollow of near-sleep she tasted the acridness of gold, left the chill of alabaster and smelled the dark, sweet stench of loam" (137). Sula succumbs to the "hollow," as Plum did at the "hole" of sleep, because she could not give adequate voice and action to her vision. Instead of flying, she descends to the loam of the very land that had marked her from birth.

Sula's death offers no "invention," only descent; it is neither a free fall nor the redeeming flight she had longed for. One clue to her decline lies in Morrison's verbal design of Sula's place of hibernation, Eva's room with its blind window, boarded up indirectly by Sula herself. Sula's paralyzing interest in watching her mother Hannah burn necessitated Eva's leap of rescue out of that window. When Sula subsequently dispossesses Eva of that room, she puts herself in the physical, but not the emotional, space for the reconciliation Eva had attempted in her failed rescue of Hannah, and, paradoxically, in her mercy killing of Plum—to keep him from descending further into the stupor of drugs, or reducing his already fragile maturity to the helpless state of an infant wanting a return to the womb. Instead of a womb, Eva offered Plum the scent and vision of the eagle's wings. Instead of flight, Eva's upper room offers Sula the best setting for the only performance she is then capable of; her foetal plunge down an imaginary birth canal or tunnel (prefiguring the town's later disaster) is a perversion of the rebirth in death that Eva had granted Plum: "The sealed window soothed her with its sturdy termination, its unassailable finality. . . . It would be here, only here, held by this blind window high above the elm tree, that she might draw her legs up to her chest, close her eyes, put her thumb in her mouth and float over and down the tunnels, just missing the dark walls, down, down until she met a rain scent and would know the water was near, and she would curl into its heavy softness and it would envelop her, carry her, and wash her tired flesh always. Always" (148–49).

Sula's plunge into the tunnel following a period of willful hibernation completes the solitude she had always wanted. This hibernation, however, had rendered her immobile, incapacitated (except in death), for Ajax's departure and Sula's recognition of her human vulnerability stun her into physical and emotional paralysis. This backfire, or boomerang, reverses the moment of moral strength Eva felt in her husband BoyBoy's desertion, and now Eva, as a discerning, combative ancestor, cannot help Sula, for Eva has been safely locked away.

Neither Sula's solitude nor tunnel plunge is a fate left to her alone. Being a product of the land, a mark of the community, she reflects the fate of others. In the collapse of the half-finished tunnel at New River Road to the clanging tune of Sula's brother in marginality, Shadrack's pied-piper parade, the town, which had made Sula both person and pariah and a source of their negatively realized pride, meets its end. Both Sula and Shadrack have presided over figurations of the land that reveal underground refuge or hibernation to be the simple burial it is, which is what Wright's Fred Daniels discovered. Hibernation, despite the subversive bravura of Ellison's invisible man, does not lead to the effective overt activity or self-assertion he had promised. Morrison's more complex rendering of place and person in the collapse of the tunnel and the spirals of grief that bind Nel to repetitions of guilt, necessitates an end to hibernation, whether underground or three floors up. In *Song of Solomon,* Morrison offers the corrective reach of the mountaintop and a triumphant surrender to the air.

SONG OF SOLOMON. "YOU SEE?" THE FARM SAID TO THEM. "SEE?
SEE WHAT YOU CAN DO?"

Whereas the framing images in *Sula* are terrestrial enclosures, those in *Song of Solomon* are celestial flights. The novel opens with Robert Smith's aborted takeoff that brings about his planned suicide, and it ends with the violent reunion between Milkman and Guitar as one of them leaps from the mountain and into the "killing" arms of the other. The difference between the flights, how their angles of ascent exceed or grasp the long-sought-for family treasure, the home and name initially giving these characters wings, is the novel's main concern.

The novel encompasses three principal organizing structures that enlarge the orbit of cultural performances suggested thus far by several key texts, including Morrison's earlier fiction. These organizational structures include the relationship between Milkman and Guitar as the problematic moral center of the novel, the conflict between family and property ties that fuels tension between Pilate and her brother Macon Dead, and finally Milkman's initiatory "errand" into and out of the wilderness. By discovering his name and performing the song that redeems him and helps him to fly, Milkman completes the unrealized gestures and dreams of Morrison's earlier characters: Pecola, Cholly, Sula, and Ajax. *Song of Solomon* is Morrison's carefully drawn map of ancestral landscape that reclaims and resurrects moribund (the family name is Dead) or hibernating personalities.

Robert Smith, insurance salesman by day and by night a member of the "underground" radical group, the Seven Days, occupies enemy territory when he climbs to the roof of No Mercy Hospital, so called because it had never admitted black patients. Smith appears to act out the words of one Negro spiritual that describes the kind of release he desires:

> Some o'dese morning's bright an' fair,
>   Way in de middle of de air
> Goin' hitch on my wings an' try de air
>   Way in de middle of de air.

Both the foreign, outer terrain of the hospital roof and the artifice involved in the "hitching" on of wings—"his wide blue silk wings curved forward around his chest" (5)—are ominous. Instead of a smooth and graceful death, Smith loses his balance, reaches for a triangle of wood jutting from the hospital's cupola, and goes "splat" (as one observer described the scene). Robert Smith's "leap" is an undignified, clumsy fall.

Smith's death sends another witness, the pregnant Ruth Foster Dead, into labor. Her son Milkman, the "little bird," whose hour of birth was accurately predicted by his aunt Pilate, who had earlier helped in his conception, becomes the first black child to be born in No Mercy. Milkman now has a more legitimate claim to the space Robert Smith had usurped.

As a real "bird," a descendant of the Byrds in Shalimar, Virginia, revealed in the ending, Milkman will not need the artifice of Robert Smith's "blue silk," Ajax's cobalt blue bottles, or Pecola's "blue" eyes. Milkman's maturation in his midwestern hometown and his departure South to discover the land of his ancestors and to sing the song of Solomon—the core subject of the novel—teach him to use his own wings. Milkman's *leap* at the novel's close is a redeeming *flight*. His journey is not an easy one; nor is the novel's moral center in the magnetic friendship between Milkman and Guitar without a healthy dose of ambiguity and role reversal. Before Pilate takes over as Milkman's veritable pilot, his first navigator through a difficult childhood and adolescence is Guitar, who as a child had also witnessed Robert Smith's fall. Guitar is best suited to be the kind of friend and adversary who can enlarge the reach of Milkman's leap "way in de middle of de air."

Guitar and Milkman do not have the same complementary personalities that make Sula and Nel appear to be one character. Although from different backgrounds, they manage to build a friendship upon mutual interests and a pendular sway of dominant and submissive roles between them as Guitar then Milkman then Guitar takes the upper hand. Older than Milkman, Guitar has the lead at first; he introduces Milkman to Pilate, whose folk conjure aided his conception and birth. Her conjure of a successful aphrodisiac had encouraged Macon and Ruth to conceive after many years of uninterest and celibacy. Pilate, who helped make Milkman's "egg," later teaches Milkman and Guitar how to make the perfect three-minute soft-boiled egg. The recipe indirectly reveals the ambiguity of love and power in their friendship and how a growing estrangement between them will be reconciled, even if in battle. "Now, the water and the egg," Pilate instructs the boys, "have to meet each other on a kind of equal standing. One can't get the upper hand over the other. So the temperature has to be the same for both" (39). In the folk logic of this equation, Milkman is the egg. What about the water? Guitar's last name is Bains, which in French means "bath" or "watering place" or both. Pilate's foolproof recipe thus becomes a formula for reconciliation; Guitar and Milkman need equal matching for either of them to assume the "perfect" control of the leap, which is the only way, as shown in *Sula,* the free fall becomes flight.

Throughout most of the novel, however, Guitar does have the upper hand. In addition to introducing Milkman to Pilate, Guitar is the one who initially guides Milkman away from his stifling, bourgeois upbringing— summers at St. Honoré Island, collecting rents for his slumlord father— and Guitar teaches Milkman the novel's core lesson: "Wanna fly, you got to give up the shit that weighs you down" (179). Until Guitar's participation in the Seven Days weakens him morally and psychologically (as had happened to mild-mannered Robert Smith) to the point where he assumes the "greed for gold" that Milkman has outgrown, Guitar, as his name suggests, is as instrumental in Milkman's development of character and cultural awareness as McKay's Banjo was for the aspiring writer Ray. That is, until Milkman finds his own voice.

The attraction of opposite social classes that initially brings Milkman and Guitar together is similar to the magnetism between Sula and Nel or the delicate class comforts that barely distinguish Pecola from Frieda and Claudia, yet allow the sisters to take Pecola under their wings. Morrison's characters appear to find stability in kinship ties and bonds of friendship that cut across class barriers and generational differences. Note the strong matrilinear network linking Eva-Hannah-Sula, for example, or the generational patterning among Pilate-Reba-Hagar. These sets of historical relationships anchor Sula and Pilate in a culture and family they use for support, particularly when the larger society rejects them as pariahs. Their hearths are comforting and inviting to Nel and Milkman, who are fleeing the stultifying middle-class repression that renders them marginal and homeless. Morrison's use of class differences as one element of mutual attraction suggests that economic conditions alone do not alienate lower or middle classes from a common culture. In *Song of Solomon* this idea is explored further when members of two different social classes represent the same family.

Macon and Pilate are brother and sister, separated after their father's murder; each inherits something different from him. Macon turns his father's love of the land and talent for farming into an obsessive ownership of property, reducing land and people to mere commodities. He advises his son Milkman: "Own things. And let the things you own own other things. Then you'll own yourself and other people too" (55). Pilate, just the opposite, already owns herself—the physical evidence of her self-possession and self-creation is her stomach without a navel. She interprets the one word uttered by her father's ghost, a regular visitor, as an admonition for performance: "Sing." Instead of acquiring property, Pilate creates song, transmitting the family lore unconsciously. The history and culture voiced here first draws Macon, then Milkman and Guitar into the charged orbit of Pilate's single-story house on Darling Street, "whose basement seemed to be rising from rather than settling into the ground" (27). Pilate's home thus moves us up out of the underground and to the mountaintop. The wings of her song first attract, then encourage full surrender to that upward motion, even for Macon, who listens surreptitiously:

They were singing some melody that Pilate was leading. A phrase that the other two were taking up and building on. Her powerful

contralto, Reba's piercing soprano in counterpoint, and the soft
voice of the girl, Hagar, who must be about ten or eleven now,
pulled him like a carpet tack under the influence of a magnet.

   Surrendering to the sound, Macon moved closer. He wanted
no conversation, no witness, only to listen and perhaps to see
the three of them, the source of that music that made him think
of fields and wild turkey and calico. (29).

As Macon peers unseen into the lives of these women, he becomes a
version of Wright's man who lived underground or of Ellison's invisible
man. Lacking Daniels's cynicism, Macon secretly yearns to come out of
hibernation and to accept fully the family he had denied in his "drive for
wealth" (28): "Near the window, hidden by the dark, he felt the irritability
of the day drain from him and relished the effortless beauty of the women
singing in the candlelight. . . . As Macon felt himself softening under the
weight of memory and music, the song died down. The air was quiet and
yet Macon Dead could not leave. He liked looking at them freely this way"
(29–30).

   Macon is the kind of invisible man Milkman refuses to be. Without
ever learning all that his nickname means (the prolonged "'sexual" nursing
from his mother and the demands of nurture he places on other women),
Milkman will develop any trait, any *device,* to differentiate himself from his
father, even to the point of affecting a limp. "Milkman feared his father,
respected him, but knew, because of the leg, that he could never emulate
him. So he differed from him as much as he dared" (63). Unlike Macon,
who listens from outside, Milkman penetrates Pilate's house and there learns
the magic in the perfect meeting of egg and water.

   Macon and Pilate vie for a controlling influence over Milkman. They
also compete over their relation to the dead father and to the farmland that
was as fertile as it was generous, "See? See what you can do?" The father
had made it the best farming in Montour County, earning him the adoration
of blacks and the emnity of the whites who eventually killed him. The land
and the family heritage become battlegrounds for the continuing struggle
between Pilate and Macon. While Macon is an owner of land and of people
(his assistant Sonny, his tenant Porter), or so he thinks, Pilate, like Cholly
Breedlove, is a "renting" black. Their different relation to the land inversely
determines how they function in the novel to help or hinder Milkman.
Macon remains dead to the past, which is celebrated and *possessed* unself-
consciously by Pilate. Macon, defeated by his father's murder, has leased
his identity to fluctuations in the real estate market and in the whims of

bank lenders out of desperation to prove his worth. Pilate, on the other hand, a restless wanderer, owns only those objects that implicitly direct her search for place (and for refuge from pariah status): rocks, a sack of human bones, and a geography book—her only legacy until she nurtures Milkman. Instead of washing her hands free of the past, she fills them with such common objects, burdens really, until Milkman's discovery shows them to be the family treasure they always were. By identifying the invisible ancestor in Pilate's song—"reading and re-reading" Pilate's oral poetry—Milkman lifts the burden of those bones from Pilate's shoulders and allows her to experience a surrender to the air that prefigures his more complete flight.

Cursed with endless wandering because the lack of a navel relegates her to pariah status in whatever community she finds herself, Pilate and her smooth stomach, like Sula and her birthmark, are objects of interpretation. Unlike Sula's artistic formlessness, Pilate has her bootlegging business, her conjure, and most importantly, her song—the same song that announced Robert Smith's presence on the hospital roof and that cushioned his awkward, suicidal descent; the same song that drew Macon to her part of town and partially out of his preferred invisibility. It is also the song neither Sula nor Cholly could sing. Like the Negro spiritual encoding messages for escape or resistance, it contains the riddle and the answer to the question of survival; it is a mystery to be unraveled, like the enigmatic advice of the grandfather in *Invisible Man*. This is the poem Milkman will hear again and again until he recites it by heart; his performance in the land of his ancestors reveals the hidden family name:

> *O Sugarman done fly away*
> *Sugarman done gone*
> *Sugarman cut across the sky*
> *Sugarman gone home . . . . (6)*

When Milkman learns the full text of the song and the history transmitted through it—"Jake the only son of Solomon"—recognizes the ancestor and the homeland Pilate perhaps had been reading about in her frayed geography book. She can now let go of the burden of bones. She buries them and her earring locket, containing her name written by her father, in a mountaintop grave. The interment of the bones also signals Pilate's end, for she is killed by a bullet intended for Milkman. Once again, she gives him life, if only for the time it takes Guitar to exchange his gun for his fists. More important, however, Pilate's death concludes her terrestrial wandering. When a bird, attracted by the glittering earring near her crumpled body, swoops down and soars away with the locket, Pilate achieves symbolic flight. She experiences the full meaning of her ancestry among the Flying Africans and of her name, no longer Pilate but *pilot* (a fulfillment that eludes LeRoi Jones's Air Force gunner and Ellison's flight trainee). The meaning of the novel's epigraph also comes clear: *"The fathers may soar / and the children may know their names."* In addition to wholeness of identity, Pilate achieves at last her rightful, celestial place.

Macon Dead, on the other hand, remains grounded in his lust for gold and in his accumulation of property. He has misread the lesson his father had learned from the land and its harvest, as heard in Morrison's thrilling rendition of the sermon the land itself delivers:

> "You see?" the farm said to them. "See? See what you can do?
> . . . . Here, this here, is what a man can do if he puts his mind
> to it and his back in it. Stop sniveling," it said. "Stop picking
> around the edges of the world. Take advantage, and if you can't
> take advantage, take disadvantage. We live here. On this planet,
> in this nation, in this country right here. Nowhere else! We got
> a home in the rock, don't you see! Nobody starving in my home;
> nobody crying in my home, and if I got a home you got one too!
> Grab it. Grab this land! Take it, hold it, my brothers, make it,
> my brothers, shake it, squeeze it, turn it, twist it, beat it, kick
> it, kiss it, whip it, stomp it . . . own it, build it, multiply it,
> and pass it on—can you hear me? Pass it on!" (235)

This land, its voice full of the language and cadence of Negro spirituals and rich with sources of identity, should offer prosperity to any family willing to use it in the ways suggested above, not merely acquire more and more of it. The land is to be used for procreation and harvest, not hibernation and greed. Thus, in many respects, Macon remains invisible to the land, to the community, to his family, and finally, to the culture that commands him to perform, not just to listen secretively. In the conflict between Macon and Pilate over the land, over history, and over Milkman, Pilate wins because she has shown Milkman a way out of the hibernation advocated by Macon's inertia. In this way, too, Milkman's struggle enlarges the orbit of geography for Afro-American identity and cultural performance beyond the cave of hibernation promoted in Ellison's *Invisible Man.*

Song of Solomon signals a major break from Ellison's territoriality in Afro-American letters, yet Morrison's thematic and imagistic challenge to Ellison begins with interesting points of comparison to his novel. These common areas of concern suggest Morrison's careful reading of Ellison and the detour she takes from his "highway," and from the theme, setting, language, and literary form he enshrined. Morrison's break becomes all the more bold, startling, and significant because the comparisons suggest that she has explored Ellison's terrain and found it lacking in the kind of cultural mobility her characters and their experiences demand.

Morrison completes the groping for avian imagery and the search for redemptive flight first articulated in slave songs and narratives and then imagined more existentially in texts by Wright, Ellison, and LeRoi Jones. Morrison's aviators, the Air Force men who frequent a local bar, inspire Milkman's envy only until he discovers that he can fly without the encumbrance of military obligations. She also manipulates and enlarges the conventions of surrealism and the *Bildungsroman,* which Ellison viewed as granting the writer freedom from the sociological predilections and realistic persuasions most readers impose upon black American fiction. This was Ellison's main criticism of Wright, but his injunction stops there. Morrison undercuts the hegemony of Ellison's preferred narrative strategy, what Robert Stepto has called "the narrative of hibernation" (193), by enlarging the structure to encompass multiple lives and points of view as her characters aim for motion, not stasis. The multiplicity of perspectives and situations in Morrison's fiction requires protagonists writ large; her novels are *Bildungsromanen* of entire communities and racial idioms rather than the voice of a single individual. What central protagonist exists develops only through the interplay between the community and the individual. Even Milkman is admonished by his father to "know the whole story" before taking sides. "And if you want to be a whole man, you have to deal with the whole truth" (70). Morrison's novels require us to read the life of a community as the text and context of an individual's articulation of voice. Milkman needs the play of the children of Shalimar to help him hear Jake's "narrative" in the song and to "close" the story of his own self-possesssion. Milkman's cultural performance when he sings the song of Solomon makes him a successful man-of-words.

Other parallels are at work and play between Morrison and Ellison. Both their protagonists struggle against an identity imposed by others. The nameless invisible man must end his passivity and willingness to be named by others, from the letters sent by Bledsoe to the slip of paper revealing the Brotherhood's name for him. Morrison's protagonist must come to terms with a nickname whose origin he never knows and with people who want to "use" him: "Somehow everybody was using him for something or as something. Working out some scheme of their own on him, making him the subject of their dreams of wealth, or lobe, or martyrdom" (165). Sonny, when he discovers Ruth's prolonged nursing of her son, announces, "A natural milkman if ever I seen one. Look out, womens. Here he come" (15). Milkman feels his name to be "dirty, intimate, and hot" (15) as he grows up to fulfill, unwittingly, Sonny's double-edged prophecy: he will take from women, but he will also be a passive, bleached, colorless (invisible?) personality until he takes charge of himself, with others. When Milkman learns through his journey to the South that names can bear witness, indeed "had meaning," he can give up his old self more easily (he loses his fine clothes and jewelry and car while on his journey) and reciprocate in lovemaking with Sweet more than he had done with any other woman ("He washed her hair. . . . He made up the bed. . . . He washed the dishes. . . . She kissed his mouth. He touched her face. She said please come back. He said I'll see you tonight" [285]). Milkman's increased awareness of the mutual responsibilities in love and self-discovery brings about his visibility.

Both novels also share a figuration of geography that shapes the protagonists' journeys. Ellison's narrative (apart from the frame) moves from the South to the North; Morrison moves from the North to the South. She alters the direction of cultural history away from simple chronology and toward a single, charged moment of multiple discoveries by emphasizing Milkman's embrace of cultural and familial geography. He arrives at the ancestral ground to become rooted in it as deep and as high as Pilate's father's bones. The protagonists in both novels also confront a riddle that invites interpretation and subversion of the nameless condition of Afro-Americans: one proffered by Ellison's protagonist's grandfather, the other by Morrison's "Sugarman" or Milkman's great-great-great grandfather, whose identity could save his life. Both narratives or novels are framed or enclosed; one by the static posture of *telling* a story through the device of prologue and epilogue, the other by dual *actions* that are dynamic performances: Smith's suicide is revised in Milkman's flight.

Although Ellison's protagonist's writing of *Invisible Man* in his underground retreat can be seen as an active deed (since it creates the space and action of the novel), Morrison offers an effective contrast: She replaces the cellar-basement environment for the invisible man's *written* performance with the mountaintop height of Milkman's *oral* performance. Also significant is their different treatment of flight. Ellison offers the folk rhyme "They picked poor robin clean" as a warning about the protagonist's grounded predicament. Morrison counteracts with the myth of the Flying Africans to show Milkman the reach and promise of the air, *if* he can ride it. Milkman becomes a true descendant of Jake, the only son of Solomon, whereas Ellison's protagonist fails to become a true blood following Trueblood's example of storytelling and rhetorical flourish. When Milkman actually sings the song of Solomon, he assumes the name that had been denied the invisible man, without which Milkman would be colorless and the land of his culture invisible to all. Milkman can now nurture others: Pilate, Ruth, Sweet, Jake, and himself. From that exchange of emotional commitment, Milkman gains the strength he needs to meet his adversary Guitar and gain an equal if not *upper* hand.

Above and beyond these various points of comparison between *Song of Solomon* and *Invisible Man* lies Morrison's most significant achievement. She extends the geographical imagery and enriches the acts of deliverance established so far in Afro-American letters. Her novel encompasses the three principal landscapes of retreat and regeneration already present in black American culture: the wilderness, the underground, and the mountaintop. Taken as part of Morrison's assessment of geography and identity in fiction, they exceed earlier attempts to fix or promote one region over another. *Song of Solomon* not only returns us to landscapes suggested in the slave songs and narratives, it also plays upon the fundamental contrast between underground and mountain stages of self-achievement, thus exposing the limits of a Wright-Ellison geography and moving us forward to other heights of self-awareness through action.

Macon and Pilate Dead, for all their successes and failures, are still connected to figures of spatial enclosures, even the imminent grave suggested by their unfortunate family name. They are also prisoners of a haunting guilt in having killed a miner at the mouth of a cave in the wilderness through which they wandered aimlessly after their father's death. Once overcoming the menacing miner—a digger of undergrounds probing for hidden treasures below—the two children are prepared to conquer other spaces, such as houses, later on. Pilate's single-story dwelling appears to rise from the basement or underground, and Macon's acquisition of property represents his rise in society. Yet both are still tied to either material goods or to the alternate meaning they can convey, which is how Fred Daniels reacted to the bank notes and diamonds in his cave. It is Milkman who eventually develops a more effective relation to the land when he confronts the wilderness. There he not only searches for the cave where the miner's gold is presumably hidden, but he is prepared for the strenuous encounter with the Shalimar woods during the nighttime hunt of the bobcat with Calvin and King Walker and the other men of the town. They hate him at first ("They looked with hatred at the city Negro who could buy a car as if it were a bottle of whiskey because the one he had was broken" [266]), but Milkman's participation in the hunt gains their fraternity and friendship. He secures

his own place in the ancestral territory apart from the claims of Pilate or
Macon.

It is not enough, however, for Milkman simply to arrive in Shalimar,
or to lose his material possession while there (the vanities that weigh him
down). He has to walk that lonesome valley, as the slave songs required,
by himself:

> There was nothing here to help him—not his money, his car,
> his father's reputation, his suit, or his shoes. In fact, they ham-
> pered him. Except for his broken watch, and his wallet with
> about two hundred dollars, all he had started out with on his
> journey was gone. . . . His watch and his two hundred dollars
> would be of no help out here, where all a man had was what he
> was born with, or had learned to use. And endurance. Eyes, ears,
> nose, taste, touch—and some other sense that he knew he did
> not have: an ability to separate out, of all the things there were
> to sense, the one that life itself might depend on. (227)

Milkman has to earn kinship by enduring the woods, the wilderness.
Like the fugitive in slave narratives, he has to renew his covenant with nature
to secure passage out of the wilderness that had invited him in. Only through
this initiatory trial in the woods of Blue Ridge County will he encounter
those figures of the landscape that will give definite meaning to the otherwise confusing names and places in the children's song:

> *Jay the only son of Solomon*
> *Come booba yalle, come booba tambee*
> *Whirl about and touch the sun*
> *Come booba yalle, come booba tambee . . .* (264)

Each step of his way puts Milkman "on land that sloped upward" (274).
Only by surviving the wilderness—which is not a foregone conclusion since
he is caught off-guard by the now crazed, nightseeing, cat-eyed Guitar,
who, with this unfair advantage, cannot "kill" Milkman yet because the
water and egg need equal matching—does Milkman learn the historical
meaning associated with two figures of landscape that lie beyond the vision
and experience of Macon or Pilate: Ryna's Gulch and Solomon's Leap, a
valley and mountaintop. These contrasting, gender-related spaces extend
from Morrison's earlier survey of cultural territory used as the framing images
in *Sula:* the hilltop Bottom leading to the collapsing tunnel. Here the
movement is reversed. Ryna's Gulch (as well as the bodies of the women
Milkman has exploited through sexual conquest) points him to Solomon's

Leap, but only after Milkman has bent his ear to the ground to hear the land's sermon or "anything the earth had to say" (279). Milkman's discovery of these new spaces and new territories, makes him the pilot to guide Pilate to the resting place for her father's bones.

In this wilderness, Milkman earns friendship with the men of Shalimar, with himself, and with the earth. Milkman discovers that he can be his own man, based on his proven skills of survival. Walking on the earth like he belonged to it, Milkman no longer needs the artificial device, the dutchman, of his limp to distinguish himself from his father. Nor does he need material possessions to differentiate himself from the kinsmen of Shalimar. Sharing at last a good-hearted laugh with them, Milkman becomes exhilarated "by simply walking the earth. Walking it like he belonged on it; like his legs were stalks, tree trunks, a part of his body that extended down down down into the rock and soil, and were comfortable there—on the earth and on the place where he walked. And he did not limp" (281). Here Milkman becomes rooted. "Back home he had never felt that way, as though he belonged to anyplace or anybody" (293). This belonging enables him to decode the children's rhyme that gives meaning to the landscape and to Milkman's ancestry. Caught without pencil or paper, Milkman cannot write the song down, as Ellison's protagonist could do with his narrative. Milkman "would just have to listen and memorize it" (303), internalize it.

When Milkman leads Pilate to Shalimar, he brings her similar home-lessness to an end: she "blended into the population like a stick of butter in a churn" (355). Together they advance to the higher ground of Solomon's Leap, both to bury the bones and to meet their separate fates. Pilate will fly without ever leaving the ground, comforted by Milkman's rendition of the song, which Morrison leaves unindented and without italics on the page to suggest that it has been refashioned in Milkman's voice and fused into the uninterrupted flow of the narrative: "Sugargirl don't leave me here / Cotton balls to choke me / Sugargirl don't leave me here / Buckra's arms to yoke me" (336). Now Milkman can ride the air. His leap of surrender is his ultimate performance, a flight he has earned by doffing his vanities and passing the test of the wilderness. His leap transcends the rootedness and the freedom he has gained. Milkman and Morrison's flight, their ride out of the wilderness, demonstrates self-mastery and perfect control.

REFERENCES

Ellison, Ralph. *Invisible Man*. Thirtieth Anniversary Edition. New York: Random House, 1982.

Morrison, Toni. *The Bluest Eye*. New York: Holt, 1970.

———. Interview by Pepsi Charles. *Nimrod* 21 and 22 (1977): 43–51.

———. " 'Intimate Things in Place': A Conversation with Toni Morrison." Interview by Robert B. Stepto. In *Chant of Saints: A Gathering of Afro-American Literature, Art, and Scholarship,* edited by Michael S. Harper and Robert B. Stepto, 213–29. Urbana: University of Illinois Press, 1979.

———. *Song of Solomon*. New York: Knopf, 1977.

———. *Sula*. New York: Knopf, 1974.

———. *Tar Baby*. New York: Knopf, 1981.

Tate, Claudia, ed. *Black Women Writers at Work*. New York: Continuum, 1983.

MARGARET ATWOOD

Haunted by Their Nightmares

Beloved is Toni Morrison's fifth novel, and another triumph. Indeed, Ms.
Morrison's versatility and technical and emotional range appear to know no
bounds. If there were any doubts about her stature as a pre-eminent American
novelist, of her own or any other generation, *Beloved* will put them to rest.
In three words or less, it's a hair-raiser.

In *Beloved,* Ms. Morrison turns away from the contemporary scene that
has been her concern of late. This new novel is set after the end of the Civil
War, during the period of so-called Reconstruction, when a great deal of
random violence was let loose upon blacks, both the slaves freed by Emancipation and others who had been given or had bought their freedom earlier.
But there are flashbacks to a more distant period, when slavery was still a
going concern in the South and the seeds for the bizarre and calamitous
events of the novel were sown. The setting is similarly divided: the countryside near Cincinnati, where the central characters have ended up, and a
slave-holding plantation in Kentucky, ironically named Sweet Home, from
which they fled 18 years before the novel opens.

There are many stories and voices in this novel, but the central one
belongs to Sethe, a woman in her mid-30's, who is living in an Ohio
farmhouse with her daughter, Denver, and her mother-in-law Baby Suggs.
Beloved is such a unified novel that it's difficult to discuss it without giving
away the plot, but it must be said at the outset that it is, among other
things, a ghost story, for the farmhouse is also home to a sad, malicious
and angry ghost, the spirit of Sethe's baby daughter, who had her throat

From *New York Times Book Review,* 13 September 1987, pp. 1, 49–50.

cut under appalling circumstances eighteen years before, when she was two.
We never know this child's full name, but we—and Sethe—think of her
as Beloved, because that is what is on her tombstone. Sethe wanted "Dearly
Beloved," from the funeral service, but had only enough strength to pay for
one word. Payment was ten minutes of sex with the tombstone engraver.
This act, which is recounted early in the novel, is a keynote for the whole
book: in the world of slavery and poverty, where human beings are mer-
chandise, everything has its price and price is tyrannical.

"Who would have thought that a little old baby could harbor so much
rage?" Sethe thinks, but it does; breaking mirrors, making tiny handprints
in cake icing, smashing dishes and manifesting itself in pools of blood-red
light. As the novel opens, the ghost is in full possession of the house, having
driven away Sethe's two young sons. Old Baby Suggs, after a lifetime of
slavery and a brief respite of freedom—purchased for her by the Sunday labor
of her son Halle, Sethe's husband—has given up and died. Sethe lives with
her memories, almost all of them bad. Denver, her teen-age daughter, courts
the baby ghost because, since her family has been ostracized by the neighbors,
she doesn't have anyone else to play with.

The supernatural element is treated, not in an "Amityville Horror,"
watch-me-make-your-flesh-creep mode, but with magnificent practicality,
like the ghost of Catherine Earnshaw in *Wuthering Heights*. All the main
characters in the book believe in ghosts, so it's merely natural for this one
to be there. As Baby Suggs says, "Not a house in the country ain't packed
to its rafters with some dead Negro's grief. We lucky this ghost is a baby.
My husband's spirit was to come back in here? or yours? Don't talk to me.
You lucky." In fact, Sethe would rather have the ghost there than not there.
It is, after all, her adored child, and any sign of it is better, for her, than
nothing.

This grotesque domestic equilibrium is disturbed by the arrival of Paul
D., one of the "Sweet Home men" from Sethe's past. The Sweet Home men
were the male slaves of the establishment. Their owner, Mr. Garner, is no
Simon Legree; instead he's a best-case slave-holder, treating his "property"
well, trusting them, allowing them choice in the running of his small
plantation, and calling them "men" in defiance of the neighbors, who want
all male blacks to be called "boys." But Mr. Garner dies, and weak, sickly
Mrs. Garner brings in her handiest male relative, who is known as "the
schoolteacher." This Goebbels-like paragon combines viciousness with intellectual pretensions; he's a sort of master-race proponent who measures the
heads of the slaves and tabulates the results to demonstrate that they are
more like animals than people. Accompanying him are his two sadistic and

repulsive nephews. From there it's all downhill at Sweet Home, as the slaves try to escape, go crazy or are murdered. Sethe, in a trek that makes the ice-floe scene in *Uncle Tom's Cabin* look like a stroll around the block, gets out, just barely; her husband, Halle, doesn't. Paul D. does, but has some very unpleasant adventures along the way, including a literally nauseating sojourn in a nineteenth-century Georgia chain gang.

Through the different voices and memories of the book, including that of Sethe's mother, a survivor of the infamous slave-ship crossing, we experience American slavery as it was lived by those who were its objects of exchange, both at its best—which wasn't very good—and at its worst, which was as bad as can be imagined. Above all, it is seen as one of the most viciously antifamily institutions human beings have ever devised. The slaves are motherless, fatherless, deprived of their mates, their children, their kin. It is a world in which people suddenly vanish and are never seen again, not through accident or covert operation or terrorism, but as a matter of everyday legal policy.

Slavery is also presented to us as a paradigm of how most people behave when they are given absolute power over other people. The first effect, of course, is that they start believing in their own superiority and justifying their actions by it. The second effect is that they make a cult of the inferiority of those they subjugate. It's no coincidence that the first of the deadly sins, from which all the others were supposed to stem, is Pride, a sin of which Sethe is, incidentally, also accused.

In a novel that abounds in black bodies—headless, hanging from trees, frying to a crisp, locked in woodsheds for purposes of rape, or floating downstream drowned—it isn't surprising that the "whitepeople," especially the men, don't come off too well. Horrified black children see whites as men "without skin." Sethe thinks of them as having "mossy teeth" and is ready, if necessary, to bite off their faces, and worse, to avoid further mossy-toothed outrages. There are a few whites who behave with something approaching decency. There's Amy, the young runaway indentured servant who helps Sethe in childbirth during her flight to freedom, and incidentally reminds the reader that the nineteenth century, with its child labor, wage slavery and widespread and accepted domestic violence, wasn't tough only for blacks, but for all but the most privileged whites as well. There are also the abolitionists who help Baby Suggs find a house and a job after she is freed. But even the decency of these "good" whitepeople has a grudging side to it, and even they have trouble seeing the people they are helping as full-fledged people, though to show them as totally free of their xenophobia and sense of superiority might well have been anachronistic.

Toni Morrison is careful not to make all the whites awful and all the blacks wonderful. Sethe's black neighbors, for instance, have their own envy and scapegoating tendencies to answer for, and Paul D., though much kinder than, for instance, the woman-bashers of Alice Walker's novel *The Color Purple,* has his own limitations and flaws. But then, considering what he's been through, it's a wonder he isn't a mass murderer. If anything, he's a little too huggable, under the circumstances.

Back in the present tense, in chapter one, Paul D. and Sethe make an attempt to establish a "real" family, whereupon the baby ghost, feeling excluded, goes berserk, but is driven out by Paul D.'s stronger will. So it appears. But then, along comes a strange, beautiful, real flesh-and-blood young woman, about twenty years old, who can't seem to remember where she comes from, who talks like a young child, who has an odd, raspy voice and no lines on her hands, who takes an intense, devouring interest in Sethe, and who says her name is Beloved.

Students of the supernatural will admire the way this twist is handled. Ms. Morrison blends a knowledge of folklore—for instance, in many traditions, the dead cannot return from the grave unless called, and it's the passions of the living that keep them alive—with a highly original treatment. The reader is kept guessing; there's a lot more to Beloved than any one character can see, and she manages to be many things to several people. She is a catalyst for revelations as well as self-revelations; through her we come to know not only how, but why, the original child Beloved was killed. And through her also Sethe achieves, finally, her own form of self-exorcism, her own self-accepting peace.

Beloved is written in an antiminimalist prose that is by turns rich, graceful, eccentric, rough, lyrical, sinuous, colloquial and very much to the point. Here, for instance, is Sethe remembering Sweet Home:

> . . . suddenly there was Sweet Home rolling, rolling, rolling out before her eyes, and although there was not a leaf on that farm that did not want to make her scream, it rolled itself out before her in shameless beauty. It never looked as terrible as it was and it made her wonder if hell was a pretty place too. Fire and brimstone all right, but hidden in lacy groves. Boys hanging from the most beautiful sycamores in the world. It shamed her— remembering the wonderful soughing trees rather than the boys. Try as she might to make it otherwise, the sycamores beat out the children every time and she could not forgive her memory for that.

In this book, the other world exists and magic works, and the prose is up to it. If you can believe page one—and Ms. Morrison's verbal authority compels belief—you're hooked on the rest of the book.

The epigraph to *Beloved* is from the Bible, Romans 9:25: "I will call them my people, which were not my people; and her beloved, which was not beloved." Taken by itself, this might seem to favor doubt about, for instance, the extent to which Beloved was really loved, or the extent to which Sethe herself was rejected by her own community. But there is more to it than that. The passage is from a chapter in which the Apostle Paul ponders, Job-like, the ways of God toward humanity, in particular the evils and inequities visible everywhere on the earth. Paul goes on to talk about the fact that the Gentiles, hitherto despised and outcast, have now been redefined as acceptable. The passage proclaims, not rejection, but reconciliation and hope. It continues: "And it shall come to pass, that in the place where it was said unto them, Ye are not my people; there shall they be called the children of the living God."

Toni Morrison is too smart, and too much of a writer, not to have intended this context. Here, if anywhere, is her own comment on the goings-on in her novel, her final response to the measuring and dividing and excluding "schoolteachers" of this world. An epigraph to a book is like a key signature in music, and *Beloved* is written in major.

DEBORAH E. McDOWELL

"The Self and the Other": Reading Toni Morrison's Sula and the Black Female Text

What shall we call our "self"? Where does it begin? Where does it end? It overflows into everything that belongs to us.
—HENRY JAMES, *Portrait of a Lady*

She has clung to Nel as the closest thing to both an other and a self, only to discover that she and Nel were not one and the same thing.
—TONI MORRISON, *Sula*[1]

In "Negro Art," an essay published in the *Crisis* in 1921, W. E. B. Du Bois described the desire of blacks for idealized literary representation. "We want everything said about us to tell of the best and highest and noblest in us . . . we fear that the evil in us will be called racial, while in others, it is viewed as individual."[2] A few years later, in 1926, Du Bois seemed himself to want to see the "best and highest and noblest" image of the black SELF in literature. Concerned because blacks were being "continually painted at their worst and judged by the public as they [were] painted," Du Bois organized a write-in symposium called "The Negro in Art: How Shall He Be Portrayed?" that ran from March to December in the *Crisis* magazine.

From *Critical Essays on Toni Morrison*, edited by Nellie Y. McKay (Boston: G. K. Hall, 1988), pp. 77–90.

The subject of intense debate, the symposium elicited applause and critiques from its respondents. Though not written directly in response to the symposium, one famous critique of its concerns was Langston Hughes's famous manifesto, published in the same year, "The Negro Artist and the Racial Mountain," in which he blasted the "Nordicized Negro intelligentsia" for demanding that black artists "be respectable, write about nice people, [and] show how good [black people] are."[3]

Roughly fifty years later, those in the vanguard of the Black Aesthetic movement described and called for black writers to inscribe the "positive" racial self in literature. In his 1977 essay "Blueprint for Black Criticism," for example, Addison Gayle appealed specifically for literary characters modeled upon such men and women as Sojourner Truth, Harriet Tubman, Martin Delaney, H. Rap Brown, and Fannie Lou Hamer—a kind of Plutarch's *Lives* of the black race. In that they offer images of "heroism, beauty, and courage," Gayle continues, "these men and women are positive" characters, functional "alternatives to the stereotypes of Blacks," and thus warriors in the "struggle against American racism."[4]

In the ten years since Gayle issued his blueprint, Afro-American literary criticism has finally seen the beginnings of a paradigm shift, one that has extended the boundaries and altered the terms of its inquiry. Falling in step with recent developments in contemporary critical theory, some critics of Afro-American literature have complicated some of our most common assumptions about the SELF, and about race as a meaningful category in literary study and critical theory.[5] These recent developments have made it difficult, if not impossible, to posit, with any assurance, a "positive" black SELF, always already unified, coherent, stable, and known.

. And yet, despite these important and sophisticated developments, Afro-American critics of Afro-American literature, in both the popular media and academic journals, continue to resist any work that does not satisfy the nebulous demand for the "positive" racial SELF. And perhaps at no time has such resistance been more determined and judgments been more harsh than now, when diehard critics, reducing contemporary black women writers to a homogenized bloc, have alleged that their portryal of black male characters is uniformly "negative."

A full inquiry into this debate, which has escaped the pages of literary journals and essay collections, and spilled over into the privileged organs of the literary establishment—the *New York Times Book Review* and the *New York Review of Books*—is not possible here, although it is in urgent need of address. But allow me to use Mel Watkins's comments from his June 1986 essay, "Sexism, Racism, and Black Women Writers," published in the *New*

York Times Book Review to represent the insistent refrain. Watkins argues that in the great majority of their novels, black women indicate that "sexism is more oppressive than racism." In these works, black males are portrayed in an "unflinchingly candid and often negative manner," almost without exception, "thieves, sadists, rapists, and ne'er-do-wells." In choosing "Black men as a target," Watkins continues, "these writers have set themselves outside a tradition," devoted to "establishing humane, positive images of Blacks" (36).[6]

It is useful here to pause and extrapolate the interlocking assumptions of Watkins's essay most relevant to my concerns. These assumptions are the struts of the dominant Afro-American critical paradigm in which 1) the world is neatly divided into black and white; 2) race is the sole determinant of being and identity, subsuming sexual difference; 3) identity is preexistent, coherent, and known; and 4) literature has the power to unify and liberate the race. This paradigm pivots on a set of oppositions—black/white, positive/negative, self/other—among an interchangeable field. The overarching preoccupation with "positive" racial representation has worked side by side with a static view of the nature of identification in the act of reading. Further, when accepted and upheld, it has resulted in substantial figurations of myth akin to Alice Walker's description: "I am Black, beautiful, and strong, and almost always right."[7] *This* is the SELF, with which our hypothetical Afro-American critic, desperately seeking flattery, is likely to identify. It is uniformly "positive" and "good" and defined in contradistinction to its OTHER, uniformly "negative" and "bad."

Easily recognizable here is the classic condition of "otherness," a subject that is itself fast becoming an industry in current critical theory and practice. And, as feminist theorists consistently and emphatically point out, the opposition of "self" to "other," and all those analogous to it, relate hierarchically and reproduce the more fundamental opposition between male and female. Man is SELF, and woman, other.[8] And in this configuration, as Shoshana Felman puts it eloquently, echoing the dutiful terms of the dominant Afro-American paradigm, woman is "the negative of the positive."[9] We face here an exponential expression of what Henry Gates has observed about Afro-American narrative more generally. He notes astutely that the irony of the Afro-American writers' "attempt to posit a 'black self' in the very Western languages in which blackness [multiply femaleness] itself is a figure of absence [is] a negation."[10]

While these observations are commonplace in feminist discourse, their usefulness to students of Afro-American literary history has not been fully interrogated. Preventing such interrogation is an almost exclusive focus on race in Afro-American literary discourse, which is often tantamount to a focus on maleness. Further preventing such investigation is what might be called an orthodoxy of victimage that unifies and homogenizes black men. In reducing their relationship to white male power and privilege as exclusively one of victimization, this orthodoxy ignores the extent to which black men share in the ideologies and practices of male privilege. The subordination (if not the absolute erasure) of black women in discourses on blackness is well known. The black SELF has been assumed male historically, of which Gloria Hull, Patricia Bell-Scott, and Barbara Smith are well aware. They do not engage in cheap and idle rhetoric in entitling their landmark anthology *All the Women Are White, All the Blacks Are Men,* for we are all too familiar with the fact that, in significant periods of their history, black women saw black men as the privileged centers of the race. While that pattern is widely evident, it stands out in noticeable relief both in Afro-American critical inquiry and in the Afro-American literary canon.[11] There, the "face" of the race, the "speaking subject," is male.[12]

While these issues need to be exposed, it will no longer suffice to leave the discourse at the point of simple descriptive exposure to which we are all inured. The next stage in the development of feminist criticism on Afro-American women writers must lead us beyond the descriptions that keep us locked in opposition and antagonism. Toni Morrison's novel, *Sula* (1973), is rife with liberating possibilities in that it transgresses all deterministic structures of opposition.

The novel invokes oppositions of good/evil, virgin/whore, self/other, but moves beyond them, avoiding the false choices they imply and dictate. As Hortense Spillers puts its eloquently, when we read *Sula,* "No Manichean analysis demanding a polarity of interest—black/white, male/female, good/bad [and I might add, positive/negative, self/other]—will do."[13] The narrative insistently blurs and confuses these and other binary oppositions. It glories in paradox and ambiguity beginning with the prologue that describes the setting, the Bottom, situated spatially in the top. We enter a new world here, a world where we never get to the "bottom" of things, a world that demands a shift from an either/or orientation to one that is both/and, full of shifts and contradictions.

In these, as well as other particulars, *Sula* opens up new literary and critical options, not only for the study of texts by Afro-American women, but for Afro-American literary study more generally. The novel certainly helps to set a new agenda for black women's social and narrative possibilities. Coming significantly on the heels of the Black Power Movement that rendered black women prone or the "queens" of the male warrior—an updated version of a familiar script—the narrative invites the reader to imagine a different script for women that transcends the boundaries of social and linguistic convention. Further, it offers a useful model of self, of identity and indentification in the reading process, a model that springs the traditional Afro-American critic from the rhetoric of opposition that has kept the discourse in arrest.

II

Day and night are mingled in our gazes . . . If we divide light from night, we give up the lightness of our mixture . . . We put ourselves into watertight compartments, break ourselves up into parts, cut ourselves in two . . . we are always one and the other, at the same time.

—Luce Irigaray[14]

To posit that we are always one and the other at the same time is to challenge effectively a fundamental assumption of Western metaphysics that has operated historically, in Afro-American literature and criticism: "the unity of the ego-centered individual self"[15] defined in opposition to an other. In *Sula,* Toni Morrison complicates and questions that assumption, evoking the very oppositions on which it has tended to rest. She transgresses and blurs the boundaries these oppositions create, boundaries separating us from others and rendering us "others" to ourselves.

Morrison's transgression begins with questioning traditional notions of SELF as they have been translated into narrative. She implicitly critiques such concepts as "protagonist," "hero," and "major character" by emphatically decentering and deferring the presence of Sula, the title character. Bearing *her* name, the narrative suggests that she is the protagonist, the privileged center, but her presence is constantly deferred. We are first introduced to a caravan of characters: Shadrack, Nel, Helene, Eva, the Deweys, Tar Baby, Hannah, and Plum before we get any sustained treatment of Sula. Economical to begin with, the novel is roughly one-third over when Sula is introduced and it continues almost that long after her death.

Not only does the narrative deny the reader a "central" character, but it also denies the whole notion of character as static *essence,* replacing it with the idea of character as *process.*[16] Whereas the former is based on the assumption that the self is knowable, centered, and unified, the latter is based on the assumption that the self is multiple, fluid, relational, and in a perpetual state of becoming. Significantly, Sula, whose eyes are "as steady and clear as rain," is associated throughout with water, fluidity. Her birth-mark, which shifts in meaning depending on the viewer's perspective, acts as a metaphor for her figurative "selves," her multiple identity. To Nel, it is a "stemmed rose"; to her children, a "scary black thing," a "black mark"; to Jude, a "copperhead" and a "rattlesnake"; to Shadrack, a "tadpole." The image of the tadpole reinforces this notion of SELF as perpetually in process. Sula never achieves completeness of being. She dies in the fetal position welcoming this "sleep of water," in a passage that clearly suggests, she is dying yet aborning (149). Morrison's reconceptualization of character has clear and direct implications for Afro-American literature and critical study, for if the self is perceived as perpetually in process, rather than a static entity always already formed, it is thereby difficult to posit its ideal or "positive" representation.

Appropriate to this conception of character as process, the narrative employs the double, a technique related, as Baruch Hoffman has observed, to the "rupturing of coherence in character."[17] It positions its doubles, Nel and Sula, in adolescence, a state of becoming when they are "unshaped, formless things" (53) "us[ing] each other to grow on," finding "in each other's eyes the intimacy they were looking for" (52). As doubles, Sula and Nel complement and flow into each other, their closeness evoked throughout the narrative in physical metaphors. Sula's return to the Bottom, after a ten-year absence is, for Nel, "like getting the use of an eye back, having a cataract removed" (95). The two are likened to "two throats and one eye" (147).

But while Sula and Nel are represented as two parts of a self, those parts are distinct; they are complementary, not identical. Although Sula and Nel might share a common vision (suggested by "one eye"), their needs and desires are distinct (they have "two throats").[18] Sula comes to understand the fact of their difference, as the epigraph to this essay suggests: "She clung to Nel as the closest thing to an *other* and a *self* only to discover that she and Nel were not one and the same thing." The relationship of other to self in this passage, and throughout the narrative, must be seen as "different but connected rather than separate and opposed," to borrow from Carole Gilligan.[19]

Sula's understanding of her relationship to Nel results from self-understanding and self-intimacy, a process that Nel's marriage to Jude in-terrupts. Like so many women writers, Morrison equates marriage with the death of the female self and imagination. Nel would be the "someone sweet, industrious and loyal to shore him up . . . the two of them would make one Jude" (83). After marriage she freezes into her wifely role, becoming one of the women who had "folded themselves into starched coffins" (122). Her definition of self becomes based on the community's "absolute" moral categories about "good" and "bad" women, categories that result in her separation from and opposition to Sula.

The narrative anticipates that opposition in one of its early descriptions of Nel and Sula. Nel is the color of "wet sandpaper," Sula is the "heavy brown" (52), a distinction that can be read as patriarchy's conventional fair lady/dark woman, virgin/whore dichotomy, one reflected in Sula's and Nel's separate matrilineages.

Sula's female heritage is an unbroken line of "manloving" women who exist as sexually desiring subjects rather than as objects of male desire. Her mother, Hannah, "ripple[s] with sex" (42), exasperating the "good" women of the community who call her "nasty." But that does not prevent her taking her lovers into the pantry for "some touching every day" (44). In contrast, Nel's is a split heritage. On one side is her grandmother, the whore of the Sundown House, and on the other her great-grandmother, who worshipped the Virgin Mary and counseled Helene "to be constantly on guard for any sign of her mother's wild blood" (17). Nel takes her great-grandmother's counsel to heart, spending her life warding off being "turn[ed] to jelly" and "custard" (22). Jelly and pudding here are metaphors of sexuality characteristic in classic blues lyrics.

Nel's sexuality is not expressed in itself and for her own pleasure, but rather, for the pleasure of her husband and in obedience to a system of ethical judgment and moral virtue, her "only mooring" (139). Because Nel's sexuality is harnessed to and only enacted within the institutions that sanction sexuality for women—marriage and family—she does not own it.[20] It is impossible for her to imagine sex without Jude. After she finds him and Sula in the sex act she describes her thighs—the metaphor for her sexuality—as "empty and dead . . . and it was Sula who had taken the life from them . . . " She concludes that "the both of them . . . left her with no thighs and no heart just her brain raveling away" (110–11).

Without Jude, Nel thinks her thighs are useless. Her sexuality is harnessed to duty and virtue in a simple cause/effect relationship as is clear from the plaintive questions she puts to an imaginary God after Jude leaves:

> even if I sew up those old pillow cases and rinse down the porch
> and feed my children and beat the rugs and haul the coal up out
> of the bin even then nobody. . . . I could be a mule or plow the
> furrows with my hands if need be or hold these rickety walls up
> with my back if need be if I knew that somewhere in this world

in the pocket of some night I could open my legs to some cowboy
lean hips but you are trying to tell me no and O my sweet Jesus
what kind of cross is that? (111)

Sula, on the other hand, "went to bed with men as frequently as she
could" (122) and assumed responsibility for her own pleasure. In her first
sexual experience with Ajax, significantly a reenactment of Hannah's sexual
rituals in the pantry, Sula "stood wide-legged against the wall and pulled
from his track-lean hips all the pleasure her thighs could hold" (125). This
is not to suggest that Sula's sexual expression is uncomplicated or unproblematic, but rather that unlike Nel's, it is not attached to anything outside
herself, especially not to social definitions of female sexuality and conventions
of duty. Although initially she "liked the sootiness of sex," liked "to think
of it as wicked" (122), she comes to realize that it was not wicked. Further,
apart from bringing her "a special kind of joy," it brought her "misery and
the ability to feel deep sorrow" and "a stinging awareness of the endings of
things" (122, 123), a feeling of "her own abiding strength and limitless
power" (123). In other words, Sula's sexuality is neither located in the realm
of "moral" abstractions nor expressed within the institution of marriage that
legitimates it for women. Rather it is in the realm of sensory experience
and in the service of the self-exploration that leads to self-intimacy. After
sex, Sula enters that "postcoital privateness in which she met herself, wel-
comed herself, and joined herself in matchless harmony" (123). Unlike Nel,
Sula has no ego and therefore feels "no compulsion . . . [to] be consistent
with herself" (119). In describing her, Morrison notes that Sula "examines
herself . . . is experimental with herself [and] perfectly willing to think the
unthinkable thing."[21] To Sula "there was only her own mood and whim"
enabling her to explore "that version of herself which she sought to reach
out to and touch with an ungloved hand," to "discover it and let others
become as intimate with their own selves as she was" (121).

Not only is sexual expression an act of self-exploration, but it is also
associated throughout the narrative with creativity as seen in the long prose
poem she creates while making love to Ajax. But significantly that creativity
is without sufficient outlet within her community. According to Morrison,
"If Sula had any sense she'd go somewhere and sing or get into show
business," implying that her "strangeness," her "lawlessness" can only be
sanctioned in a world like the theater.[22] Because of her community's rigid
norms for women, Sula's impulses cannot be absorbed. Without an "art
form," her "tremendous curiosity and her gift for metaphor" become destructive (121). Without art forms, Sula is the artist become her own work

of art.[23] As she responds defiantly to Eva's injunction that she make babies to settle herself, "I don't want to make somebody else. I want to make myself" (92).

Because she resists self-exploration, such creativity is closed to Nel. She has no "sparkle or splutter," just a "dull glow" (83). Her imagination has been driven "underground" from years of obeying the normative female script. She "belonged to the town and all of its ways" (120). The narrative strongly suggests that one cannot belong to the community and preserve the imagination, for the orthodox vocations for women—marriage and motherhood—restrict if not preclude imaginative expression.

Obedience to community also precludes intimacy with self for women. Nel rejects this intimacy that involves confronting what both Sula and Shadrack have confronted: the unknown parts of themselves. In turning her back on the unknown, Nel fails to grow, to change, or to learn anything about herself until the last page of the novel. She thinks that "hell is change" (108). "One of the last true pedestrians" in the Bottom, Nel walks on the road's shoulder (on its edge, not on the road), "allowing herself to accept rides only when the weather required it" (166).

Nel fits Docherty's description of the type of character who is "fixed and centered up on one locatable ego," blocking "the possibility of authentic response, genuine statement." According to this ego-centered schema, "the self can only act in accord with a determined and limited 'characteristic' response" (80). Whereas Sula is an ambiguous character with a repertoire of responses along a continuum and thus cannot be defined as either totally "good" or "bad," Nel's is a limited response: "goodness," "rightness," as her name "Wright" suggests. As it is classically defined for women "goodness" is sexual faithfulness, self-abnegation, and the idealization of marriage and motherhood.

After years of nursing the belief that Sula has irreparably wronged her and violated their friendship, Nel goes to visit Sula on her deathbed as any "good woman" would do. Virtue, "her only mooring," has hidden "from her the true motives for her charity" (139). Their conversation, after years of estrangement, is peppered with references to good and evil, right and wrong. Nel protests, "I was good to you, Sula, why don't that matter?" And Sula reponds in her characteristically defiant way "Being good to somebody is just like being mean to somebody. Risky. You don't get nothing for it." Exasperated because "talking to [Sula] about right and wrong" (144–45) was impossible, Nel leaves but not before Sula has the last word. And significantly, that last word takes the form of a question, an uncertainty, not an unambiguous statement of fact or truth:

"How you know?" Sula asked.

"Know what?" Nel still wouldn't look at her.

"About who was good. How you know it was you?"

"What you mean?"

"I mean maybe it wasn't you. Maybe it was me."

In the space of the narrative Nel has another twenty-five years to deflect the contemplation of Sula's question through desperate acts of goodness: visits to "the sick and shut in," the category on the back page of black church bulletins that pull on the chords of duty. But on one such mission to visit Eva, Nel is confronted with not only the question but the more *unsettling* suggestion of guilt.

"Tell me how you killed that little boy."

"What? What little boy?"

"The one you threw in the water . . ."

"I didn't throw no little boy in the river. That was Sula."

"You, Sula. What's the difference?"

After years of repression, Nel must own her complicity in Chicken Little's drowning, a complicity that is both sign and symbol of the disowned piece of herself. She recalls the incident in its fullness, remembering "the good feeling she had when Chicken's hands slipped" (170) and "the tranquillity that follow[ed] [that] joyful stimulation" (170). That remembrance makes space for Nel's psychic reconnection with Sula as a friend as well as symbol of that disowned self. Significantly, that reconnection occurs in the cemetery, a metaphor for Nel's buried shadow. The "circles and circles of sorrow" she cried at the narrative's end prepare her for what Sula strained to experience throughout her life: the process of mourning and remembering that leads to intimacy with the self, which is all that makes intimacy with others possible.

And the reader must mourn as Nel mourns, must undergo the process of development that Nel undergoes.[24] And as with Nel, that process begins with releasing the static and coherent conception of SELF and embracing what Sula represents: the self as process and fluid possibility. That embrace makes possible an altered understanding of the nature of identification in the reading process.

III

Recent theories of the act of reading have enriched and complicated— for the good—our understanding of what takes place in the act of reading.

They have described the reading process as dialogical, as an interaction between a reader (a SELF) and an OTHER, an interaction in which neither remains the same.[25] In light of this information, we can conceive the act of reading as a process of self-exploration that the narrative strategies of *Sula* compel. What strategies does the narrative employ to generate that process? It deliberately miscues the reader, disappointing the very expectations the narrative arouses, forcing the reader to shift gears, to change perspective. Though these strategies might well apply to all readers, they have specific implications for Afro-American critics.

Sula threatens the readers' assumptions and disappoints their expectations at every turn. It begins by disappointing the reader's expectations of a "realistic" and unified narrative documenting black/white confrontation. Although the novel's prologue, which describes a community's destruction by white greed and deception, gestures toward "realistic" documentation, leads the reader to expect "realistic" documentation of a black community's confrontation with an oppressive white world, the familiar and expected plot is in the background. In the foreground are the characters whose lives transcend their social circumstances. They laugh, they dance, they sing, and are "mightily preoccupied with earthly things—and each other" (6). The narrative retreats from linearity privileged in the realist mode. Though dates entitle the novel's chapters, they relate only indirectly to its central concerns and do not permit the reader to use chronology in order to interpret its events in any cause/effect fashion. In other words, the story's forward movement in time is deliberately nonsequential and without explicit reference to "real" time. It roves lightly over historical events, dates, and details as seen in the first chapter. Titled "1919," the chapter begins with a reference to World War II, then refers, in quick and, paradoxically, regressive succession, to National Suicide Day, instituted in 1920, then backwards to Shadrack running across a battlefield in France in World War I.

In addition, the narrative forces us to question our readings, to hold our judgment in check, and to continually revise it. Susan Blake is on the mark when she says that "the reader never knows quite what to think" of characters and events in *Sula*: "whether to applaud Eva's self-sacrifice or deplore her tyranny, whether to admire Sula's freedom or condemn her heartlessness."[26] The narrative is neither an apology for Sula's destruction nor an unsympathetic critique of Nel's smug conformity. It does not reduce a complex set of dynamics to a simple opposition or choice between two "pure" alternatives.

Among the strategies Morrison uses to complicate choice and block judgment are the dots within dots (. . . .) in the narrative that mark time breaks and function as stop signs. They compel the reader to pause, think back, evaluate the narrative's events, and formulate new expectations in light of them, expectations that are never quite fulfilled.[27] The Afro-American critic, wanting a world cleansed of uncertainty and contradictions and based on the rhetorical polarities—positive and negative—might ask in frustration, "Can we ever determine the right judgment?" The narrative implies that that answer can only come from within, from exploring all parts of the SELF. As Nel asks Eva in the scene mentioned earlier, "You think I'm guilty?" Eva whispers, "Who would know that better than you?" (169).

Not only does the narrative disappoint the reader's expectations of correct answers and appropriate judgment, but it also prevents a stable and unified reading of the text, though I have fabricated one here by tracing a dominant thread in the narrative: the relationship between self and other. But in exploring this relationship, Morrison deliberately provides echoing passages that cancel each other out, that thwart the reader's desire for stability and consistency:

> She had clung to Nel as the closest thing to both an other and a self, only to discover that she and Nel were not one and the same thing.

But the following passage, which comes much later in the narrative, effectively cancels this passage out: Sula learned that

> there was no other that you could count on . . . [and] there was no *self* to count on either.

The novel's fragmentary, episodic, elliptical quality helps to thwart textual unity, to prevent a totalized interpretation. An early reviewer described the text as a series of scenes and glimpses, each "written . . . from scratch." Since none of them has anything much to do with the ones that preceded them, "we can never piece the glimpses into a coherent picture."[28] Whatever coherence and meaning resides in the narrative, the reader must struggle to create.

The gaps in the text allow for the reader's participation in the creation of meaning in the text. Morrison has commented on the importance of the "affective and participatory relationship between the artist and the audience," and her desire "to have the reader work *with* the author in the construction of the book." She adds, "What is left out is as important as what is there."[29] The reader must fill in the narrative's many gaps, for instance: Why is there no funeral for either Plum or Hannah? What happens to Jude? Where *was* Eva during her eighteen-month absence from the Bottom? What really happened to her leg? How does Sula support herself after she returns from her ten-year absence?

The reader's participation in the meaning-making process helps to fill in the gaps in the text, as well as to bridge the gaps separating the reader *from* the text. This returns us full circle to the beginning of this essay: the boundary separating some Afro-American readers from the black text that opposes a single unified image of the black SELF.

As Norman Holland and others have noted, each reader has a vision of the world arising from her/his identity theme. In the act of reading, the reader tries to re-create the text according to that identity theme. Holland continues, as we read, we use the "literary work to symbolize and finally to replicate ourselves,"[30] to reflect ourselves, to affirm ourselves by denying or demeaning the other. But, writing in a different context, Holland usefully suggests that, "one of literature's adaptive functions . . . is that it allows us to loosen boundaries between self and not self."[31]

Transgressing that boundary and viewing identity and the self in relation, rather than coherent, separate, and opposed, permits an analogous view of identification in the reading process. Just as the self is fluid, dynamic, and formed in relation, so is identification a process involving a relationship between the SELF and the "otherness" of writers, texts, and literary characters.

If we would approach that "unified" black community splintered, many argue, by black women writers' imaginative daring, those boundaries and the rigid identity themes and fantasies holding them up must be crossed. After all, as *Sula* playfully suggests, our conceptions of who we are never include all that we are anyway. One answer, then, to the epigraph: "What shall we call our 'self'?" is we shall call ourselves by many names. Our metaphors of self cannot then rest in stasis, but will glory in difference and overflow into everything that belongs to us.

NOTES

[1] Toni Morrison, *Sula* (New York: New American Library, 1973), 119. Subsequent references are to this edition and will be indicated parenthetically in the text.

[2] W. E. B. Du Bois, "Negro Art," *Crisis* (June 1921): 55–56.

[3] Langston Hughes, "The Negro Artist and the Racial Mountain," in *Five Black Writers*, ed. Donald B. Gibson (New York: New York University Press, 1970), 227–28.

[4] Addison Gayle, "Blueprint for Black Criticism," *First World* (January/February 1977): 44.

[5] See three essays by Henry Louis Gates, Jr.: "Preface to Blackness: Text and Pretext," in *Afro-American Literature: The Reconstruction of Instruction*, ed. Dexter Fischer and Robert Stepto (New York: MLA, 1979), 44–69; "Criticism in the Jungle," in *Black Literature and Literary*

Theory, ed. Henry Gates (New York: Methuen, 1984), 1–24; and "Writing 'Race' and the Difference It Makes," *Critical Inquiry* 12 (Autumn 1985): 1–20. For critiques of the issue on " 'Race,' Writing and Difference," in which the last essay appears, see *Critical Inquiry* 13 (Autumn 1986).

[6] Mel Watkins, "Sexism, Racism, and Black Women Writers," *New Yook Times Book Review* (15 June 1986): 36. For similar discussions see Darryl Pinckney, "Black Victims, Black Villains," *New York Review of Books* 34 (29 January 1987): 17–20 and Richard Barksdale, "Castration Symbolism in Recent Black American Fiction," *College Language Association Journal* 29 (June 1986): 400–13.

[7] Alice Walker, "The Unglamorous but Worthwhile Duties of the Black Revolutionary Artist, or of the Black Writer Who Simply Works and Writes," in *In Search of Our Mothers' Gardens* (New York: Harcourt Brace Jovanovich, 1983), 137.

[8] Although a whole field of binary oppositions can be viewed as analogous to the male/female opposition, Cary Nelson rightly cautions against so rigid a reading. He argues persuasively that when such dualities are considered in cultural and historical context, the basic male/female opposition breaks down and the qualities associated with each side are often reversed. See "Envoys of Otherness: Difference and Continuity in Feminist Criticism," in *For Alma Mater: Theory and Practice in Feminist Scholarship*, ed. Paula Treichler et al. (Urbana: University of Illinois Press, 1985), 91–118.

[9] Shoshana Felman, "Women and Madness: The Critical Phallacy," *Diacritics* 5 (Winter 1975): 3.

[10] See Gates, "Criticism in the Jungle," 7.

[11] The historical equation of blackness with maleness in discourses on blackness and in the development of the Afro-American literary canon is an issue calling urgently for examination. Although I cannot address it here in any detail it is the subject of my essay-in-progress forthcoming in *Black American Literature Forum*. For a discussion of how this equation has worked out in discourses on slavery see Deborah Gray White, *Ar'n't I a Woman: Female Slaves in the Plantation South* (New York: Norton, 1985). White examines slave women whose experiences are neglected, more often than not, from scholarship on slavery. According to White, the pattern began with the publication of Stanley Elkins's *Slavery: A Problem in American Institutional and Intellectual Life* (Chicago: University of Chicago Press, 1959) in which he posited his controversial "Sambo" thesis of male infantilism and incompetence which historians have since focussed their energies on negating. That focus has effectively eclipsed black women from view.

[12] See Robert Stepto, *From Behind the Veil: A Study of Afro-American Narrative* (Urbana: University of Illinois Press, 1979), who defines the Afro-American narrative tradition in almost exclusively male terms. See also Henry Gates's preface to the special issue of *Critical Inquiry*, " 'Race,' Writing, and Difference," in which he describes the beginning of that tradition: the writings of John Gronniosaw, John Marrant, Olaudah Equiano, Ottabah Cugoano, and John Jea, all male. They, he argues, posited both "the individual 'I' of the Black author as well as the collective 'I' of the race. Text created author; and Black authors, it was hoped would create or re-create the image of the race in European discourse" (11).

[13] Hortense Spillers, "A Hateful Passion, a Lost Love," *Feminist Studies* 9 (Summer 1983): 296.

[14] Luce Irigaray, *This Sex Which Is Not One* (Ithaca: Cornell University Press, 1985), 217.

[15] Thomas Docherty, *Reading (Absent) Character: Toward a Theory of Characterization in Fiction* (Oxford: Clarendon Press, 1983), 265.

[16] I am adapting Docherty's distinction between "character as a 'becoming' rather than as an 'essence.' " See Docherty, *Reading (Absent) Character*, 268.

[17] Baruch Hoffman, *Character in Literature* (Ithaca: Cornell University Press, 1985), 79.

[18] I borrow this point from Judith Kegan Gardiner, "The (US)es of (I)dentity: A Response to Abel on '(E)merging Identities,' " *Signs* 6 (Spring 1981): 439.

[19] Carole Gilligan, *In a Different Voice* (Cambridge: Harvard University Press, 1982), 147.

[20] In *The Bluest Eye* Morrison is similarly concerned with those women who view sex as a marital duty rather than a source of their own pleasure. Called the Mobile women, they try to rid themselves of the "dreadful funkiness of passion," give their "bod[ies] sparingly and partially," and hope that they will "remain dry between [their] legs" (68–69).

[21] Toni Morrison, "Intimate Things in Place," *Massachusetts Review* (Autumn 1977): 477.

[22] See Bettye J. Parker, "Complexity: Toni Morrison's Women—An Interview Essay" in *Sturdy Black Bridges: Visions of Black Women in Literature*, ed. Roseann P. Bell, Bettye J. Parker and Beverly Guy-Sheftall (New York: Anchor/Doubleday, 1979), 256.

[23] For a discussion of this theme in other Morrison novels see Renita Weems, " 'Artists without Art Form': A Look at One Black Woman's World of Unrevered Black Women," *Conditions: Five* 2 (Autumn 1979): 46–58.

[24] *Sula* is an intensely elegiac novel about loss, grieving, and the release of pain. The epigraph signals the concern. "It is sheer good fortune to miss somebody long before they leave you." It implies that leave-taking and loss are inevitable. At the end of the book Shadrack gives over to his grief for Sula, and when he does, he ceases to fill his life with compulsive activity. At Chicken Little's funeral, the women grieve for their own painful childhoods, the "most devastating pain there is" (65). The narrator grieves for a community that has become increasingly atomistic with the passage of time. Barbara Christian also sees these qualities in the novel, reading the epilogue as "a eulogy to the Bottom." See "Community and Nature: The Novels of Toni Morrison," *Journal of Ethnic Studies* 7 (Winter 1980): 64–78.

[25] Wolfgang Iser, for example, discusses the two "selves" that interact in the reading process: one, the reader's own self or "disposition"; the other, that offered by the text. See *The Act of Reading* (Baltimore: Johns Hopkins, 1978), 37. For a thorough overview and synthesis of theories of reading see Susan R. Suleiman, "Introduction: Varieties of Audience-Oriented Criticism," in *The Reader in the Text*, ed. Susan Suleiman and Inge Crosman (Princeton: Princeton University Press, 1980), 3–45.

[26] Susan Blake, "Toni Morrison," in *Dictionary of Literary Biography* (Detroit: Gale Research Co., 1984), 191.

[27] I am indebted here to Jerome Beaty's afterward to *Sula* in *The Norton Introduction to the Short Novel*, 2d ed. (1987), 699.

[28] Christopher Lehmann-Haupt, Review of *Sula*, *New York Times* 123 (7 January 1974): 29.

[29] "Rootedness: The Ancestor as Foundation," in *Black Women Writers: A Critical Evaluation*, ed. Mari Evans (New York: Anchor/Doubleday, 1984), 341.

[30] "UNITY IDENTITY TEXT SELF," *PMLA* 90 (1975): 816. See also Jean Kennard, "Ourself behind Ourself: A Theory for Lesbian Readers," in *Gender and Reading*, ed. Elizabeth Flynn and Patrocinio Schweikart (Baltimore: Johns Hopkins University Press, 1986), 63–80.

[31] See *Dynamics of Literary Response* (New York: Oxford University Press, 1968), 101.

ROGER SALE

Toni Morrison's Beloved

Among the score of American novels of last year that I read, *the* book is Toni Morrison's *Beloved*. Not without hue and cry: there was Stanley Crouch's very sour review in *The New Republic,* which itself caused a storm, and I have had some heated conversations about it with my colleague, Charles Johnson, whose *Being and Race: Black Writing since 1970* reveals a fine shrewd mind on every page. Not without reservation either. *Beloved* was written in the palace of Art, its ways with history are like those of *Nostromo* or Ford's *Fifth Queen* series, its verbal texture is as rich as that of *Mrs. Dalloway,* and Morrison is thereby heir to more problems than she perhaps knows. No matter. This is a major book.

Here are the opening sentences:

> 124 was spiteful. Full of a baby's venom. The women in the house knew it and so did the children. For years each put up with the spite in his own way, but by 1873 Sethe and her daughter Denver were its only victims. The grandmother, Baby Suggs, was dead, and the sons, Howard and Buglar, had run away by the time they were thirteen years old—as soon as merely looking in a mirror shattered it (that was the signal for Buglar); as soon as two tiny hand prints appeared in the cake (that was it for Howard).

Finish the book and reread this and you know that 124 is a house, Sethe and Denver are the central characters, Baby Suggs is the most memorable

From *Massachusetts Review* 29, No. 1 (Spring 1988): 81–86.

minor character since one of Faulkner's, Howard and Buglar never reappear, and the baby with the venom "is" the "almost crawling? baby" *and* the Beloved of the title.

But the art is right there for the first-time readers. Morrison tosses many balls in the air in these five sentences without telling us which ones to make sure to watch. She gives us many different ways of dealing with time—"for years," "by 1873," "thirteen years old," without telling us how, or how soon, each might matter. By the time we have gotten to Howard and the hand prints, Morrison has so enmeshed us in verbal machinery that it is not easy to remember, let alone feel any impact from "spiteful" in the first sentence or "venom" in the second. What did Howard see in the hand prints, or Buglar in the mirror? How many years had these boys put up with the spite of the baby's venom? Everything in Morrison's way of rendering creates distance, a sense that she will in her own sweet time tell us all she thinks we need to know and no more. And, by the end of the novel the hand prints and the face are still unclear to me, and I've read *Beloved* twice, once aloud.

So Stanley Crouch is out of court when he calls the novel a soap opera. In a soap we are supposed to respond, fully, directly, and right now, to each scene put in front of us, while for long stretches of *Beloved* we simply don't know how to do this, because we don't know yet what we're seeing. Crouch is just finding an easy way to put the book down. For the same reason, he is quite mistaken when he suggests this is like a Holocaust novel (for Concentration Camps read Slavery). There are horrible images of things that happened to slaves here, no question. Sethe is held down and milked by some young men, one of her companions is bridled and bitted like a mule and spends a horrible stretch in a chain gang, another is burned alive after being caught trying to escape. But Morrison's art makes us gasp at these moments, then insists we not organize our feeling as if for protest or other action, but instead move back into the heavy verbal texture of her fiction.

There is a fundamental objection to writers and books where the author is so openly and powerfully in control; it is the one made by Lawrence to Mann and Flaubert about the will of the artist to be superior to the materials being created and worked with. In this respect, I felt no difficulty with *Beloved,* no sense that it is the intent of Morrison's art to show off its own ability and power. She works very much, though in her own way, in the service of person, scene, situation, life; it's just that her way is not that of dramatic realism.

I can, however, state a similar objection that may prove more germane. Morrison is so constantly telling you and not telling you, telling you a bit more but leaving you wondering if you've missed something, that she encourages, almost forces, readers to read too fast, to rush ahead to the clarifying moments. The book became a page turner for me the first time through. My guess is that the result will be some enthralled readers who will end up unsure what they have read, and perhaps a smaller number—and my money is on their being mostly men—of unenchanted ones who end up praising Morrison's lyric gifts and claiming that as a novel it is mostly a trick. So some of the hue and cry may be built into the nature of Morrison's art and its relation to its readers. Not everyone is going to find out how beautifully this book reads when read slowly, and in small doses.

That said, let the rest be praise:

> "Where I was before I came here, that place is real. It's never going away. Even if the whole farm—every tree and grass blade of it dies . . . if you go there—you who never was there—if you go there and stand in the place where it was, it will happen again; it will be there for you, waiting for you. So, Denver, you can't ever go there. Never. Because even though it's all over— over and done with—it's going to always be there waiting for you. That's how come I had to get all my children out. No matter what."

And that's how come Sethe is willing to murder her children rather than have them taken back when a slavecatcher comes after they've escaped and are living at 124, in a house not far from Cincinnati.

Not since time past, present, and future in "Burnt Norton," maybe, has someone played such games for us about time. But Eliot offers us propositions, and Sethe gives us, at once, insistent perplexity and insistent assurance. The farm is Sweet Home, Kentucky, where Sethe was a slave; she is speaking to Denver, who was born after Sethe escaped. That Sweet Home lives for Sethe, and would even if it were in fact destroyed, we understand as memory. But Sethe has another word, "rememory," that seems at times just another word like "remember," but here it is Seth's memory as it would happen to Denver if she went to Sweet Home. "It will be . . . waiting for you," so "You can't never go there" or else you will know what happened to me there.

As a proposition I'm not sure what to make of it, what I "believe." But *Beloved* is not concerned with propositions but with experience, and at this point (we are on p. 37) we have two propositions that for Sethe are experiences: "124 was spiteful. Full of a baby's venom," and "That's how come I had to get all my children out" of Sweet Home and of my memory of my life as a slave. She is saying, in effect, though I doubt if even the shrewdest reader can take it in, "You are living in this spiteful house, full of a baby's venom, because *that* rememory is preferable to the one you would, or will, face the moment you see Sweet Home and my rememory of it." There seems something a little crazy here, though we are far from knowing if that is an appropriate word. But if we cannot take it in, we can engage in the story, in our finding out.

Now let me add Paul D, who has been engaged in a counter activity, the keeping dead of memory as much as Sethe is keeping memory alive. Paul D was a slave at Sweet Home, he is the one who is bitted like a mule, who endures the chain gang, who escapes and is told, since it is February, "follow the tree flowers" that will keep telling him where north is. He spends eighteen years wandering, all the time learning to forget, and not to know what he once felt:

> It was some time before he could put Alfred, Georgia, Sixo, schoolteacher, Halle, his brothers, Sethe, Mister, the taste of iron, the sight of butter, the smell of hickory, notebook paper, one by one, into the tobacco tin lodged in his chest. By the time he got to 124 nothing in this world could pry it open.

It would be fun to show how all the items on that list come into the novel even as Paul D is trying to lock them away into the tobacco tin in his chest. But that would take too long, and I must settle for saying that when Paul D comes to 124, he senses immediately that the house is spiteful, haunted with rememory, though he is told little about the baby's venom. Dedicated to killing the past, he exorcises the ghost of the house: "Holding the table by two legs, he bashed it about, wrecking everything, screaming back at the screaming house. 'You want to fight, come on! God damn it! She got enough without you. She got enough!' " Then "it was gone," Paul D takes Sethe up to her bed, and the next day Sethe begins to think she might be able to plan her days, her life, ahead a little. But shortly thereafter the mysterious Beloved appears, an intent young woman who is just the age the baby with the venom would have been had Sethe not murdered her to keep her from the slavecatcher. So the house is once again haunted.

The rest of the novel shows the struggle of Beloved and Paul D for Sethe, who loves Paul D but who is so ravaged by guilt and her rememory, that for a long stretch Paul D must leave 124 and let Beloved reign there, so it is not Paul D but Denver who finally sets in motion the events that bring the story to its climax. When Stanley Crouch comes to his senses, he will have to examine his motives in linking Morrison and *Beloved* with Alice Walker and *The Color Purple* concerning their treatment of black men. Since Morrison not only treats Paul D with admiration and respect—at a number of points one is grateful indeed for his presence among a group of women who seem almost lunatic—but reserves for him some of her most lavish and loving prose. My guess is that Crouch's feelings follow a logic similar to this: *The Color Purple* is a not very good novel that was adored by black women and white folks; it looks as though the same thing will happen with *Beloved;* if I can suggest that Morrison is "not good about" black men too, maybe I can get away with calling *Beloved* trite and sentimental; Morrison has a lot more talent than Walker, and I need to stop this stampede—call them "feminists" as if that *were* a dirty word—soon. Crouch got one thing right: *The Color Purple* is not a very good novel, though I see no reason to call it a bad novel, and in any event, it is irrelevant to consideration of *Beloved.* And among the things Crouch could not dare do in his review is quote from the scenes between Paul D and the Underground Railroad worker with the wonderful name of Stamp Paid.

It is Toni Morrison's ambition to create a form, and a storytelling, that keeps alive the struggle to remember, the need to forget, and the inability to forget. Something terrible happened, and keeps happening, and it is not entirely clear what, or even when. Though the events of *Beloved* could be arranged to make a drama, though there is a grand climatic scene, the book is elegy, pastoral, sad, sweet, mysterious.

I trace part of a thread: way back, about as far back as the novel's memory goes, a slave named Halle got permission from his owner to work for pay on Sundays so that, years later, after Halle had married Sethe, he could buy freedom for his mother, Baby Suggs. With the help of the whites who own the house, Baby Suggs had come to live at 124—so that 124 is where Halle and Sethe will come after they escape, except they are separated and Sethe arrives alone. Baby Suggs had "decided that, because slave life had 'busted her legs, back, head, eyes, hands, kidneys, womb and tongue,' she had nothing left to make a living with but her heart," and she becomes a preacher:

> The company watched her from the trees. They knew she was ready when she put her stick down. Then she shouted, "Let the children come!" and they ran from the trees toward her.
>
> "Let your mothers hear you laugh," she told them, and the woods rang. The adults looked on and could not help smiling.
>
> Then "Let grown men come," she shouted. They stepped out one by one from among the ringing trees.
>
> "Let your wives and children see you dance," she told them, and groundlife shuddered under their feet.
>
> Finally, she called the women to her. "Cry," she told them.

"For the living and the dead. Just cry." And without covering
their eyes the women let loose.

It started that way: laughing children, dancing men, crying
women and then it got mixed up. Women stopped crying and
danced; men sat down and cried; children danced, women
laughed, children cried until, exhausted and riven, all and each
lay about the Clearing damp and gasping for breath. In the silence
that followed, Baby Suggs, holy, offered up to them her great
big heart.

But this rememory, called up because Paul D's arrival, which killed the
ghost, forced Sethe to tell herself she would never see Halle again: "Why
now, with Paul D instead of the ghost, was she breaking up? getting scared?
needing Baby? The worst was over, wasn't it?"

No, because other parts of the past can reach out and clutch like the
tentacles of an octopus, because Beloved is there to cast a spell over Sethe,
because Denver must finally seize the day, because Paul D, who had locked
the tobacco tin of his past in his chest, must come to remember. Yet there
does come a time when the worst indeed is over:

"Sethe," Paul D says, "me and you, we got more yesterday
than anybody. We need some kind of tomorrow."

He leans over and takes her hand. With the other he touches
her face. "You your best thing, Sethe. You are." His holding
fingers are holding hers.

"Me? Me?"

Paul D is strong here because he has remembered what another slave
had said, twenty years ago, about his woman, "She is a friend of my mind,"
and so Paul D can know what Sethe is for him. And she, bewildered, loved,
can now forget. It's a long and beautiful tale.

THEODORE O. MASON, JR.

The Novelist as Conservator: Stories and Comprehension in Toni Morrison's Song of Solomon

> I am not experimental, I am simply trying to re-create something out of an old art form in my books—the something that defines what makes a book "black." And that has nothing to do with whether the people in the books are black or not. The open-ended quality that is sometimes a problematic in the novel form reminds me of the uses to which stories are put in the black community. The stories are constantly being retold, constantly being imagined within a framework. And I hook into this like a life-support system, which for me, is the thing out of which I come.
>
> —TONI MORRISON, "An Interview with Toni Morrison"

Perhaps no black writer, man or woman, has attracted as much attention in the last decade as novelist Toni Morrison. She has been claimed as a spokeswoman in her fiction for any number of points of view, including Marxist and feminist. Others have tried to characterize her as a postmodern fictionalist whose work reveals the deep fissures in our comfortable illusion that the world outside the text has some kind of innate coherence apart from that conferred by language. Most of these claims tend to "modernize" or "postmodernize" Toni Morrison's work by seeing her as a reviser of past

From *Contemporary Literature* 29, No. 4 (Winter 1988): 564–80.

traditions in fiction which have been predominantly male, or white, or upper-class.[1] While parts of her five novels[2] do indeed display such revisionist inclinations, much of the current criticism about her fiction misses her profoundly traditional view of the relation between literature and culture.

Morrison is certainly not an apologist for the status quo either stylistically or ideologically. Nevertheless, most attempts to see Morrison's work as technically disjunctive run afoul of the fundamentally antiexperimental quality of her prose and of her unwillingness to be readily categorized either as an innovator or a traditionalist. Although some have termed her work "magical realism" (Lange 173), her novels tend to be fairly representational and not especially technically innovative. Morrison's work relies on fundamentally linear plotting, the use of rounded characters, and a generally mimetic conception of the novel.

Morrison's stature depends upon a great deal more, certainly, than simply a reluctance to forsake time-honored methods of fiction. Perhaps better said, Morrison is an example of the novelist as *conservator*. She is a writer particularly interested in depicting, and thereby preserving and perpetuating, the cultural practices of black communities. Her work displays a commitment to the capacity of fiction to provide ways of maintaining and communicating important cultural values which otherwise might be lost. The novelist, then, is not a figure isolated from history and culture but rather is someone who conserves cultural forms and practices by depicting them in the public act of fiction.

Shortly after publishing *Song of Solomon,* Toni Morrison commented on the future of the novel:

> Novels aren't dying! People *crave* narration. Magazines only sell because they have stories in them, not because somebody wants to read those ads. . . . People want to hear a story. . . . That's the way they learn things. That's the way human beings organize their human knowledge—fairy tales, myths. All narration. And that's why the novel is so important. ("Seams" 58)

Perhaps just as significantly, fiction is a way of knowing, not only for readers but for the creators of fictions, especially in their role as contributors to culture: "After I had published, it was sort of a compulsive thing because it was a way of knowing, a way of thinking that I found really necessary" ("Seams" 56). In much of what Morrison writes, stories are represented as ways of creating sense out of the chaos of reality, for her characters and for readers as well, by providing significant information about reality. Fictions, then, have a powerful epistemological effect, acting as a method of constructing and construing the world. Fictions certainly achieve part of their value by way of aesthetic fineness. They also allow us opportunities for certain sorts of imaginative play. But in Morrison's work, fictions also accrue value by way of a limited kind of instrumentality— they provide information for living.[3]

The emphasis on the connection between history and fiction helps answer the criticism of Morrison's work that it unnecessarily problematizes Afro-American cultural patterns by representing them as anarchic and frequently violent. Morrison's fiction represents human experience as something whose meaning is organized by human faculties of understanding rather than as something possessing meaning in itself. The situation of black people is especially problematic since the inevitable flux of real experience becomes complicated by political, social, and economic oppression. One of the more interesting aspects of Morrison's fiction is the examination of this existential and ideological flux, to be made sense of by means of the story.

Morrison's emphasis on the capacity of the story to create history makes difficult her characterization as a writer at odds with so much of the literary tradition that precedes her. Her technical emphasis on suggestion and evocation rather than brute representation is a function of seeing experience as needing relative clarification. In this regard, the processes of her fiction mirror her belief in the constructive nature of human subjectivity. Morrison forces the reader to fill in the spaces—to create a sense of history by means of apprehending a fiction. She does this by a conscious play between two pairs of values: opacity and transparency and rigidity and fluidity. The essence of her fiction is to set these opposites in motion, forcing her characters (and her readers) to take obscuring opacities and try to make them transparent, and paralyzing rigidities and make them more fluid. Rather than emphasizing the deconstructive aspect of language, Morrison seem more interested in its constructive function. She consistently emphasizes our ability to make legitimate sense out of the world by means of narrative, although she is certainly aware of the imperfect nature of communication.

The emphasis on the constructive power of language has a long history in the Afro-American literary tradition. When Frederick Douglass "steals" language in chapter 7 of *Narrative of the Life of Frederick Douglass, an American Slave* (1845), for example, it is one of the most important moments in Afro-American literary history. There Douglass finds a method with which to carve out an identity. This he does in part by creating a character in an autobiographical fiction who "stands for" Frederick Douglass, the man. Perhaps more importantly, the acquisition of language helps Douglass wrest from the dominant white world a modicum of control over his own life. He

accomplishes this by gaining access to different and broader kinds of knowledge than he previously was able to obtain—one way of "taking the ell,"
as Mr. Auld, his master, would say (40). The taking of this "ell" represents
a special danger, because acquiring the power of language and knowledge
implies that Douglass will soon acquire the capacity to analyze, argue, and
persuade, to reveal the sordid contradiction of a democracy whose very
foundation is chattel slavery. He also finds a way of aiding his escape since
he can now forge passes or "protections" which allow him to move about
with a greater degree of freedom (86–87).

Additionally, Douglass steals the capacity to create a *public* identity
that is social, political, and historical. This identity achieves an authenticity
precisely because it "rises" from Douglass himself rather than being im-
pressed on him from the outside. For dominant cultures, such a connection
between identity and language is a commonplace, though certainly not an
afterthought; it is an entitlement—part of the perquisites of holding economic, social, and political power. Douglass's *Narrative* is an attempt to
wrest a part of this power for himself by rewriting and re-creating history.
For members of "subject" cultures, whose methods of expressing or actual-
izing self are severely limited and fraught with the aura of inauthenticity,
the very substantial ability to control and express one's identity by means
of language is hard won and doubly valued. This overwhelmingly important
fact accounts for the significance of developing and controlling language and
of finding one's own voice in the Afro-American literary tradition. The
tremendous significance of telling one's own story in one's own language
accounts in part also for the inclination toward autobiographical narrative
in the Afro-American tradition.

Morrison's *Song of Solomon,* a narrative at some remove from Douglass's
work and not explicitly or overtly autobiographical, reveals this emphasis
on language as a constituting agent and on story as a means of fixing identity.
Even from as early as the second page of this novel Morrison makes the
emphasis on the role of language in everyday life clear. To the black populace,
the street on which Dr. Foster lives comes to be known as Doctor Street,
rather than the official Mains Avenue, for reasons of habituation and convenience. It is, moreover, a name that develops out of the reality of the
lives of the black Southside residents—a way of impressing the authority
of the people on the landscape. It "acquired a quasi-official status," though
this condition soon changed:

> Some of the city legislators, whose concern for appropriate names
> and the maintenance of the city's landmarks was the principal

part of their political life, saw to it that "Doctor Street" was never used in any official capacity. And since they knew that only Southside residents kept it up, they had notices posted in the stores, barbershops, and restaurants in that part of the city saying that the avenue running northerly and southerly from Shore Road fronting the lake to the junction of routes 6 and 2 leading to Pennsylvania, and also running parallel to and between Rutherford Avenue and Broadway, had always been and would always be known as Mains Avenue and not Doctor Street.

It was a genuinely clarifying public notice because it gave Southside residents a way to keep their memories alive and please the city legislators as well. They called it Not Doctor Street, and were inclined to call the charity hospital at its northern end No Mercy Hospital since it was 1931 . . . before the first colored expectant mother was allowed to give birth inside its wards and not on its steps. (4)

More than anything else, this early passage concerns a conflict between two kinds of narrative authority. The black residents of Southside exercise control over their environment by reserving the capacity to name it, to assign it a value, and to indicate its quality. Authentic social practice is at the root of this particular naming process. As distinguished from the authenticity gained from a close connection with real life, an abstract inauthenticity characterizes the language of the city fathers, who attempt to impose a false clarity on the landscape. Morrison deftly indicates this by stringing together six lines of official language which aim to fix the landscape in a web of artificial abstractions bearing no relationship to the lives of the people of Southside, nor any to the "quality" of the landscape itself.[4]

The political life of these city fathers is wrapped up in the process of artificial symbolization. It is a means of controlling a potentially subversive black population, by reserving the capacity to name and control the world and to define history. Opposed to this, Southside residents exercise a subversion of their own, turning the language of official power back on itself, retaining some measure of control in a world where the real sources of power are apparently beyond them.[5] Black life in this universe is characterized by an inversion of some of the conditions of white life. To survive, one must apparently play by the rules established by white economic and political power yet invert their meaning to subvert their strength and dominance.

But more generally, life in Southside is characterized by a precarious kind of anarchy:

> Here was the wilderness of Southside. Not the poverty or dirt
> or noise, not just extreme unregulated passion where even love
> found its way with an ice pick, but the absence of control. Here
> one lived knowing that at any time, anybody might do anything.
> Not wilderness where there was system, or the logic of lions,
> trees, toads, and birds, but wild wilderness where there was none.
> (138)

This anarchy occasions an especial need for Southsiders to create fictions by
which to run their lives, for they are caught between the destructive rigidity
of the city fathers and the equally destructive fluidity of their neighborhood.

In *Song of Solomon*, Toni Morrison depicts her characters' efforts to
mediate the opposites of fluidity and rigidity by means of the story in order
to explore the central conflict informing all of her works—the fate of more
or less rigid ways of understanding and of creating meaning in a "universe"
characterized by extreme fluidity. Three major types of "stories" dominate
the novel: those that enhance reality, those that seek to control reality, and
those that try to substitute for reality. At least one more category of story
or narrative is possible—narratives that mirror reality. But the anarchy of
Southside would militate against the prevalence of mimetic stories in the
narrative, especially if the function of a story generally is to establish a
bearable stability. A narrative which mirrored the anarchy of Southside would
have the virtue of accuracy, certainly, but it is hard to see what psychological
advantages such a narrative could provide its "author," or in what way it
could alleviate the destructive fluidity of the novel's setting.

Narratives that enhance reality, such as Ruth Foster Dead's, depend
upon emblems or other literary devices to generate a stability and continuity
otherwise lacking. The water spot on Ruth's table becomes an emblem of
middle-class stability:

> Like the keeper of the lighthouse and the prisoner, she regarded
> it as a mooring, a checkpoint, some stable visual object that
> assured her that the world was still there; that this was life and
> not a dream. That she was alive somewhere, inside, which she
> acknowledged to be true only because a thing she knew intimately
> was out there, outside herself. (11)

Ruth requires this visible token of continuity and regularity, even if it is
only a spot; even if, as Morrison implies, it provides some sort of imprisonment just as it provides guidance.

This excessive dependence on external signs of continuity and the combination of guidance and imprisonment are echoed in the overtones of Ruth's unnatural affection for both her father and her son. Though Morrison intentionally leaves the details cloudy, one finds little reason to doubt Macon's suspicion that his wife's relationship with her father was little short of incestuous. Ruth's psychopathological attraction to her father represents too great a need for parental support and guidance and illuminates her dependence on fairly fast and steady modes of being. Similarly her nursing of Milkman becomes a "balm," some form of protection against the outside world. But instead of being either the keeper of the lighthouse or the inmate of the prison, she becomes a figure out of a fairy tale—the miller's daughter in "Rumpelstiltskin."

As any of these three figures, Ruth places herself in the midst of a story which "clarifies" her present life. The spot on the table is really a discoloration left by years of centerpieces—signs to Ruth of the Fosters' gentility. It works, therefore, in two ways. Because the spot is really the sign of something not there, it signifies an absence which Ruth turns into a kind of presence, turning it into a temporarily safe harbor. In the re-creation of the fairy tale, she replays a magical transition from poverty to wealth which presumably re-creates the gentility whose emblem is the missing centerpiece. Ruth plays the central and characteristically isolated role in all three versions of her plight, as the solitary figure on a seaside landscape, the prisoner in her cell, or the threatened heroine soon to be rescued.

A similar enhancement is characteristic of even a minor character such as Corinthians Dead, who fixes on the Latinate *amanuensis* (with its attendant class implications) to make her life as Mary-Michael Graham's maid more consonant with her self-image. The term plays a role in a drama Corinthians creates, and it serves Ruth's purposes as well, since *amanuensis,* much like the centerpiece, maintains at least the surface of gentility. Until she is released from this story by her association with Porter, Corinthians remains as caught by the terms with which she chooses to define her life as the rest of the characters. In the instances of both Ruth and Corinthians we discover Morrison's recognition of the ease with which human lives can turn rigid under the pressures of everyday life. The discontinuity so characteristic of life can lead the psychologically unready or ill-equipped to a critical sort of stasis destructive of themselves and of others.[6]

Stories that seek to control reality also try to emend experience in a significant way. But rather than fixing on a single part, word, or emblem alone and letting that stand for the whole in a kind of synecdoche, stories that control seek to take over other narratives as models, even if that process requires an extreme alteration of the values of the model. For example,

Macon fetishizes his property holdings as well as their emblem—his ring of keys. The keys and the houses as well are symbols in a fiction which seeks to control the world—the narrative Macon has tried to build to avoid the fate of his father, whose story concerns a pastoral paradise stolen away by greedy white neighbors. To avoid his father's fate—a violent death—Macon tries to create a similar story chronicling possession and ownership, but with a different ending. Macon says to Milkman, "Own things. And let the things you own own other things. Then you'll own yourself and other people too" (55). Ownership is his mode of defense against the depredations of an intrinsically antagonistic white world. His desire for control transforms the world in his eyes into a universe to be bought and protected (though not cared for and harvested, as in his father's story). But the threat of the white world is still ubiquitous and extracts from Macon a surrender to the values of conspicuous consumption. Macon's story differs significantly from his father's not only in that it is set in the city rather than in the country; the relationship between the important symbols and their users is changed, too. Macon's father husbands his land and his animals, even when he eats the latter; Macon himself owns things and leases them—a relationship far more characteristic of advanced stages of capitalism than the economic relationships in the pastoral idyll of his father. In the instances of Ruth and Macon, their desire for safety has rigidified and become abstract—has become exclusively idea rather than thing—and made them either psychopathologically dependent or inhumanly cold and indifferent to the fates of others.

Surprisingly, the character who creates a story most similar to Macon's is Guitar Bains. Morrison establishes Guitar as superficially opposite—his violent radicalism contrasting with Macon's capitulation to white middle-class values. But this explicit conflict of political values masks a greater informing similarity. Both characters remain infected by a nearly single-mindedly rigid pursuit of the informing goals of their fictions—property and revenge. In response to the injuries caused by the white world, both Guitar and Macon create fictive strategies designed to protect themselves. Ironically, each in his own way is controlled by the very white world he wishes to fight. The whims of consumer fashion and the marketplace control Macon, as do his internalized conceptions of propriety and appropriate social behavior. Guitar, on the other hand (the rest of the Days as well), finds himself subject to the dictates of the same white violence he claims to abhor and has pledged himself to combat. The irony of the Days' mode of revenge, that the violence of whites against blacks is returned to whites in kind, in fact turns back against the Days in an important reversal. Despite their avowed stand against passivity, in a perverse way the Days remain dependent on the action of whites. The particular black people certain whites kill and how they are killed determine the conduct of their lives. The single-minded pursuit of this kind of revenge "freezes" Guitar up, turning him against his former friend, making him unable to see beyond the story that controls his life.

Stories which seek to enhance reality and those which seek to control it both rely on some implied, if limited, connection with the outside world or with other fictions. There is something beyond itself which each fiction tries to mediate. The third type of story, that which seeks to substitute for reality, is the hermetic fiction—a story which enforces its own authority over and against the authority of other fictions or the outside world. Assuredly, all three types of narrative try to take the place of the reality. But the hermetic fiction differs from the previous forms by way of the totality of its substitution and the comprehensiveness of it scope. The dominant hermetic fiction in *Song of Solomon* belongs to Milkman, created by his response to the conditions of life in Southside and in his family.

Milkman has no significant history and no real sense of the future. Though ritual drives on Sunday afternoons are a way for the Deads to establish an identity, they work otherwise for the young boy: "For the little boy it was simply a burden . . . riding backward made him uneasy. It was like flying blind, and not knowing where he was going—just where he had been—troubled him" (31–32). The visual distortion caused by the constant motion of the car is an emblem for a kind of perceptual distortion in Milkman's sense of his own being and in his sense of history. There is no future to be seen for him; the present recedes so quickly into the past that it has no real meaning. The physical remoteness of the past is further an expression of the distance between Milkman and anything like a buttressing sense of self and place—a knowledge of history. The metaphor of the automobile is especially important since the car and the ride as well are elements in a story woven by Macon Dead that serves his purposes more than those of any other character. The pastoral tale of the family farm has transposed into the business novel of the twentieth century. But the car, the primary symbol in that tale—aside from the keys and the houses—becomes disabling for Milkman rather than enabling, turning into a symbol of imprisonment and limitation rather than their opposites.

When Milkman accidentally "pisses" on his sister Lena, Morrison reinforces Milkman's orientation toward the past: "It was becoming a habit—this concentration on things behind him. Almost as though there were no future to be had" (35). But what looks like a useful confrontation with his past and an interest in his relation to that past is really Milkman's unac-

knowledged confrontation with a mystery he is incapable of knowing. His
glance backward is a gesture toward that which he cannot fathom. He has
neither a sufficient sense of himself nor a full enough understanding of his
connections with others to give him a context in which to place his perception
of the past.

Milkman's identity is a mass of fragments which never coheres into a
whole: "It was all very tentative, the way he looked, like a man peeping
around a corner or someplace he is not supposed to be, trying to make up
his mind whether to go forward or to turn back" (70). Paradoxically, this
indeterminacy leads to a crucial rigidity which is purely defensive. He cannot
see himself as part of a whole because he cannot understand the nature of
the "part" he would constitute. Depicted as truly lost, Milkman has no
sense of purpose other than his immediate wishes for comfort. The boredom
and estrangement Milkman feels are precisely functions of this vacuum in
Southside and the vacuum in Milkman's character.

The possible curative for this condition of emptiness and estrangement
is for Milkman to create a fiction by which to organize his life. As we have
seen, all significant characters in this novel have their stories, the fictions
by which they live. But not all fictions are equal—the rigidity of some
suggests the way in which the anarchy of Southside is met by the solipsism
and the vanity of the hermetic fiction. In these hermetic fictions, consciousness reigns supreme—legislating other fictions out of existence. Enhancing
fictions and controlling fictions tend to resemble hermetic ones, especially
the more involved and self-reflexive they become. At that point, they share
both the qualities and the specific failures of hermetic narratives. The hermetic fiction fails in part because it is too enclosed and fixed. It exalts the
ego of its creator but cannot clarify the outside world in any significant way.
An extremely significant example of this comes early in the novel, after
Milkman strikes his father for abusing his mother:

> Just as the father brimmed with contradictory feelings as he crept
> along the wall—humiliation, anger, and a grudging feeling of
> pride in his son—so the son felt his own contradictions. There
> was the pain and shame of seeing his father crumple before any
> man—even himself. Sorrow in discovering that the pyramid was
> not a five-thousand-year wonder of the civilized world, myste-
> riously and permanently constructed by generation after genera-
> tion of hardy men who had died in order to perfect it, but that
> it had been made in the back room at Sears, by a clever window
> dresser, of papier-mâché, guaranteed to last for a mere lifetime.

He also felt glee. A snorting, horse-galloping glee as old as desire. He had won something and lost something in the same instant. Infinite possibilities and enormous responsibilities stretched out before him, but he was not prepared to take advantage of the former, or accept the burden of the latter. So he cock-walked around the table. . . . (68)

In this brief passage, Morrison outlines the essential dynamic of Milkman's story and the dynamic of so many of the stories belonging to other characters as well. "Cock-walking" around the table by way of establishing his power is Milkman's ready and easy response to a very difficult emotional and psychological situation. Morrison has revealed Macon's essential weakness by demystifying him, by making him just as capable of being struck as he is capable of striking. Significantly, Milkman understands or apprehends this event by means of a revelatory story. In the tale, a wonder of the world is unmasked as a product of consumer fashion, made merely out of flour paste. The king whom Milkman has overthrown is actually feeble. But rather than accustom himself to the new truth about his father and in doing so accept certain possibilities and responsibilities, Milkman merely takes recourse in the comforting simplicity of his ego. Ruth's stories, along with Guitar's and Macon's, share this tendency, too. Each story places its author at the center of a self-glorifying narrative either as heroine or victim.

The egocentricity of the hermetic fiction leads to a second failure— the sealing off of the "author" from other human consciousness. This isolation is emphasized throughout the novel. At a point early in *Song* as Milkman walks down the street, he finds himself on a crowded sidewalk and moving in the opposite direction from everyone else. He cannot fathom why he doesn't walk on the other side of the street where no one seems to be (78). In fact, though the symbolism is a bit labored, Milkman is just as alone as he would be on that deserted sidewalk. Not so surprisingly, the movement of the novel is marked by Milkman's progressive revelation that his persistent ignorance is a function of being locked inside his own story, sealed off from other people and other stories (279–80). Similarly, Macon's "story" estranges him from his sister Pilate. Further, each of the Seven Days avoids all of the most intimate forms of human contact, just as Guitar comes to be isolated from his best friend.

The persistent isolation prevalent in Milkman's story leads him to a further failure—the dehumanizing distance which characterizes Macon and Guitar. One can see this in his similar tendency to turn value into commodity. From his watch to his car to Hagar, the things or people Milkman comes in contact with remain so distanced from him that all achieve the status of object and are represented as such by Morrison. Even his parents are characters in a "story" which involves him just barely, if at all. This isolation constitutes a defense for Milkman that amounts merely to "pissing" on people—another name for the sort of exploitation practiced by Macon. Lena says to Milkman at the end of Part I that Macon "displayed us, then he splayed us. All our lives were like that: he would parade us like virgins through Babylon, then humiliate us like whores in Babylon" (218). Significantly, Lena identifies Milkman with his father and with a metaphorical sort of incest (not unlike Ruth's exploitation of Milkman, though the particulars are different). Both men see the world as some collection of things to be used not for themselves but for some form of exchange value.

The hermetic fiction's inherent egocentricity and its tendency toward isolation and distance lead to a disabling vanity. The peacock serves as Morrison's central metaphor for the problematic of vanity. Of the peacock, Guitar says: "Like vanity. Can't nobody fly with all that shit. Wanna fly, you got to give up the shit that weighs you down" (180). The irony, of course, is that at this point in the novel the vainest of the characters are both Guitar and Milkman. They achieve this state by being so thoroughly wrapped up in their own stories that they fail to hear other stories and fail to acknowledge that they play roles in other fictions.[7]

Vanity is alleviated ultimately by the power of the story properly considered and by the historicity of comprehension. As I mentioned earlier, the essential problem facing so many of the characters in the novel is working their way out of a blindness into something that resembles partial sight, if not insight. Stories facilitate this process by asserting an essential commonality between teller and listener, by engaging characters in stories other than their own. Further, they take the disparate fact and fit it into some relatively coherent framework. For example, Morrison regularly breaks up the flow of her narrative by disclosing a piece of information "too soon." She offers a disjunctive fact or observation and follows it with the story which under other circumstances would have preceded it: "Macon decided it was of no importance, and less and less often did he get angry enough to slap her. Particularly after the final time, which became final because his son jumped up and knocked him back into the radiator" (63). Morrison smooths over the disjunction by narrating the story in which the radiator plays and important part.

Stories can force a liberating movement in part because no story is ever original. All the stories in this novel are a merging of and an interpretation of other stories, which suggests a further joining of the tellers and the subjects of the other stories. Regrettably, the stories of other people, that shaping of the world in fiction by other people, have no effect on Milkman. After Macon explains the circumstances of Dr. Foster's death to his son, Milkman

> felt curiously disassociated from all that he had heard. As though a stranger that he'd sat down next to on a park bench had turned to him and begun to relate some intimacy. He was entirely sympathetic to the stranger's problems—understood perfectly his view of what had happened to him—but part of his sympathy came from the fact that he himself was not involved or in any way threatened by the stranger's story. (74–75)

Milkman curiously operates under the fiction that the world is simply a projection of and emanation from his own ego—therefore it has a coherence much different from the perceptual and psychological anarchy of the world he sees. The question he phrases, "Couldn't I be a whole man without knowing all that?" (77), suggests his fundamental unwillingness to see beyond the horizon of his own perceptual landscape.

When Milkman does move outside of his own landscape all he wishes to hear are the painless fictions, the unproblematic ones: "Above all he wanted to escape what he knew, escape the implications of what he had been told. And all he knew in the world about the world was what other people had told him" (120). Milkman's desire only for happiness and not unhappiness (280), like his vanity, insulates him from the pain of others, and from his own pain, by letting him create in the fashion he chooses the only story which affects him. The novel, however, insists on the significance of shared history communicated by shared stories, shared traditions, and shared experience.

If stories fail when they become too enclosed and self-reflexive, they tend to succeed when they reveal a sense of humane openness. The instructive example is provided by Pilate Dead. Her story, which falls in the middle of the novel, is much like Milkman's insofar as it chronicles a movement from isolation to community. Because she lacks a navel, Pilate is ostracized by many of the people she meets on her travels through Pennsylvania and Virginia. She overcomes this ostracism by means of the power of love and self-knowledge. Her story begins with the heroine being cast out of family and society but ends with her reconstructing the necessary intimacy between people in her relationship with Reba and Hagar, and also with Ruth and Milkman. At one point she remarks in a bit of foreshadowing that it's most likely that a woman will save Milkman's life (150). In fact she already has saved Milkman (as a baby) from his father; and she will do so again in the concluding sections of the novel by demonstrating the value of love and human connection: "She gave up, apparently, all interest in table manners or hygiene, but acquired a deep concern for and about human relationships. . . . She was a natural healer, and among quarreling drunks and fighting women she could hold her own" (150). Hers is the model story, controlled by the recognition of the validity of other fictions and other people; it is the text which informs the later development of Milkman's story.

Once Milkman begins his trek back to the South, he becomes aware of the implications of shared experience. He notes a significant difference in his response to the telling of a familiar story: "Maybe it was being there in the place where it happened that made it seem so real. . . . Here in the parsonage, sitting in a cane-bottomed chair near an upright piano and drinking homemade whiskey poured from a mayonnaise jar, it was real" (233). At home hearing Pilate or Macon talk about these things everything seemed only "exotic." Putting the reality of Danville into the category of the exotic only distances it from Milkman's perception of things. Being grounded in such a world is so foreign to him (in all the senses of the word) that Milkman has conceived of it as a place beyond his capacity to know. But being grounded in the milieu of the story has the effect of circumventing Milkman's vanity and self-possession.

Milkman's invigorated sense of closeness extends to the people of Shalimar as well as to the story he hears: "He was curious about these people. He didn't feel close to them, but he did feel connected, as though there was some cord or pulse or information they shared" (296). The connection Milkman shares is a function of his newfound sense of shared history, which lends context and contours to his life.

Although Morrison sets Milkman's revelation within the context of something that exists before language, there is a very strong sense in her novel that without language, history does not exist. Milkman in glimpsing a prelinguistic realm sees only the facticity of life that he can more clearly express by means of the story, which he does later in the novel:

> No, it was not language; it was what there was before language. Before things were written down. Language in the time when men and animals did talk to one another, when a man could sit down with an ape and the two converse; when a tiger and a man could share the same tree, and each understood the other; when men ran *with* wolves, not from or after them. (281)

He gains direction and purpose and even a greater sense of his own life. Later,

> Really laughing, . . . he found himself exhilarated by simply walking the earth. Walking it like he belonged on it; like his legs were stalks, tree trunks, a part of his body that extended down down down into the rock and soil, and were comfortable there—on the earth and on the place where he walked. And he did not limp. (284)

The comfort Milkman feels and the restoration he experiences are a sign of his being grounded, metaphorically speaking, in a reality other than that which he himself has created. The tremendous emphasis on the oral, traditional aspect of language, where one speaks rather than writes, re-emphasizes the communal nature of the history-creating act. For it is certainly true that there is no history outside of that which we create out of our minds and with our language. The story "is" in some important sense the history we experience.

At the end of the novel when Milkman realizes that the children in Shalimar are singing a song about his own family, he recognizes the essential temporality and atemporality of the story. By breaking down the barrier of time, stories enable us to experience precisely the temporality they violate.[8] Without that violation we would experience the isolation of radical historicism, where past time is irrevocably separated from us. Stories, however, allow us to experience the past as both present and past, enabling us to see ourselves in the light of other perspectives. A story is "dislocating" because it has the capacity to pull us out of one particular place in time; but it is more importantly "locating" since it allows us to fix that place within the larger continuum of human history. More than anything else, Morrison emphasizes this essential continuity between past and present achieved by means of the story. Experience itself may somehow be radically disjunctive, but it is made far less so by the power of the story and by the knowledge stories communicate to tellers and hearers.

In this respect, knowledge is not individual so much as it is communal, in the same sense that knowledge and experience are more continuous than discontinuous. Morrison emphasizes the tremendously social aspect of knowledge and identity. Language in her view is not a fundamentally unreliable tool we use to understand reality; it is not a system which is abysmally referential only to itself. The fluidity of language is a value, not so much because it leads us back to play but because it facilitates the serious work which is the essence of life. We need stories and novels not only because they are ways of "organizing human knowledge"; they are also the rituals by which we create individual and communal identity.

Within this cultural context, the novelist preserves and reconstructs important cultural patterns. As Morrison has observed, part of the novelist's project, or at the very least part of her personal project, is to determine the cultural basis of language use—"what makes a book 'black.' " The humane story, that which engenders a useful intersubjectivity, at least in *Song of Solomon,* is characterized by a persistent open-endedness. This open-endedness Morrison conspicuously mirrors in the quality of her novel's conclusion, where we leave Milkman yet alive, about to embrace his brother. Just as crucial is the sense in which stories are shown not to be finite, shown to be constantly in cycle and regularly revoiced. This constant revoicing and consequent emending of stories (as well as the necessary following of stories) constitutes a significant component of culture.

In this view, the novelist is not simply a linguist or semiotician or even literary critic whose interest is solely in the pattern of language use abstractly considered. Rather, the novelist is both recorder and creator of significant history within an ongoing pattern of culturally conditioned linguistic exchange. This pattern of exchange and influence is not limited to the conditions of a narrowly defined intertextuality. The pattern itself is as open-ended and as susceptible to influence as the stories which constitute the pattern; susceptible particularly to the influence of experience as lived and not merely to the influence of experience as written down.

NOTES

[1] See, for example, the essays by Jane Bakerman, Cynthia Davis, and Susan Willis.
[2] *The Bluest Eye* (1970), *Sula* (1974), *Song of Solomon* (1977), *Tar Baby* (1981), and *Beloved* (1987).
[3] This instrumentality is different from the sort which used to be claimed as a value for Afro-American literature. In the earlier usage, a text had *instrumental* value because it could be seen as a tool or a weapon in a political movement for social change. A novel written by a black writer could be construed to make an argument for the humanity of all black people. At the same time the novel served as an example of that humanity, since its author could be seen to be someone obviously possessed of feeling, intelligence, and insight. As I use it, *instrumentality* refers to a relation between reader, text, and world that is more generalized and not especially informed by a vision of fiction as a tool for political liberation. *Instrumentality* refers more to the process of reading and not at all to the suasion of a presumably antagonistic or indifferent white audience.
[4] Morrison uses the same strategy when she parodies the "Dick and Jane" reading primers in *The Bluest Eye.*
[5] Ironically, Southsiders seem to be arch antipostmoderns, as far as some kinds of language use are concerned. The relation between language and being is here admittedly complex, but Southsiders are evidently convinced that the quality of one's actions implies a certain way of describing or naming those actions. The arbitrariness of the sign is limited by the

conditions of life as lived. Early in the novel, Pilate introduces Milkman to Hagar as her brother (rather than cousin), because one treats a relative that close as though he were a brother (43–44).

[6] Morrison has touched on this issue before in *Sula*. Nel, who represents the principle of order, requires a balancing anarchy which she gets from Sula Peace. Neither is whole without the other. It takes Sula's death to reveal to Nel, for whom disorder is anathema, that some sort of irregularity or discontinuity is necessary, if not beneficial. The townspeople in Bottom are certainly more aware of this than Nel. The evil characterized by Sula has two important effects in the town. Sula accustoms the residents to the reality and the inevitability of evil. Additionally, her presence has a salutary effect on the life of the town.

[7] Assuredly, the value of self-esteem is offered as the antidote to a poisonous vanity. Corinthians's liberation is achieved at the cost of considerable vanity, but "in place of vanity she now felt a self-esteem that was quite new" (202).

[8] For an important discussion of the relationship between fiction and history, see Louis Mink's "History and Fiction as Modes of Comprehension." Mink establishes a connection between historical narrative and the fictional story: "History does not as such differ from fiction, therefore, insofar as it essentially depends on and develops our skill and subtlety in following stories. History *does* of course differ from fiction insofar as it is obligated to rest upon evidence of the occurrence in real space and time of what it describes and insofar as it must grow out of a critical assessment of the received materials of history, including the analyses and interpretations of other historians. But researches of historians, however arduous and technical, only increase the amount and precision of knowledge of facts which remain contingent and discontinuous. It is by being assigned to stories that they become intelligible and increase understanding by going beyond 'What?' and 'When?' to 'How?' and 'Why?' " (111–12). All modes of comprehension "are ways of grasping together in a single mental act things which are not experienced together, or even capable of being so experienced, because they are separated by time, space, or logical kind. And the ability to do this is a necessary (although not a sufficient) condition of *understanding*" (113). Stories ameliorate the isolating facticity of events, putting them in streams of perception which lend them a relative coherence—a function of seeing these events both synchronically and diachronically.

WORKS CITED

Bakerman, Jane. "Failures of Love: Female Initiation in the Novels of Toni Morrison." *American Literature* 52 (1981): 541–63.

Davis, Cynthia. "Self, Society, and Myth in Toni Morrison's Fiction." *Contemporary Literature* 23 (1983): 323–42.

Douglass, Frederick. *Narrative of the Life of Frederick Douglass, an American Slave*. 1845. Garden City, NY: Anchor, 1973.

Lange, Bonnie Shipman. "Toni Morrison's Rainbow Code." *Critique: Studies in Modern Fiction* 24 (1983): 173–81.

Mink, Louis. "History and Fiction as Modes of Comprehension." *New Directions in Literary History*. Ed. Ralph Cohen. Baltimore: Johns Hopkins University Press, 1974. 107–24.

Morrison, Toni. "An Interview with Toni Morrison." With Nellie McKay. *Contemporary Literature* 24 (1983): 413–29.

————. "The Seams Can't Show: An Interview with Toni Morrison." With
Jane Bakerman. *Black American Literature Forum* 12 (1978): 56–60.
————. *Song of Solomon.* New York: New American Library, 1977.
Willis, Susan. "Eruptions of Funk: Historicizing Toni Morrison." *Black
American Literature Forum* 16 (1982): 34–42. Rpt. in *Black Literature
and Literary Theory.* Ed. Henry Louis Gates, Jr. New York: Methuen,
1984. 263–83.

MARILYN SANDERS MOBLEY

A Different Remembering: Memory, History and Meaning in Toni Morrison's Beloved

The slave woman ought not to be judged by the same standards as others.
—HARRIET JACOBS, *Incidents in the Life of a Slave Girl*

. . . when we get a little farther away from the conflict, some brave and truth-loving man, with all the facts before him . . . will gather . . . the scattered fragments . . . and give to those who shall come after us an impartial history of this the grandest moral conflict of the century. {For} Truth is patient and time is just.
—FREDERICK DOUGLASS[1]

Every age re-accentuates in its own way the works of its most immediate past.
—MIKHAIL BAKHTIN, "Discourse in the Novel"

In 1974 Toni Morrison edited an often overlooked publication called *The Black Book*.[2] This collection of memorabilia represents 300 years of black history, and not only records the material conditions of black life from slavery to freedom, but also exhibits the black cultural production that grew out of and in spite of these conditions. Compiled in scrapbook fashion, it contains everything from bills of sale for slaves to jazz and poetry. Through diverse

---

Published for the first time in this volume.

images of black life presented in such items as photos of lynchings, share-cropping families and slave-made quilts, and encoded in excerpts from such sources as slave narratives, folk sayings and black newspapers, *The Black Book* tells a complex story of oppression, resistance and survival. More importantly, it was published at a moment in American history when many feared that the Black Power movement of the 1960s and early 1970s would be reduced to faddish rhetoric and mere image rather than understood for its cultural and political implications. Morrison herself feared the movement propounded a kind of historical erasure or denial of those aspects of the past which could not be easily assimilated into its rhetorical discourse or into the collective consciousness of black people as a group. She feared, for example, that the rhetoric of the movement, in its desire to create a new version of history that would affirm the African past and the heroic deeds of a few great men, had inadvertently bypassed the equally heroic deeds of ordinary African-Americans who had resisted and survived the painful traumas of slavery. In other words, she questioned what she perceived to be a romanticization of both the African past and the American past that threatened to devalue 300 years of black life on American soil before it was fully recorded, examined or understood for its complexity and significance. Thus, *The Black Book* was a literary intervention in the historical dialogue of the period to attest to "Black life as lived" experience.[3]

What is particularly pertinent, however, is that in the process of editing *The Black Book,* Morrison discovered the story that would become the basis of her fifth novel, *Beloved.*[4] Indeed, on the tenth page of *The Black Book* is a copy of a news article, "A Visit to the Slave Mother Who Killed Her Child," that documents the historical basis for what would later become Morrison's most challenging fictional project.[5] Although the relevance of history informs all her novels from *The Bluest Eye* to *Tar Baby,* it is in *Beloved* that history simultaneously becomes both theme and narrative process.[6] In other words, *Beloved* dramatizes the complex relationship between history and memory by shifting from lived experience as documented in *The Black Book* to remembered experience as represented in the novel.

Yet the intertextual relationship between *The Black Book* and *Beloved* is not the only one that can illuminate the compelling intricacies of this novel. Several reviewers place it in the American literary tradition with intertextual connections to Harriet Beecher Stowe's *Uncle Tom's Cabin* (1852). Others compare Morrison's narrative strategies to those of William Faulkner, who incidentally, along with Virginia Woolf, was the subject of her master's thesis. Certainly, the thematics of guilt and the complex fragmentation of time that shape Morrison's fiction are inherent in Faulkner's writing, as well as in the work of many other white authors of the American literary tradition. Yet Morrison's own expressed suspicions of critical efforts to place her in a white literary tradition are instructive. She explains:

> Most criticism . . . justifies itself by identifying black writers with some already accepted white writer . . . I find such criticism dishonest because it never goes into the work on its own terms. It comes from some other place and finds content outside of the work and wholly irrelevant to it to support the work . . . It's merely trying to place the book into an already established literary tradition.[7]

With Morrison's own comments in mind, I would like to suggest that the intertextual relationship between *Beloved* and the slave narratives—the genre that began the African-American literary tradition in prose—offers significant interpretative possibilities for entering the hermeneutic circle of this novel. More specifically, I would like to argue that Morrison uses the trope of memory to revise the genre of the slave narrative and thereby to make the slave experience it inscribes more accessible to contemporary readers. In other words, she uses memory as the metaphorical sign of the interior life to explore and represent dimensions of slave life that the classic slave narrative omitted. By so doing, she seeks to make slavery accessible to readers for whom slavery is not a memory, but a remote historical fact to be ignored, repressed or forgotten. Thus, just as the slave narratives were a form of narrative intervention designed to disrupt the system of slavery, *Beloved* can be read as a narrative intervention that disrupts the cultural notion that the untold story of the black slave mother is, in the words of the novel, "the past something to leave behind."[8]

One of the first observations often made about the slave narratives is the striking similarities that exist among the hundreds of them that were written. In the "Introduction" to *The Classic Slave Narratives*, Henry Louis Gates, Jr., accounts for this phenomenon by reminding us that

> when the ex-slave author decided to write his or her story, he or she did so only after reading and rereading the telling stories of other slave authors who preceded them.[9]

While we cannot know exactly which narratives Morrison read, it is certain that she read widely in the genre and that she is familiar with the two most popular classics—Frederick Douglass's *Narrative* (1845) and Harriet Jacobs's *Incidents in the Life of a Slave Girl* (1861).[10] As prototypical examples of the genre, they adhere to the narrative conventions carefully delineated and described by James Olney. According to him, the vast majority of narratives begin with the three words "I was born" and proceed to provide information about parents, siblings, the cruelty of masters, mistresses and overseers, barriers to literacy, slave auctions, attempts, failures and successes at escaping, name changes, and general reflections on the peculiar institution of slavery.[11] As Valerie Smith points out, however, the important distinction between the narratives of Douglass and Jacobs is that while his narrative not only concerns "the journey from slavery to freedom but also the journey from slavery to manhood," her narrative describes the sexual exploitation that challenged the womanhood of slave women and tells the story of their resistance to that exploitation.[12] *Beloved* contains all these characteristics with several signifying differences. While the classic slave narrative draws on memory as though it is a monologic, mechanical conduit for facts and incidents, Morrison's text foregrounds the dialogic characteristics of memory along with its imaginative capacity to construct and reconstruct the significance of the past. Thus, while the slave narrative characteristically moves in a chronological, linear narrative fashion, *Beloved* meanders through time, sometimes circling back, other times moving vertically, spirally out of time and down into space. Indeed, Morrison's text challenges the Western notion of linear time that informs American history and the slave narratives. It engages the reader not just with the physical, material consequences of slavery, but with the psychological consequences as well. Through the trope of memory, Morrison moves into the psychic consequences of slavery for women, who, by their very existence, were both the means and the source of production. In the words of the text, the slave woman was "property that reproduced itself without cost" (228). Moreover, by exploring this dimension of slavery, Morrison produces a text that is at once very different from and similar to its literary antecedent with its intervention in the cultural, political and social order of black people in general and of black women in particular. What the reader encounters in this text is Morrison as both writer and reader, for inscribed in her writing of the novel is her own "reading"—a revisionary rereading—of the slave's narrative plot of the journey from bondage to freedom. In the process of entering the old text of slavery from "a new critical direction," Morrison discovers what Adrienne Rich refers to as a "whole new psychic geography to be explored," and what Morrison herself identifies as the "interior life of black people under those circumstances."[13] Ultimately, *Beloved* responds to Fredric Jameson's dictum to "always historicize" by illustrating the dynamics of the act of interpretation that memory performs on a regular basis at any given historical moment.[14]

Unlike the slave narratives which sought to be all-inclusive eyewitness accounts of the material conditions of slavery, Morrison's novel exposes the unsaid of the narratives, the psychic subtexts that lie within and beneath the historical facts. In the author's words, she attempts to leave "spaces so the reader can come into it."[15] Critic Steven Mallioux refers to such hermeneutic gaps as places where the text must be "supplemented by its readers before its meaning can be discovered."[16] By examining the use of memory in *Beloved*, we can not only discover to what extent she revises the slave narrative, but also explore how her narrative poetics operate through memory and history to create meaning.

The actual story upon which the novel is based is an 1855 newspaper account of a runaway slave from Kentucky named Margaret Garner. When she realizes she is about to be recaptured in accordance with the Fugitive Slave Law, she kills her child rather than allow it to return to a "future of servitude."[17] Indeed, the story itself involves a conflation of past, present and future in a single act. In the novel, Margaret Garner becomes Sethe, a fugitive slave whose killing of her two-year-old daughter, Beloved, haunts her first as a ghost and later as a physical reincarnation. But time is not so much conflated as fragmented in the fictional rendering of the tale. Moreover, the text contains not only Sethe's story or version of the past, but those of her friend and eventual lover, Paul D, her mother-in-law, Baby Suggs, her remaining child, a daughter named Denver, and later, Beloved herself. Each of their fragments amplifies or modifies Sethe's narrative for the reader. In that the fragments constitute voices which speak to and comment on one another, the text illustrates the call and response pattern of the African-American oral tradition.[18]

The setting of the novel is 1873 in Cincinnati, Ohio, where Sethe resides in a small house with her daughter, Denver. Her mother-in-law, Baby Suggs, has recently died and her two sons, Howard and Buglar, have left home, unable to live any longer in a ghost-haunted house with a mother who seems oblivious or indifferent to the disturbing, disruptive presence. Sethe seems locked in memories of her escape from slavery, the failure of her husband, Halle, to show up at the planned time of escape, her murder of her child, and the Kentucky plantation referred to by its benevolent white slave owner as Sweet Home. One of the Sweet Home men, Paul D, inadvertently arrives on her porch after years of wandering, locked in his own guilt, alienation and shame from the psychic scars of slavery. They become lovers, but more importantly, his arrival initiates the painful plunge into the past through the sharing of their individual stories, memories and experiences. Unable to tolerate the presence of the ghost, however, he drives it away, only to be driven away himself by his inability to cope with Sethe's

obsession with Denver, whom he calls a "room-and-board witch" (165). A
bond of affection unites Sethe, Denver and Beloved until Denver realizes
that her mother has become oblivious to her and has begun to devote her
attention exclusively to Beloved. As she watches her mother deteroriate
physically and mentally in the grips of overwhelming guilt and consuming
love, Denver realizes she must abandon the security of home to get help for
her mother and to rid their lives of Beloved once and for all. With the help
of the black community, she eventually rescues her mother and Beloved
vanishes.

What this cursory synopsis of the plot cannot account for is the ways
in which Sethe modifies, amplifies and subverts her own memory of the
murder that serves as the locus of the narrative. In fact, even in freedom
she lives in a kind of psychic bondage to the task of "keeping the past at
bay" (43). While she had murdered Beloved to save her from the future,
she raises Denver by "keeping her from the past" (43). The two different
manifestations of maternal love are just one source of the novel's narrative
tension that evolves from Sethe's response to slavery. The more compelling
source of tension lies in the complexity Morrison brings to the normal
property of literature Frank Kermode refers to as the "secrecy of narrative."[19]
While all texts develop to a certain extent by secrecy or by what informtion
they withhold and gradually release to the reader, the text of *Beloved* moves
through a series of narrative starts and stops that are complicated by Sethe's
desire to forget or "disremember" the past (118). Thus, at the same time
that the reader seeks to know "the how and why" (120) of Sethe's infanticide,
Sethe seeks to withhold that information not only from everyone else, but
even from herself. Thus, the early sections of the novel reveal the complex
ways in which memories of the past disrupt Sethe's concerted attempt to
forget.

The first sign of this tension between remembering and forgetting
occurs on the second page of the text in a scene where Denver and Sethe
attempt to call the ghost forth. When Denver grows impatient with the
seeming reluctance of the ghost to make its presence felt, Sethe cautions
her by saying: "You forgetting how little it is . . . She wasn't even two
years old when she died" (4). Denver's expression of surprise that a baby
can throw such a "powerful spell" is countered in the following passage:

> 'No more powerful than the way I loved her,' Sethe answered
> and there it was again. The welcoming cool of unchiseled head-
> stones; the one she selected to lean against on tiptoe, her knees
> wide open as any grave. Pink as a fingernail it was, and sprinkled

with glittering chips . . . Counting on the stillness of her own
soul, she had forgotten the other one: the soul of her baby girl. (5)

In this passage we have several things occurring at once. First, Sethe's
verbalization of love triggers her memory of selecting a tombstone for the
baby she murdered. The phrase "there it was again" signals that this is a
memory that recurs and that brings the ambivalent emotions of consolation
and anguish. Second, the memory of the tombstone triggers her memory of
the shameful circumstances of getting it engraved. In this memory, the
reality of gender and oppression converge, for the engraver offers to place
seven letters—the name "Beloved"—on the headstone in exchange for sex.
She also remembers that for ten more minutes, she could have gotten the
word "dearly" added. Thirdly, this memory raises the issue around which
the entire novel is constructed and which is the consequence and/or responsibility that she must carry for her actions.

Throughout the novel there are similar passages that signal the narrative
tension between remembering and forgetting. At various points in the text,
a single phrase, a look or the most trivial incident rivets Sethe's attention
to the very details of the past she is least ready to confront. In the words
of the text, "she worked hard to remember as close to nothing as was safe"
(6). In another place the text refers to the "serious work of beating back the
past" (73). Moreover, a mindless task such as folding clothes takes on grave
significance, as the following passage suggests: "She had to do something
with her hands because she was remembering something she had forgotten
she knew. Something privately shameful that had seeped into a slit in her
mind" (61). Morrison even includes vernacular versions of words to suggest
the slaves' own preoccupation with mnemonic processes. For example, at
one point "rememory" is used as a noun, when Sethe refers to what Paul D
stirs up with his romantic attention to her. Later, the same word is used as
a verb, when Sethe begins to come to terms with the past through her
relationship with Beloved. She allows her mind to be "busy with the things
she could forget" and thinks to herself: "Thank God I don't have to rememory
or say a thing" (191). Even the vernacular word for forgetting, "disremember" (118), calls our attention to its binary opposite of remembering.

When Paul D arrives at Sethe's home on 124 Bluestone, Denver seeks
to frighten this unwanted guest away by telling him they have a "lonely
and rebuked" ghost on the premises (13). The obsolete meaning of rebuked—
repressed—not only suggests that the ghost represents repressed memory,
but that, as with anything that is repressed, it eventually resurfaces or returns
in one form or another. Paul D's arrival is a return of sorts in that he is

reunited with Sethe, his friend from Mr. Garner's Sweet Home plantation. His presence signals an opportunity to share both the positive and negative memories of life there. On the one hand, he and Sethe talk fondly of the "headless bride back behind Sweet Home" and thus share a harmless ghost story of a haunted house. On the other hand, when they remember Sweet Home as a place, they regard it with ambivalence and admit that "it wasn't sweet and it sure wasn't home" (14). Sethe warns against a total dismissal of it, however, by saying: "But it's where we were [and it] comes back whether we want it to or not" (14).

What also comes back through the stories Paul D shares are fragments of history Sethe is unprepared for such as the fact that years ago her husband had witnessed the white boys forcibly take milk from her breasts, but had been powerless to come to her rescue or stop them. Furthermore, his personal stories of enduring a "bit" (69) in his mouth—the barbaric symbol of silence and oppression that Morrison says created a perfect "labor force"—along with numerous other atrocities, such as working on the chain gang, introduce elements of the classic slave narrative into the text. Perhaps more importantly, these elements comprise the signs of history that punctuate the text and that disrupt the text of the mind which is both historical and ahistorical at the same time.

I believe the meaning of Morrison's complex use of the trope of memory becomes most clear in what many readers regard as the most poetic passages in the text. These passages appear in sections two through five of Part Two, where we have a series of interior monologues that become a dialogue among the three central female characters. The first is Sethe's, the second is Denver's, the third is Beloved's and the last one is a merging of all three. Beloved's is the most intriguing, for the text of her monologue contains no punctuation. Instead, there are literal spaces between groups of words that signal the timelessness of her presence as well as the unlived spaces of her life. Earlier in the novel, Sethe even refers to Beloved as "her daughter [who had] . . . come back home from the timeless place" (182). Samples of phrases from Beloved's monologue reveal the meaning of her presence: "[H]ow can I say things that are pictures   I am not separate from her   there is no place where I stop   her face is my own . . . all of it is now   it is always now" (210). These words suggest not only the seamlessness of time, but the inextricability of the past and present, of ancestors and their progeny. In the last interior "dialogue," the voices of Sethe, Denver and Beloved blend to sugget not only that it is always now, but to suggest that the past, present and future are all one and the same.

In an article entitled "Rediscovering Black History," written on the occasion of the publication of the *The Black Book,* Toni Morrison speaks of the "complicated psychic power one had to exercise to resist devastation."[20] She was speaking, of course, not just of slavery, but of the Black existence in America after slavery as well. *Beloved* and all her novels, to a certain extent, bear witness to this psychic power. It must be stated as I conclude, however, that my intertextual reading of this novel as a revision of the slave narrative should not be construed as an attempt to diminish the form and content of the slave narratives themselves in any way. It is, instead, a recognition of the truth that Gates offers in the introduction to *The Slave's Narrative:*

> Once slavery was abolished, no need existed for the slave to write himself [or herself] into the human community through the action of first-person narration. As Frederick Douglass in 1855 succinctly put the matter, the free human being "cannot see things in the same light with the slave, because he does not and cannot look from the same point from which the slave does" . . . The nature of the narratives, and their rhetorical strategies and import, changed once slavery no longer existed.[21]

Beloved is a complex, contemporary manifestation of this shift. In a larger sense, however, it is what Mikhail Bakhtin calls a "reaccentuation" of the past (in this case, the past of slavery) to discover newer aspects of meaning embedded in the classic slave narrative.[22] Morrison's purpose is not to convince white readers of the slave's humanity, but to address black readers by inviting us to return to the very part of our past that many have repressed, forgotten or ignored. At the end of the novel, after the community has helped Denver rescue her mother from Beloved's ferocious spell by driving her out of town, Paul D returns to Sethe "to put his story next to hers" (273). Despite the psychic healing that Sethe undergoes, however, the community's response to her healing is encoded in the choruslike declaration on the last two pages of the text, that this was "not a story to pass on" (274). Yet, as readers, if we understand Toni Morrison's ironic and subversive vision at all, we know that our response to the text's apparent final call for silence and forgetting is not that at all. Instead, it is an ironic reminder that the process of consciously remembering not only empowers us to tell the difficult stories that must be passed on, but it also empowers us to make meaning of our individual and collective lives as well.

NOTES

[1] Quoted in the opening epigraph of Charles T. Davis and Henry Louis Gates, Jr., eds., *The Slave's Narrative* (New York: Oxford University Press, 1985).

[2] Middleton A. Harris, comp., *The Black Book* (New York: Random House, 1974). A shorter version of the text of this essay was presented at the annual convention of the Modern Language Association of America on December 29, 1988, in New Orleans, Louisiana. I am grateful to my colleagues of the First Draft Club—Carolyn Brown, Evelyn Hawthorne, Ann Kelly and especially, Claudia Tate—for their generous response to this essay.

[3] Toni Morrison, "Behind the Making of *The Black Book*," *Black World* 23 (February 1974): 86–90. Compiled by Middleton A. Harris, *The Black Book* does not identify Morrison as its editor. In this article, however, she not only discusses her role as editor, but describes the project of producing the book as an act of professional service and personal mission: "I was scared that the world would fall away before somebody put together a thing that got close to the way we really were" (90). Ironically, although *The Black Book* omits any mention of Morrison as its editor, it names her parents, Ramah Wofford and George Carl Wofford, in the acknowledgments, as two of the people who contributed to the text "with stories, pictures, recollections and general aid."

[4] See Amanda Smith, "Toni Morrison," *Publishers Weekly*, 21 August 1987, 51. This article is a report on an interview with Morrison a month before the publication of *Beloved*.

[5] See Harris, *Black Book*, 10.

[6] Toni Morrison, *The Bluest Eye* (New York: Holt, Rinehart and Winston, 1970); *Sula* (New York: Knopf, 1973); *Song of Solomon* (New York: Knopf, 1977) and *Tar Baby* (New York: Knopf, 1981). Of the first four novels, *Song of Solomon* is most clearly engaged with the subject of history. Specifically, it connects the African past with the lived life of African-Americans from slavery to the recent past of the 1960s.

[7] Claudia Tate, ed., *Black Women Writers at Work* (New York: Continuum, 1984), 122.

[8] Toni Morrison, *Beloved* (New York: Knopf, 1988), 256. All subsequent references to this novel are cited in the text parenthetically. The term "narrative intervention" is one I borrow from Hazel Carby's analysis of the uses of fiction in moments of historical crisis. See Hazel Carby, *Reconstructing Womanhood: The Emergence of the Afro-American Woman Novelist* (New York: Oxford University Press, 1987), 121–44.

[9] Henry Louis Gates, Jr., ed., *The Classic Slave Narratives* (New York: New American Library, 1987), x.

[10] Frederick Douglass, *The Narrative of the Life of Frederick Douglass* (New York: Signet, 1968); Harriet Jacobs, *Incidents in the Life of a Slave Girl*, ed. Jean Fagan Yellin (Cambridge: Harvard University Press, 1987).

[11] See James Olney, " 'I Was Born': Slave Narratives, Their Status as Autobiography and as Literature," *Callaloo* 7 (Winter 1984): 46–73. Reprinted in Davis and Gates, *The Slave's Narrative*, 148–75.

[12] Valerie Smith, *Self-Discovery and Authority in Afro-American Narrative* (Cambridge: Harvard University Press, 1987), 34. See also Mary Helen Washington, ed., *Invented Lives: Narratives of Black Women 1860–1960* (Garden City: Doubleday/Anchor, 1987), 3–15.

[13] Adrienne Rich, "When We Dead Awaken: Writing as Re-Vision," *College English* 34 (October 1972): 18–26; Morrison's words are quoted in Smith, *Publishers Weekly*, 51.

[14] Fredric Jameson, *The Political Unconscious: Narrative as a Socially Symbolic Act* (Ithaca: Cornell University Press, 1981), 9.

[15] Tate, *Black Women Writers*, 125.

[16] Steven Mallioux, *Interpretive Conventions: The Reader in the Study of American Fiction* (Ithaca: Cornell University Press, 1982), 170.

[17] See Helen Dudar, "Toni Morrison: Finally Just a Writer," *The Wall Street Journal*, 30 September 1987, 34. This is one of several newspaper articles to appear around the time of *Beloved*'s publication in which Morrison discussed the actual story upon which the novel is based.

[18] See Sherley Anne Williams, "The Blues Roots of Contemporary Afro-American Poetry," in Dexter Fisher and Robert Stepto, eds., *Afro-American Literature: The Reconstruction of In-*

struction (New York: Modern Language Association of America), 73. In the novel, the statements of individual characters shape the "call" to which other characters offer a "response" by sharing their versions of the past. This pattern of call and reponse then shapes the collective story of slavery that binds the members of the community together. This pattern resonates with similar patterns found in the blues and other forms of African-American oral expression.

[19] Frank Kermode, *The Genesis of Secrecy: On the Interpretation of Narrative* (Cambridge: Harvard University Press, 1979), 144.

[20] Toni Morrison, "Rediscovering Black History," *New York Times Magazine,* 11 August 1974, 18.

[21] Davis and Gates, *The Slave's Narrative,* xiii.

[22] Mikhail Bakhtin, "Discourse in the Novel," *The Dialogic Imagination,* Michael Holquist, ed., Caryl Emerson and Michael Holquist, trs. (Austin: University of Texas Press, 1981), 421.

TONI MORRISON

Unspeakable Things Unspoken:
The Afro-American Presence
in American Literature

I

I planned to call this paper "Canon Fodder," because the terms put me in mind of a kind of trained muscular response that appears to be on display in some areas of the recent canon debate. But I changed my mind (so many have used the phrase) and hope to make clear the appropriateness of the title I settled on.

My purpose here is to observe the panoply of this most recent and most anxious series of questions concerning what should or does constitute a literary canon in order to suggest ways of addressing the Afro-American presence in American Literature that require neither slaughter nor reification — views that may spring the whole literature of an entire nation from the solitude into which it has been locked. There is something called American literature that, according to conventional wisdom, is certainly not Chicano literature, or Afro-American literature, or Asian-American, or Native American, or . . . It is somehow separate from them and they from it, and in spite of the efforts of recent literary histories, restructured curricula and anthologies, this separate confinement, be it breached or endorsed, is the subject of a large part of these debates. Although the terms used, like the vocabulary of earlier canon debates, refer to literary and/or humanistic value, aesthetic criteria, value-free or socially anchored readings, the contemporary battle plain is most often understood to be the claims of others against the whitemale origins and definitions of those values; whether those definitions

From *Michigan Quarterly Review* 28, No. 1 (Winter 1989): 9–34.

reflect on eternal, universal and transcending paradigm or whether they constitute a disguise for a temporal, political and culturally specific program.

Part of the history of this particular debate is located in the successful assault that the feminist scholarship of men and women (black and white) made and continues to make on traditional literary discourse. The male part of the whitemale equation is already deeply engaged, and no one believes the body of literature and its criticism will ever again be what it was in 1965: the protected preserve of the thoughts and works and analytical strategies of whitemen.

It is, however, the "white" part of the question that this paper focuses on, and it is to my great relief that such terms as "white" and "race" can enter serious discussion of literature. Although still a swift and swiftly obeyed call to arms, their use is no longer forbidden.[1] It may appear churlish to doubt the sincerity, or question the proclaimed well-intentioned self-lessness of a 900-year-old academy struggling through decades of chaos to "maintain standards." Yet of what use is it to go on about "quality" being the only criterion for greatness knowing that the definition of quality is itself the subject of much rage and is seldom universally agreed upon by everyone at all times? Is it to appropriate the term for reasons of state; to be in the position to distribute greatness or withhold it? Or to actively pursue the ways and places in which quality surfaces and stuns us into silence or into language worthy enough to describe it? What is possible is to try to recognize, identify and applaud the fight for and triumph of quality when it is revealed to us and to let go the notion that only the dominant culture or gender can make those judgments, identify that quality or produce it.

Those who claim the superiority of Western culture are entitled to that claim only when Western civilization is measured thoroughly against other civilizations and not found wanting, and when Western civilization owns up to its own sources in the cultures that preceded it.

A large part of the satisfaction I have always received from reading Greek tragedy, for example, is in its similarity to Afro-American communal structures (the function of song and chorus, the heroic struggle between the claims of community and individual hubris) and African religion and philosophy. In other words, that is part of the reason it has quality for me— I feel intellectually at home there. But that could hardly be so for those unfamiliar with my "home," and hardly a requisite for the pleasure they take. The point is, the form (Greek tragedy) makes available these varieties of provocative love because *it* is masterly—not because the civilization that is its referent was flawless or superior to all others.

One has the feeling that nights are becoming sleepless in some quarters, and it seems to me obvious that the recoil of traditional "humanists" and some post-modern theorists to this particular aspect of the debate, the "race" aspect, is as severe as it is because the claims for attention come from that segment of scholarly and artistic labor in which the mention of "race" is either inevitable or elaborately, painstakingly masked; and if all of the ramifications that the term demands are taken seriously, the bases of Western civilization will require re-thinking. Thus, in spite of its implicit and explicit acknowledgement, "race" is still a virtually unspeakable thing, as can be seen in the apologies, notes of "special use" and circumscribed definitions that accompany it[2]—not least of which is my own deference in surrounding it with quotation marks. Suddenly (for our purposes, suddenly) "race" does not exist. For three hundred years black Americans insisted that "race" was no usefully distinguishing factor in human relationships. During those same three centuries every academic discipline, including theology, history, and natural science, insisted "race" was *the* determining factor in human development. When blacks discovered they had shaped or become a culturally formed race, and that it had specific and revered difference, suddenly they were told there is no such thing as "race", biological or cultural, that matters and that genuinely intellectual exchange cannot accommodate it.[3] In trying to come to some terms about "race" and writing, I am tempted to throw my hands up. It always seemed to me that the people who invented the hierarchy of "race" when it was convenient for them ought not to be the ones to explain it away, now that it does not suit their purposes for it to exist. But there *is* culture and both gender and "race" inform and are informed by it. Afro-American culture exists and though it is clear (and becoming clearer) how it has responded to Western culture, the instances where and means by which it has shaped Western culture are poorly recognized or understood.

I want to address ways in which the presence of Afro-American literature and the awareness of its culture both resuscitate the study of literature in the United States and raise that study's standards. In pursuit of that goal, it will suit my purposes to contextualize the route canon debates have taken in Western literary criticism.

I do not believe this current anxiety can be attributed solely to the routine, even cyclical arguments within literary communities reflecting unpredictable yet inevitable shifts in taste, relevance or perception. Shifts in which an enthusiasm for and official endorsement of William Dean Howells, for example, withered; or in which the legalization of Mark Twain in critical court rose and fell like the fathoming of a sounding line (for which he may or may not have named himself); or even the slow, delayed but steady swell of attention and devotion on which Emily Dickinson soared to what is now, surely, a permanent crest of respect. No. Those were discoveries, reappraisals of individual artists. Serious but not destabilizing. Such accommodations were simple because the questions they posed were simple: Are there one hundred sterling examples of high literary art in American literature and no more? One hundred and six? If one or two fall into disrepute, is there space, then, for one or two others in the vestibule, waiting like girls for bells chimed by future husbands who alone can promise them security, legitimacy—and in whose hands alone rests the gift of critical longevity? Interesting questions, but, as I say, not endangering.

Nor is this detectable academic sleeplessness the consequence of a much more radical shift, such as the mid-nineteeth century one heralding the authenticity of American literature itself. Or an even earlier upheaval—receding now into the distant past—in which theology and thereby Latin, was displaced for the equally rigorous study of the classics and Greek to be followed by what was considered a strangely arrogant and upstart proposal: that English literature was a suitable course of study for an aristocratic education, and not simply morally instructive fodder designed for the working classes. (The Chaucer Society was founded in 1848, four hundred years after Chaucer died.) No. This exchange seems unusual somehow, keener. It has a more strenuously argued (and felt) defense and a more vigorously insistent attack. And both defenses and attacks have spilled out of the academy into the popular press. Why? Resistance to displacement within or expansion of a canon is not, after all, surprising or unwarranted. That's what canonization is for. (And the question of whether there should be a canon or not seems disingenuous to me—there always is one whether there should be or not—for it is in the interests of the professional critical community to have one.) Certainly a sharp alertness as to *why* a work is or is not worthy of study is the legitimate occupation of the critic, the pedagogue and the artist. What is astonishing in the contemporary debate is not the resistance to displacement of works or to the expansion of genre within it, but the virulent passion that accompanies this resistance and, more importantly, the quality of its defense weaponry. The guns are very big; the trigger-fingers quick. But I am convinced the mechanism of the defenders of the flame is faulty. Not only may the hands of the gun-slinging cowboy-scholars be blown off, not only may the target be missed, but the subject of the conflagration (the sacred texts) is sacrificed, disfigured in the battle. This canon fodder may kill the canon. And I, at least, do not intend to live without Aeschylus or William Shakespeare, or James or Twain or Hawthorne, or Melville, etc., etc., etc. There must be some way to enhance canon readings without enshrining them.

When Milan Kundera, in *The Art of the Novel,* identified the historical territory of the novel by saying "The novel is Europe's creation" and that "The only context for grasping a novel's worth is the history of the European novel," the *New Yorker* reviewer stiffened. Kundera's "personal 'idea of the novel,' " he wrote, "is so profoundly Eurocentric that it's likely to seem exotic, even perverse, to American readers. . . . *The Art of the Novel* gives off the occasional (but pungent) whiff of cultural arrogance, and we may feel that Kundera's discourse . . . reveals an aspect of his character that we'd rather not have known about. . . . In order to become the artist he now is, the Czech novelist had to discover himself a second time, as a European. But what if that second, grander possibility hadn't been there to be discovered? What if Broch, Kafka, Musil—all that reading—had never been a part of his education, or had entered it only as exotic, alien presence? Kundera's polemical fervor in *The Art of the Novel* annoys us, as American readers, because we feel defensive, excluded from the transcendent 'idea of the novel' that for him seems simply to have been there for the taking. (If only he had cited, in his redeeming version of the novel's history, a few more heroes from the New World's culture.) Our novelists don't discover cultural values within themselves; they invent them."[4]

Kundera's views, obliterating American writers (with the exception of William Faulkner) from his own canon, are relegated to a "smugness" that Terrence Rafferty dissociates from Kundera's imaginative work and applies to the "sublime confidence" of his critical prose. The confidence of an exile who has the sentimental education of, and the choice to become, a European.

I was refreshed by Rafferty's comments. With the substitution of certain phrases, his observations and the justifiable umbrage he takes can be appropriated entirely by Afro-American writers regarding their own exclusion from the "transcendent 'idea of the novel.' "

For the present turbulence seems not to be about the flexibility of a canon, its range among and between Western countries, but about its miscegenation. The word is informative here and I do mean its use. A powerful ingredient in this debate concerns the incursion of third-world or so-called minority literature into a Eurocentric stronghold. When the topic of third world culture is raised, unlike the topic of Scandinavian culture, for example, a possible threat to and implicit criticism of the reigning equilibrium is seen to be raised as well. From the seventeenth century to the twentieth, the arguments resisting that incursion have marched in predictable sequence: 1) there is no Afro-American (or third world) art. 2) it exists but is inferior. 3) it exists and is superior when it measures up to the "universal" criteria of Western art. 4) it is not so much "art" as ore—rich are—that requires a Western or Eurocentric smith to refine it from its "natural" state into an aesthetically complex form.

A few comments on a larger, older, but no less telling academic struggle—an extremely successful one—may be helpful here. It is telling because it sheds light on certain aspects of this current debate and may locate its sources. I made reference above to the radical upheaval in canon building that took place at the inauguration of classical studies and Greek. This canonical re-routing from scholasticism to humanism, was not merely radical, it must have been (may I say it?) savage. And it took some seventy years to accomplish. Seventy years to eliminate Egypt as the cradle of civilization *and* its model and replace it with Greece. The triumph of that process was that Greece lost its own origins and became itself original. A number of scholars in various disciplines (history, anthropology, ethnobotany, etc.) have put forward their research into cross-cultural and intercultural transmissions with varying degress of success in the reception of their work. I am reminded of the curious publishing history of Ivan van Sertima's work, *They Came Before Columbus,* which researches the African presence in Ancient America. I am reminded of Edward Said's *Orientalism,* and especially the work of Martin Bernal, a linguist, trained in Chinese history, who has defined himself as an interloper in the field of classical civilization but who has offered, in *Black Athena,* a stunning investigation of the field. According to Bernal, there are two "models" of Greek history: one views Greece as Aryan or European (the Aryan Model); the other sees it as Levantine—absorbed by Egyptian and Semitic culture (the Ancient Model). "If I am right," writes Professor Bernal, "in urging the overthrow of the Aryan Model and replacement by the Revised Ancient one, it will be necessary not only to rethink the fundamental bases of 'Western Civilization' but also to recognize the penetration of racism and 'continental chauvinism' into all our historiography, or philosophy of writing history. The Ancient Model had no major 'internal' deficiencies or weaknesses in explanatory power. It was overthrown for external reasons. For eighteenth and nineteenth century Romantics and racists it was simply intolerable for Greece, which was seen not merely as the epitome of Europe but also as its pure childhood, to have been the result of the mixture of native Europeans and *colonizing*

Africans and Semites. Therefore the Ancient Model had to be overthrown and replaced by something more acceptable."[5]

It is difficult not to be persuaded by the weight of documentation Martin Bernal brings to his task and his rather dazzing analytical insights. What struck me in his analysis were the *process* of the fabrication of Ancient Greece and the *motives* for the fabrication. The latter (motive) involved the concept of purity, of progress. The former (process) required mis-reading, pre-determined selectivity of authentic sources, and—silence. From the Christian theological appropriation of Israel (the Levant), to the early nineteenth-century work of the prodigious Karl Müller, work that effectively dismissed the Greeks' own record of their influences and origins as their "Egyptomania," their tendency to be "wonderstruck" by Egyptian culture, a tendency "manifested in the 'delusion' that Egyptians and other non-European 'barbarians' had possessed superior cultures, from which the Greeks had borrowed massively,"[6] on through the Romantic response to the Enlightenment, and the decline into disfavor of the Phoenicians, "the essential force behind the rejection of the tradition of massive Phoenician influence on early Greece was the rise of racial—as opposed to religious—antisemitism. This was because the Phoenicians were correctly perceived to have been culturally very close to the Jews."[7]

I have quoted at perhaps too great a length from Bernal's text because *motive,* so seldom an element brought to bear on the history of history, is located, delineated and confronted in Bernal's research, and has helped my own thinking about the process and motives of scholarly attention to and an appraisal of Afro-American presence in the literature of the United States.

Canon building is Empire building. Canon defense is national defense. Canon debate, whatever the terrain, nature and range (of criticism, of history, of the history of knowledge, of the definition of language, the universality of aesthetic principles, the sociology of art, the humanistic imagination), is the clash of cultures. And *all* of the interests are vested.

In such a melee as this one—a provocative, healthy, explosive melee—extraordinarily profound work is being done. Some of the controversy, however, has degenerated into *ad hominem* and unwarranted speculation on the personal habits of artists, specious and silly arguments about politics (the destabilizing forces are dismissed as merely political; the status quo sees itself as not—as though the term "*a*political" were only its prefix and not the most obviously political stance imaginable since one of the functions of political ideology is to pass itself off as immutable, natural and "innocent"), and covert expressions of critical inquiry designed to neutralize and disguise the political interests of the discourse. Yet much of the research and analysis has rendered speakable what was formerly unspoken and has made humanistic studies, once again, the place where one has to go to find out what's going on. Cultures, whether silenced or monologistic, whether repressed or repressing, seek meaning in the language and images available to them.

Silences are being broken, lost things have been found and at least two generations of scholars are disentangling received knowledge from the apparatus of control, most notably those who are engaged in investigations of French and British Colonialist Literature, American slave narratives, and the delineation of the Afro-American literary tradition.

Now that Afro-American artistic presence has been "discovered" actually to exist, now that serious scholarship has moved from silencing the witnesses and erasing their meaningful place in and contribution to American culture, it is no longer acceptable merely to imagine us and imagine for us. We have always been imagining ourselves. We are not Isak Dinesen's "aspects of nature," nor Conrad's unspeaking. We are the subjects of our own narrative, witnesses to and participants in our own experience, and, in no way coincidentally, in the experience of those with whom we have come in contact. We are not, in fact, "other." We are choices. And to read imaginative literature by and about us is to choose to examine centers of the self and to have the opportunity to compare these centers with the "raceless" one with which we are, all of us, most familiar.

II

Recent approaches to the reading of Afro-American literature have come some distance; have addressed those arguments, mentioned earlier (which are not arguments, but attitudes), that have, since the seventeenth century, effectively silenced the autonomy of that literature. As for the charge that "there is no Afro-American art," contemporary critical analysis of the literature and the recent surge of reprints and re-discoveries have buried it, and are pressing on to expand the traditional canon to include classic Afro-American works where generically and chronologically appropriate, and to devise strategies for reading and thinking about these texts.

As to the second silencing charge, "Afro-American art exists, but is inferior," again, close readings and careful research into the culture out of which the art is born have addressed and still address the labels that once passed for stringent analysis but can no more: that it is imitative, excessive, sensational, mimetic (merely), and unintellectual, though very often "moving," "passionate," "naturalistic," "realistic" or sociologically "revealing."

These labels may be construed as compliments or pejoratives and if valid, and shown as such, so much the better. More often than not, however, they are the lazy, easy brand-name applications when the hard work of analysis is deemed too hard, or when the critic does not have access to the scope the work demands. Strategies designed to counter this lazy labeling include the application of recent literary theories to Afro-American literature so that non-canonical texts can be incorporated into existing and forming critical discourse.

The third charge, that "Afro-American art exists, but is superior only when it measures up to the 'universal' criteria of Western art," produces the most seductive form of analysis, for both writer and critic, because comparisons are a major form of knowledge and flattery. The risks, nevertheless, are twofold: 1) the gathering of a culture's difference into the skirts of the Queen is a neutralization designed and constituted to elevate and maintain hegemony. 2) circumscribing and limiting the literature to a mere reaction to or denial of the Queen, judging the work soley in terms of its referents to Eurocentric criteria, or its sociological accuracy, political correctness or its pretense of having no politics at all, cripple the literature and infantilize the serious work of imaginative writing. This response-oriented concept of Afro-American literature contains the seeds of the next (fourth) charge: that when Afro-American art is worthy, it is because it is "raw" and "rich," like ore, and like ore needs refining by Western intelligences. Finding or imposing Western influences in/on Afro-American literature has value, but when its sole purpose is to *place* value only where that influence is located it is pernicious.

My unease stems from the possible, probable, consequences these approaches may have upon the work itself. They can lead to an incipient orphanization of the work in order to issue its adoption papers. They can confine the discourse to the advocacy of diversification within the canon and/ or a kind of benign co-existence near or within reach of the already sacred texts. Either of these two positions can quickly become another kind of silencing if permitted to ignore the indigenous created qualities of the writing. So many questions surface and irritate. What have these critiques made of the work's own canvas? Its paint, its frame, its framelessness, its spaces? Another list of approved subjects? Of approved treatments? More self-censoring, more exclusion of the specificity of the culture, the gender, the language? Is there perhaps an alternative utility in these studies? To advance power or locate its fissures? To oppose elitist interests in order to enthrone egalitarian effacement? Or is it merely to rank and grade the readable product as distinct from the writeable production? Can this criticism reveal ways in which the author combats and confronts received prejudices and even creates *other terms* in which to rethink one's attachment to or intolerance of the material of these works? What is important in all of this is that the critic not be engaged in laying claim on behalf of the text to his or her own dominance and power. Nor to exchange his or her professional anxieties for the imagined turbulence of the text. "The text should become a problem of passion, not a pretext for it."

There are at least three focuses that seem to me to be neither reactionary nor simply pluralism, nor the even simpler methods by which the study of Afro-American literature remains the helpful doorman into the halls of sociology. Each of them, however, requires wakefulness.

One is the development of a theory of literature that truly accommodates Afro-American literature: one that is based on its culture, its history, and the artistic strategies the works employ to negotiate the world it inhabits.

Another is the examination and re-interpretation of the American canon, the founding nineteenth-century works, for the "unspeakable things unspoken"; for the ways in which the presence of Afro-Americans has shaped the choices, the language, the structure—the meaning of so much American literature. A search, in other words, for the ghost in the machine.

A third is the examination of contemporary and/or non-canonical literature for this presence, regardless of its category as mainstream, minority, or what you will. I am always amazed by the resonances, the structural gear-shifts, and the *uses* to which Afro-American narrative, persona and idiom are put in contemporary "white" literature. And in Afro-American literature itself the question of difference, of essence, is critical. What makes a work "Black"? The most valuable point of entry into the question of cultural (or racial) distinction, the one most fraught, is its language—its unpoliced, seditious, confrontational, manipulative, inventive, disruptive, masked and unmasking language. Such a penetration will entail the most careful study, one in which the impact of Afro-American presence on modernity becomes clear and is no longer a well-kept secret.

I would like to touch, for just a moment, on focuses two and three.

We can agree, I think, that invisible things are not necessarily "not-there"; that a void may be empty, but is not a vacuum. In addition, certain absences are so stressed, so ornate, so planned, they call attention to themselves; arrest us with intentionality and purpose, like neighborhoods that are defined by the population held away from them. Looking at the scope of American literature, I can't help thinking that the question should never have been "Why am I, an Afro-American, absent from it?" It is not a particularly interesting query anyway. The spectacularly interesting question

is "What intellectual feats had to be performed by the author or his critic
to erase me from a society seething with my presence, and what effect has
that performance had on the work? What are the strategies of escape from
knowledge? Of willful oblivion? I am not recommending an inquiry into
the obvious impulse that overtakes a soldier sitting in a World War I trench
to think of salmon fishing. That kind of pointed "turning from," deliberate
escapism or transcendence may be life-saving in a circumstance of immediate
duress. The exploration I am suggesting is, how does one sit in the audience
observing, watching the performance of Young America, say, in the nineteenth century, say, and reconstruct the play, its director, its plot and its
cast in such a manner that its very point never surfaces? Not why. How?
Ten years after Tocqueville's prediction in 1840 that " 'Finding no stuff for
the ideal in what is real and true, poets would flee to imaginary regions
. . . ' in 1850 at the height of slavery and burgeoning abolitionism, American
writers chose romance." Where, I wonder, in these romances is the shadow
of the presence from which the text has fled? Where does it heighten, where
does it dislocate, where does it necessitate novelistic invention; what does
it release; what does it hobble?

The device (or arsenal) that serves the purpose of flight can be Ro-
manticism versus verisimilitude; new criticism versus shabbily disguised and
questionably sanctioned "moral uplift"; the "complex series of evasions,"
that is sometimes believed to be the essence of modernism; the perception
of the evolution of art; the cultivation of irony, parody; the nostalgia for
"literary language"; the rhetorically unconstrained textuality versus socially
anchored textuality, and the undoing of textuality altogether. These critical
strategies can (but need not) be put into service to reconstruct the historical
world to suit specific cultural and political purposes. Many of these strategies
have produced powerfully creative work. Whatever *uses* to which Roman-
ticism is put, however suspicious its origins, it has produced an incontestably
wonderful body of work. In other instances these strategies have succeeded
in paralyzing both the work and its criticism. In still otehrs they have led
to a virtual infantilization of the writer's intellect, his sensibility, his craft.
They have reduced the mediations on theory into a "power struggle among
sects" reading unauthored and unauthorable material, rather than an outcome
of reading *with* the author the text both construct.

In other words, the critical process has made wonderful work of some
wonderful work, and recently the means of access to the old debates have
altered. The problem now is putting the question. Is the nineteenth century
flight from blackness, for example, successful in mainstream American literature? Beautiful? Artistically problematic? Is the text sabotaged by its own

proclamations of "universality"? Are there ghosts in the machine? Active but unsummoned presences that can distort the workings of the machine and can also *make* it work? These kinds of questions have been consistently put by critics of Colonial Literature vis-à-vis Africa and India and other third world countries. American literature would benefit from similar critiques. I am made melancholy when I consider that the act of defending the Eurocentric Western posture in literature as not only "universal" but also "race-free" may have resulted in lobotomizing that literature, and in diminishing both the art and the artist. Like the surgical removal of legs so that the body can remain enthroned, immobile, static—under house arrest, so to speak. It may be, of course, that contemporary writers deliberately exclude from their conscious writerly world the subjective appraisal of groups perceived as "other," and whitemale writers frequently abjure and deny the excitement of framing or locating their literature in the political world. Nineteenth-century writers, however, would never have given it a thought. Mainstream writers in Young America understood their competition to be national, cultural, but only in relationship to the Old World, certainly not vis-à-vis an ancient race (whether Native American or African) that was stripped of articulateness and intellectual thought, rendered, in D. H. Lawrence's term, "uncreate." For these early American writers, how could there be competition with nations or peoples who were presumed unable to handle or uninterested in handling the written word? One could write about them, but there was never the danger of their "writing back." Just as one could speak to them without fear of their "talking back." One could even observe them, hold them in prolonged gaze, without encountering the risk of being observed, viewed, or judged in return. And if, on occasion, they were themselves viewed and judged, it was out of a political necessity and, for the purposes of art, could not matter. Or so thought Young America. It could never have occurred to Edgar Allan Poe in 1848 that I, for example, might read "The Gold Bug" and watch his efforts to render my grandfather's speech to something as close to braying as possible, an effort so intense you can see the perspiration—and the stupidity—when Jupiter says "I knows," and Mr. Poe spells the verb "nose."[8]

Yet in spite or because of this monologism there is a great, ornamental, prescribed absence in early American literature and, I submit, it is instructive. It only seems that the canon of American literature is "naturally" or "inevitably" "white." In fact it is studiously so. In fact these absences of vital presences in Young American literature may be the insistent fruit of the scholarship rather than the text. Perhaps some of these writers, although under current house arrest, have much more to say than has been realized.

Perhaps some were not so much transcending politics, or escaping blackness, as they were transforming it into intelligible, accessible, yet artistic modes of discourse. To ignore this possibility by never questioning the strategies of transformation is to disenfranchise the writer, diminish the text and render the bulk of the literature aesthetically and historically incoherent—an exorbitant price for cultural (whitemale) purity, and, I believe, a spendthrift one. The re-examination of founding literature of the United States for the unspeakable unspoken may reveal those texts to have deeper and other meanings, deeper and other power, deeper and other significances.

One such writer, in particular, it has been almost impossible to keep under lock and key is Herman Melville.

Among several astute scholars, Michael Rogin has done one of the most exhaustive studies of how deeply Melville's social thought is woven into his writing. He calls our attention to the connection Melville made between American slavery and American freedom, how heightened the one rendered the other. And he has provided evidence of the impact on the work of Melville's family, milieu, and, most importantly, the raging, all-encompassing conflict of the time: slavery. He has reminded us that it was Melville's father-in-law who had, as judge, decided the case that made the Fugitive Slave Law law, and that other evidence in *Moby-Dick* also suggests the impact of Shaw's ruling on the climax of Melville's tale. Melville conceived the final confrontation between Ahab and the white whale some time in the first half of 1851. He may well have written his last chapters only after returning from a trip to New York in June. [Judge Shaw's decision was handed down in April, 1851.] When New York anti-slavery leaders William Seward and John van Buren wrote public letters protesting the *Sims* ruling, the New York *Herald* responded. Its attact on "The Anti-Slavery Agitators" began: "Did you ever see a whale? Did you ever see a mighty whale struggling?" . . .[9]

Rogin also traces the chronology of the whale from its "birth in a state of nature" to its final end as commodity.[10] Central to his argument is that Melville in *Moby-Dick* was being allegorically and insistently political in his choice of the whale. But within his chronology, one singular whale transcends all others, goes beyond nature, adventure, politics and commodity to an abstraction. What is this abstraction? This "wicked idea"? Interpretation has been varied. It has been viewed as an allegory of the state in which Ahab is Calhoun, or Daniel Webster; an allegory of capitalism and corruption, God and man, the individual and fate, and most commonly, the single allegorical meaning of the white whale is understood to be brute, indifferent Nature, and Ahab the madman who challenges that Nature.

But let us consider, again, the principal actor, Ahab, created by an author who calls himself Typee, signed himself Tawney, identified himself as Ishmael, and who had written several books before *Moby-Dick* criticizing missionary forays into various paradises.

Ahab loses sight of the commercial value of his ship's voyage, its point, and pursues an idea in order to destroy it. His intention, revenge, "an audacious, immitigable and supernatural revenge," develops stature—maturity—when we realize that he is not a manmourning his lost leg or a scar on his face. However intense and dislocating his fever and recovery had been after his encounter with the white whale, however satisfactorily "male" this vengeance is read, the vanity of it is almost adolescent. But if the whale is more than blind, indifferent Nature unsubduable by masculine aggression, if it is as much its adjective as it is its noun, we can consider the possibility that Melville's "truth" was his recognition of the moment in America when whiteness became ideology. And if the white whale is the ideology of race, what Ahab has lost to it is personal dismemberment and family and society and his own place as a human in the world. The trauma of racism is, for the racist and the victim, the severe fragmentation of the self, and has always seemed to me a cause (not a symptom) of psychosis—strangely of no interest to psychiatry. Ahab, then, is navigating between an idea of civilization that he renounces and an idea of savergery he must annihilate, because the two cannot co-exist. The former is based on the latter. What is terrible in its complexity is that the idea of savagery is not the missionary one: it is white racial ideology that is savage and if, indeed, a white, nineteeth-century, American male took on not abolition, not the amelioration of racist institutions or their laws, but the very concept of whiteness as an inhuman idea, he would be very alone, very desperate, and very doomed. Madness would be the only appropriate description of such audacity, and "he heaves me," the most succinct and appropriate description of that obsession.

I would not like to be understood to argue that Melville was engaged in some simple and simple-minded black/white didacticism, or that he was satanizing white people. Nothing like that. What I am suggesting is that he was overwhelmed by the philosophical and metaphysical inconsistencies of an extraordinary and unprecedented idea that had its fullest manifestation in his own time in his own country, and that that idea was the successful assertion of whiteness as ideology.

On the *Pequod* the multiracial, mainly foreign, proletariat is at work to produce a commodity, but it is diverted and converted from that labor to Ahab's more significant intellectual quest. We leave whale as commerce and confront whale as metaphor. With that interpretation in place, two of the most famous chapters of the book become luminous in a completely new way. One is Chapter 9, The Sermon. In Father Mapple's thrilling rendition of Jonah's trials, emphasis is given to the purpose, "To preach the Truth to the face of Falsehood! That was it!" Only then the reward "Delight"— which strongly calls to mind Ahab's lonely necessity. "Delight is to him . . . who against the proud gods and commodores of this earth, ever stand forth his own inexorable self. . . . Delight is to him whose strong arms yet support him, when the ship of this base treacherous world has gone down beneath him. Delight is to him who gives no quarter in the truth and kills, burns, and destroys all *sin* though he pluck it out from under the robes of Senators and Judges. Delight—top-gallant delight is to him who acknowledges no law or lord, but the Lord his God, and is only a *patriot to heaven*" [italics mine]. No one, I think, has denied that the sermon is designed to be prophetic, but it seems unremarked what the nature of the sin is—the sin that must be destroyed, regardless. Nature? A sin? The terms do not apply. Capitalism? Perhaps. Capitalism fed greed, lent itself inexorably to corruption, but probably was not in and of itself sinful to Melville. Sin suggests a moral outrage within the bounds of man to repair. The concept of racial superiority would fit seamlessly. It is difficult to read those words ("destruction of sin," "patriot to heaven") and not hear in them the description of a different Ahab. Not an adolescent male in adult clothing, a maniacal egocentric, or the "exotic plant" that V. S. Parrington thought Melville was. Not even a morally fine liberal voice adjusting, balancing, compromising with racial institutions. But another Ahab: the only white male American heroic enough to try to slay the monster that was devouring the world as he knew it.

Another chapter that seems freshly lit by this reading is Chapter 42. The Whiteness of the Whale. Melville points to the do-or-die significance of his effort to say something unsayable in this chapter. "I almost despair," he writes, "of putting it in a comprehensive form. It was the whiteness of the whale that above all things appalled me. But how can I hope to explain myself here; and yet in some dim, random way, explain myself I must, *else all these chapters might be naught*" [italics mine]. The language of this chapter ranges between benevolent, beautiful images of whiteness and whiteness as sinsister and shocking. After dissecting the ineffable, he concludes: "Therefore . . . symbolize whatever grand or gracious he will by whiteness, no man can deny that in its profoundest *idealized significance* it calls up a peculiar apparition to the soul." I stress "idealized significance" to emphasize and make clear (if such clarity needs stating) that Melville is not exploring white *people,* but whiteness idealized. Then, after informing the reader of his "hope to light upon some chance clue to conduct us to the hidden course we seek," he tries to nail it. To provide the key to the "hidden course." His struggle to do so is gigantic. He cannot. Nor can we. But in nonfigurative language, he idealifies the imaginative tools needed to solve the problem: "subtlety appeals to subtlety, and without imagination no man can follow another into the halls." And his fainal observation reverberates with personal trauma. "This visible [colored] world seems formed in love, the invisible [white] spheres were formed in fright." The necessity for whiteness as provileged "natural" state, the invention of it, was indeed formed in fright.

"Slavery," writes Rogin, "confirmed Melville's isolation, decisively established in *Moby-Dick,* from the dominant consciousness of his time."[11] I differ on this point and submit that Melville's hostility and repugnance for slavery would have found company. There were many white Americans of his acquaintance who felt repelled by slavery, wrote journalism about it, spoke about it, legislated on it and were active in abolishing it. His attitude to slavery alone would not have condemned him to the almost autistic separation visited upon him. And if he felt convinced that blacks were worthy of being treated like whites, or that capitalism was dangerous—he had company or could have found it. But to question the very notion of white progress, the very idea of racial superiority, of whiteness as privileged place in the evolutionary ladder of humankind, and to meditate on the fraudulent, self-destroying philosophy of that superiority, to "pluck it out from under the robes of Senators and Judges," to drag the "judge himself to the bar,"— that was dangerous, solitary, radical work. Especially then. Especially now. To be "only a patriot to heaven" is no mean aspiration in Young America for a writer—or the captain of a whaling ship.

A complex, heaving, disorderly, profound text is *Moby-Dick,* and among its several meanings it seems to me this "unspeakable" one has remained the "hidden course," the truth in the Face of Falsehood." To this day no novelist has so wrestled with its subject. To this day literary analyses of canonical texts have shied away from that perspective: the informing and determining Afro-American presence in traditional American literature. The chapters I have made reference to are only a fraction of the instances where the text surrenders such insights, and points a helpful finger toward the ways in which the ghost drives the machine.

Melville is not the only author whose works double their fascination and the power when scoured for this presence and the writerly strategies taken to address or deny it. Edgar Allan Poe will sustain such a reading. So will Nathaniel Hawthorne and Mark Twain; and in the twentieth century, Willa Cather, Ernest Hemingway, F. Scott Fitzgerald, and William Faulkner, to name a few. Canonical American literature is begging for such attention.

It seems to me a more than fruitful project to produce some cogent analysis showing instances where early American literature identifies itself, risks itself, to assert its antithesis to blackness. How its linguistic gestures prove the intimate relationship to what is being nulled by implying a full descriptive apparatus (identity) to a presence-that-is-assumed-not-to-exist. Afro-American critical inquiry can do this work.

I mentioned earlier that finding or imposing Western influences in/on Afro-American literature had value provided the valued process does not become self-anointing. There is an adjacent project to be undertaken—the third focus in my list: the examination of contemporary literature (both the sacred and the profane) for the impact Afro-American presence has had on the structure of the work, the linguistic practice, and fictional enterprise in which it is engaged. Like focus two, this critical process must also eschew the pernicious goal of equating the fact that presence with the achievement of the work. A work does not get better because it is responsive to another culture; nor does it become automatically flawed because of that responsiveness. The point is to clarify, not to enlist. And it does not "go without saying" that a work written by an Afro-American is automatically subsumed by an enforcing Afro-American presence. There is a clear flight from blackness in a great deal of Afro-American literature. In others there is the duel with blackness, and in some cases, as they say, "You'd never know."

III

It is on this area, the impact of Afro-American culture on contemporary American literature, that I now wish to comment. I have already said that works by Afro-Americans can respond to this presence (just as non-black works do) in a number of ways. The question of what constitutes the art of a black writer, for whom that modifer is more search than fact, has some urgency. In other words, other than melanin and subject matter, what, in fact, may make me a black writer? Other than my own ethnicity—what is going on in my work that makes me believe it is demonstrably inseparable from a cultural specificity that is Afro-American?

Please forgive the use of my own work in these observations. I use it not because it provides the best example, but because I know it best, know what I did and why, and know how central these queries are to me. Writing is, *after* all, an act of language, its practice. But *first* of all it is an effort of the will to discover.

Let me suggest some of the ways in which I activate language and ways in which that language activates me. I will limit this perusal by calling attention only to the first sentences of the books I've written, and hope that in exploring the choices I made, prior points are illuminated.

The Bluest Eye begins "Quiet as it's kept, there were no marigolds in the fall of 1941." The sentence, like the one that open each succeeding book, is simple, uncomplicated. Of all the sentences that begin all the books, only two of them have dependent clauses; the other three are simple sentences and two are stripped down to virtually subject, verb, modifier. Nothing fancy here. No words need looking up; they are ordinary, everyday words. Yet I hoped the simplicity was not simply-minded, but devious, even loaded. An that the process of selecting each word, for itself and its relationship to the others in the sentence, along with the rejection of others for their echoes, for what is determined and what is not determined, what is almost there and what must be gleaned, would not theatricalize itself, would not erect a proscenium—at least not a noticeable one. So important to me was this unstaging, that in this first novel I summarized the whole of the book on the first page. (In the first edition, it was printed in its entirety on the jacket).

The opening phrase of this sentence, "Quiet as it's kept," had several attractions for me. First, it was a phrase familiar to me as a child listening to adults; to black women conversing with one another; telling a story, an anecdote, gossip about some one or event within the circle, the family, the neighborhood. The words are conspiratorial. "Shh, don't tell anyone else," and "No one is allowed to know this." It is a secret between us and a secret that is being kept from us. The conspiracy is both held and withheld, exposed and sustained. In some sense it was precisely what the act of writing the book was: the public exposure of a private confidence. In order fully to comprehend the duality of that position, one needs to think of the immediate political climate in which the writing took place, 1965–1969, during great social upheaval in the life of black people. The publication (as opposed to the writing) involved the exposure; the writing was the disclosure of secrets, secrets "we" shared and those withheld from us by ourselves and by the world outside the community.

"Quiet as it's kept," is also a figure of speech that is written, in this instance, but clearly chosen for how speakerly it is, how it speaks and bespeaks a particular world and its ambience. Further, in addition to its "back fence" connotation, its suggestion of illicit gossip, of thrilling revelation, there is also, in the "whisper," the assumption (on the part of the reader) that the teller is on the inside, knows something others do not, and is going to be generous with this privileged information. The intimacy I was aiming for, the intimacy between the reader and the page, could start up immediately because the secret is being shared, at best, and eavesdropped upon, at the least. Sudden familiarity or instant intimacy seemed crucial to me then, writing my first novel. I did not want the reader to have time to wonder "What do I have to do, to give up, in order to read this? What defense do I need, what distance maintain?" Because I know (and the reader does not — he or she has to wait for the second sentence) that this is a terrible story about things one would rather not know anything about.

What, then, is the Big Secret about to be shared? The thing we (reader and I) are "in" on? A botanical aberration. Pollution, perhaps. A skip, perhaps, in the natural order of things: a September, an autumn, a fall without marigolds. Bright common, strong and sturdy marigolds. When? In 1941, and since that is a momentous year (the beginning of World War II for the United States), the "fall" of 1941, just before the declaration of war, has a "closet" innuendo. In the temperate zone where there is a season known as "fall" during which one expects marigolds to be at their peak, in the months before the beginning of U.S. participation in World War II, something grim is about to be divulged. The next sentence will make it clear that the sayer, the one who knows, is a child speaking, mimicking the adult black women on the porch or in the back yard. The opening phrase is an effort to be grown-up about this shocking information. The point of view of a child alters the priority an adult would assign the information. "We thought it was because Pecola was having her father's baby that the marigolds did not grow" foregrounds the flowers, backgrounds illicit, traumatic, incomprehensible sex coming to its dreaded fruition. This foregrounding of "trivial" information and backgrounding of shocking knowledge secures the point of view but gives the reader pause about whether the voice of children can be trusted at all or is more trustworthy than an adult's. The reader is thereby protected from a confrontation too soon with the painful details, while simultaneously provoked into a desire to know them. The novelty, I thought, would be in having this story of female violation revealed from the vantage point of the victims or could-be victims of rape—the persons no one inquired of (certainly not in 1965)—the girls themselves. And since the victim does not have the vocabulary to understand the violence or its context, gullible, vulnerable girl friends, looking back as the knowing adults they pretended to be in the beginning, would have to do that for her, and would have to fill those silences with their own reflective lives. Thus, the opening provides the stroke that announces something more than a secret shared, but a silence broken, a void filled, an unspeakable thing spoken at last. And they draw the connection between a minor destabilization in seasonal flora with the insignificant destruction of a black girl. Of course "minor" and "insignificant" represent the outside world's view—for the girls both phenomena are earthshaking depositories of information they spend that whole year of childhood (and afterwards) trying to fathom, and cannot. If they have any success, it will be in transferring the problem of fathoming to the presumably adult reader, to the inner circle of listeners. At the least they have distributed the weight of these problematical questions to a larger constituency, and justified the public exposure of a privacy. If the conspiracy that the opening words announce is entered into by the reader, then the book can be seen to open with its close: a speculation on the disruption of "nature," as being a social disruption with tragic individual consequences in which the reader, as part of the population of the text, is implicated.

However a problem, unsolved, lies in the central chamber of the novel. The shattered world I built (to complement what is happening to Pecola), its pieces held together by seasons in childtime and commenting at every turn on the incompatible and barren white family primer, does not in its present form handle effectively the silence at its center. The void that is Pecola's "unbeing." It should have had a shape—like the emptiness left by a boom or a cry. It required a sophistication unavailable to me, and some deft manipulation of the voices around her. She is not *seen* by herself until she hallucinates a self. And the fact of her hallucination becomes a point of outside-the-book conversation, but does not work in the reading process.

Also, although I was pressing for a female expressiveness (a challenge that re-surfaced in *Sula*), it eluded me for the most part, and I had to content myself with female personae because I was not able to secure throughout the work the feminine subtext that is present in the opening sentence (the women gossiping, eager and aghast in "Quiet as it's kept"). The shambles this struggle became is most evident in the section on Pauline Breedlove where I resorted to two voices, hers and the urging narrator's, both of which are extremely unsatisfactory to me. It is interesting to me that where I thought I would have the most difficulty subverting the language to a feminine mode, I had the least: connecting Cholly's "rape" by the whitemen to his own of his daughter. This most masculine act of aggression becomes feminized in my language, "passive," and, I think, more accurately repellent when deprived of the male "glamor of shame" rape is (or once was) routinely given.

The points I have tried to illustrate are that my choices of language (speakerly, aural, colloquial), my reliance for full comprehension on codes embedded in black culture, my effort to effect immediate co-conspiracy and intimacy (without any distancing, explanatory fabric), as well as my (failed) attempt to shape a silence while breaking it are attempts (many unsatisfactory) to transfigure the complexity and wealth of Afro-American culture into a language worthy of the culture.

In *Sula,* it's necessary to concentrate on *two* first sentences because what survives in print is not the one I had intended to be the first. Originally the book opened with "Except for World War II nothing ever interfered with National Suicide Day." With some encouragement, I recognized that it was a false beginning. *"In medias res"* with a vengeance, because there was no *res* to be in the middle of—no implied world in which to locate the specificity and the resonances in the sentence. More to the point, I knew I was writing a second novel, and that it too would be about people in a black community not just foregrounded but totally dominant; and that it was about black women—also foregrounded and dominant. In 1988, certainly, I would not need (or feel the need for) the sentence—the short section—that now opens *Sula.* The threshold between the reader and the black-topic text need not be the safe, welcoming lobby I persuaded myself it needed at that time. My preference was the demolition of the lobby altogether. As can be seen from *The Bluest Eye,* and in every book I have written, only *Sula* has this "entrance." The others refuse the "presentation"; refuse the seductive safe harbor; the line of demarcation between the sacred and the obscene, public and private, them and us. Refuse, in effect, to cater to the diminished expectations of the reader, or his or her alarm heightened by the emotional luggage one carries into the black-topic text. (I should remind you that *Sula* was begun in 1969, while my first book was in proof, in a period of extraordinary political activity.)

Since I had become convinced that the effectiveness of the original beginning was only in my head, the job at hand became how to construct an alternate beginning that would not force the work to genuflect and would complement the outlaw quality in it. The problem presented itself this way: to fashion a door. Instead of having the text open wide the moment the cover is opened (or, as in *The Bluest Eye,* to have the book stand exposed before the cover is even touched, much less opened, by placing the complete "plot" on the first page—and finally on the cover of the first edition), here I was to posit a door, turn its knob and beckon for some four or five pages. I had determined not to mention any characters in those pages, there would be no people in the lobby—but I did, rather heavy-handedly in my view, end the welcome aboard with the mention of Shadrack and Sula. It was a craven (to me, still) surrender to a worn-out technique of novel writing: the overt announcement to the reader whom to pay attention to. Yet the bulk of the opening I finally wrote is about the community, a view of it, and the view is not from within (this is a door, after all) but from the point of view of a stranger—the "valley man" who might happen to be there on some errand, but who obviously does not live there and to and for whom all this is mightily strange, even exotic. You can see why I despise much of this beginning. Yet I tried to place in the opening sentence the signature terms of loss: "There used to be a neighborhood here; not any more." That may not be the world's worst sentence, but it doesn't "play," as they say in the theater.

My new first sentence became "In that place, where they tore the nightstand and blackberry patches from their roots to make room for the Medallion City Golf Course, there was once a neighborhood." Instead of my original plan, here I am introducing an outside-the-circle reader into the circle. I am translating the anonymous into the specific, a "place" into a "neighborhood," and letting a stranger in through whose eyes it can be viewed. In between "place" and "neighborhood" I now have to squeeze the specificity and the *difference;* the nostalgia, the history, and the nostalgia for the history; the violence done to it and the consequences of that violence. (It took three months, those four pages, a whole summer of nights.) The nostalgia is sounded by "once"; the history and a longing for it is implied in the connotation of "neighborhood." The violence lurks in having something torn out by its roots—it will not, cannot grow again. It consequences are that what has been destroyed is considered weeds, refuse necessarily removed in urban "development" by the unspecified but no less known "they" who do not, cannot, afford to differentiate what is displaced, and would not care that this is "refuse" of a certain kind. Both plants have darkness in them: "black" and "night." One is unusual (nightshade) and has two darkness words: "night" and "shade." The other (blackberry) is common. A familiar plant and an exotic one. A harmless one and a dangerous one. One produces a nourishing berry; one delivers toxic ones. But they both thrived there together, *in that place when it was a neighborhood.* Both are gone now, and the description that follows is of the other specific things, in this black community, destroyed in the wake of the golf course. Golf course conveys what it is not, in this context: not houses, or factories, or even a public park, and certainly not residents. It is a manicured place where the likelihood of the former residents showing up is almost nil.

I want to get back to those berries for a moment (to explain, perhaps, the length of time it took for the language of that section to arrive). I always thought of Sula as quintessentially black, metaphysically black, if you will, which is not melanin and certainly not unquestioning fidelity to the tribe. She is new world black and new world woman extracting choice from choicelessness, responding inventively to found things. Improvisational. Daring, disruptive, imaginative, modern, out-of-the-house, outlawed, unpolicing, uncontained and uncontainable. And dangerously female. In her final conversation with Nel she refers to herself as a special kind of black person woman, one with choices. Like a redwood, she says. (With all due respect to the dream landscape of Freud, trees have always seemed feminine to me.) In any case, my perception of Sula's double-dose of *chosen* blackness and *biological* blackness is in the presence of those two words of darkness in "nightshade" as well as in the uncommon quality of the vine itself. One variety is called "enchanter," and the other "bittersweet" because the berries taste bitter at first and then sweet. Also nightshade was thought to counteract witchcraft. All of this seemed a wonderful constellation of signs for Sula. And "blackberry patch" seemed equally appropriate for Nel: nourishing, never needing to be tended or cultivated, once rooted and bearing. Reliably sweet but thorn-bound. Her process of becoming, heralded by the explosive dissolving of her fragilely-held-together ball of string and fur (when the thorns of her self-protection are removed by Eva), puts her back in touch with the complex, contradictory, evasive, independent, liquid modernity Sula insisted upon. A modernity which overturns pre-war definitions, ushers in the Jazz Age (an age *defined* by Afro-American art and culture), and requires new kinds of intelligences to define oneself.

The stage-setting of the first four pages is embarrassing to me now, but the pains I have taken to explain it may be helpful in identifying the strategies one can be forced to resort to in trying to accommodate the mere fact of writing about, for and out of black culture while accommodating and responding to mainstream "white" culture. The "valley man's" guidance into the territory was my compromise. Perhaps it "worked," but it was not the work I wanted to do.

Had I begun with Shadrack, I would have ignored the smiling welcome and put the reader into immediate confrontation with his wound and his scar. The difference my preferred (original) beginning would have made would be calling greater attention to the traumatic displacement this most wasteful capitalist war had on black people in particular, and throwing into relief the creative, if outlawed, determination to survive it whole. Sula as (feminine) solubility and Shadrack's (male) fixative are two extreme ways of dealing with displacement—a prevalent theme in the narrative of black people. In the final opening I replicated the demiurge of discriminatory, prosecutorial racial oppression in the loss to commerical "progress" of the village, but the references to the community's stability and creativeness (music, dancing, craft, religion, irony, wit all referred to in the "valley man's" presence) refract and subsume their pain while they are in the thick of it. It is a softer embrace than Shadrack's organized, public madness— his disruptive remembering presence which helps (for a while) to cement the community, until Sula challenges them.

"The North Carolina Mutual Life Insurance agent promised to fly from Mercy to the other side of Lake Superior at 3:00."

This declarative sentence is designed to mock a journalistic style; with a minor alteration it could be the opening of an item in a small-town newspaper. It has the tone of an everyday event of minimal local interest. Yet I wanted it to contain (as does the scene that takes place when the agent fulfills his promise) the information that *Song of Solomon* both centers on and radiates from.

The name of the insurance company is real, a well known black-owned company dependent on black clients, and in its corporate name are "life" and "mutual"; *agent* being the necessary ingredient of what enables the relationship between them. The sentence also moves from North Carolina to Lake Superior—geographical locations, but with a sly implication that the move from North Carolina (the south) to Lake Superior (the north) might not actually involve the progress to some "superior state"—which, of course, it does not. The two other significant words are "fly," upon which the novel centers and "Mercy," the name of the place from which he is to fly. Both constitute the heartbeat of the narrative. Where is the insurance man flying to? The other side of Lake Superior is Canada, of course, the historic terminus of the escape route for black people looking for asylum. "Mercy," the other significant term, is the grace note; the earnest though, with one exception, unspoken wish of the narrative's population. Some grant it; some never find it; one, at least, makes it the text and cry of her extemporaneous sermon upon the death of her granddaughter. It touches, turns and returns to Guitar at the end of the book—he who is least deserving of it—and moves him to make it his own final gift. It is what one wishes for Hagar; what is unavailable to and unsought by Macon Dead, senior; what his wife learns to demand from him, and what can never come from the white world as is signified by the inversion of the name of the hospital from Mercy to "no-Mercy." It is only available from within. The center of the narrative is flight; the springboard is mercy.

But the sentence turns, as all sentences do, on the verb: promised. The insurance agent does not declare, announce, or threaten his act. He promises, as though a contract is being executed—faithfully—between himself and others. Promises broken, or kept; the difficulty of ferreting out loyalties and ties that bind or bruise wend their way throughout the action and the shifting relationships. So the agent's flight, like that of the Solomon in the title, although toward asylum (Canada, or freedom, or home, or the company of the welcoming dead), and although it carries the possibility of failure and the certainty of danger, is toward change, an alternative way, a cessation of things-as-they-are. It should not be understood as a simple desperate act, the end of a fruitless life, a life without gesture, without examination, but as obedience to a deeper contract with his people. It is his commitment to them, regardless of whether, in all its details, they understand it. There is, however, in their response to his action, a tenderness, some contrition, and mounting respect ("They didn't know he had it in him.") and an awareness that the gesture enclosed rather than repudiated themselves. The note he leaves asks for forgiveness. It is tacked on his door as a mild invitation to whomever might pass by, but it is not an advertisement. It is an almost Christian declaration of love as well as humility of one who was not able to do more.

There are several other flights in the work and they are motivationally different. Solomon's the most magical, the most theatrical and, for Milkman, the most satisfying. It is also the most problematic—to those he left behind. Milkman's flight binds these two elements of loyalty (Mr. Smith's) and abandon and self-interest (Solomon's) into a third thing: a merging of fealty and risk that suggests the "agency" for "mutual" "life," which he offers at the end and which is echoed in the hills behind him, and is the marriage of surrender and domination, acceptance and rule, commitment to a group *through* ultimate isolation. Guitar recognizes this marriage and recalls enough of how he himself is to put his weapon down.

The journalistic style at the beginning, its rhythm of a familiar, hand-me-down dignity is pulled along by an accretion of detail displayed in a meandering unremarkableness. Simple words, uncomplex sentence structures, persistent understatement, highly aural syntax—but the ordinariness of the language, its colloquial, vernacular, humorous and, upon occasion, parabolic quality sabotage expectations and mask judgments when it can no longer defer them. The composition of red, white and blue in the opening scene provides the national canvas/flag upon which the narrative works and against which the lives of these black people must be seen, but which must not overwhelm the enterprise the novel is engaged in. It is a composition of color that heralds Milkman's birth, protects his youth, hides its purpose and through which he must burst (through blue Buicks, red tulips in his waking dream, and his sisters' white stockings, ribbons and gloves) before discovering that the gold of his search is really Pilate's yellow orange and the glittering metal of the box in her ear.

These spaces, which I am filling in, and can fill in because they were planned, can conceivably be filled in with other significances. That is planned as well. The point is that into these spaces should fall the ruminations of the reader and his or her invented or recollected or misunderstood knowingness. The reader as narrator asks the questions the community asks, and both reader and "voice" stand among the crowd, within it, with privileged intimacy and contact, but without any more privileged information that the crowd has. The egalitarianism which places us all (reader, the novel's population, the narrator's voice) on the same footing reflected for me the force of flight and mercy, and the precious, imaginative yet realistic gaze of black people who (at one time, anyway) did not mythologize what or whom it mythologized. The "song" itself contains this unblinking evaluation of the miraculous and heroic flight of the legendary Solomon, an unblinking gaze which is lurking in the tender but amused choral-community response to the agent's flight. Sotto (but not completely) is my own giggle (in Afro-American terms) of the proto-myth of the journey to manhood. Whenever characters are cloaked in Western fable, they are in deep trouble; but the African myth is also contaminated. Unprogressive, unreconstructed, self-born Pilate is unimpressed by Solomon's flight and knocks Milkman down when, made new by his appropriation of his own family's fable, he returns to educate her with it. Upon hearing all he has to say, her only interest is filial. "Papa? . . . I've been carryin' Papa?" And her longing to hear the song, finally, is a longing for balm to die by, not a submissive obedience to history—anybody's.

The opening sentence of *Tar Baby,* "He believed he was safe," is the second version of itself. The first, "He thought he was safe," was discarded because "thought" did not contain the doubt I wanted to plant in the reader's mind about whether or not he really was—safe. "Thought" came to me at once because it was the verb my parents and grandparents used when describing what they had dreamed the night before. Not "I dreamt," or "It seemed" or even "I saw or did" this or that—but "I thought." It gave the dream narrative distance (a dream is not "real") and power (the control implied in *thinking* rather than *dreaming*). But to use "thought" seemed to undercut the faith of the character and the distrust I wanted to suggest to the reader. "Believe" was chosen to do the work properly. And the person who does the believing is, in a way, about to enter a dream world, and convinces himself, eventually, that he is in control of it. He believed; was convinced. And although the word suggests his conviction, it does not reassure the reader. If I had wanted the reader to trust his person's point of view I would have written "He was safe." Or, "Finally, he was safe." The unease about this view of safety is important because safety itself is the desire of each person in the novel. Locating it, creating it, losing it.

You may recall that I was interested in working out the mystery of a piece of lore, a folk tale, which is also about safety and danger and the skills needed to secure the one and recognize and avoid the other. I was not, of course, interested in re-telling the tale; I suppose that is an idea to pursue, but it is certainly not interesting enough to engage me for four years. I have said, elsewhere, that the exploration of the Tar Baby tale was like stroking a pet to see what the anatomy was like but not to disturb or distort its mystery. Folk lore may have begun as allegory for natural or social phenomena; it may have been employed as a retreat from contemporary issues in art, but folk lore can also contain myths that re-activate themselves endlessly through providers—the people who repeat, reshape, reconstitute and re-interpret them. The Tar Baby tale seemed to me to be about masks. Not masks as covering what is to be hidden, but how masks come to life, take life over, exercise the tensions between itself and what it covers. For Son, the most effective mask is none. For the others the construction is careful and delicately borne, but the masks they make have a life of their own and collide with those they come in contact with. The texture of the novel seemed to want leanness, architecture that was worn and ancient like a piece of mask sculpture: exaggerated, breathing, just athwart the representational life it displaced. Thus, the first and last sentences had to match, as the exterior planes match the interior, concave ones inside the mask. Therefore "He believed he was safe" would be the twin of "Lickety split, lickety split, lickety lickety split." This close is 1) the last sentence of the folk tale. 2) the action of the character. 3) the indeterminate ending that follows from the untrustworthy beginning. 4) the complimentary meter of its twin sister [u u/u u/with u u u/u u u/], and 5) the wide and marvelous space between the contradiction of those two images: from a dream of safety to the sound of running feet. The whole mediated world in between. This masked and unmasked; enchanted, disenchanted; wounded and wounding world is played out on and by the varieties of interpretation (Western and Afro-American) the Tar Baby myth has been (and continues to be) subjected to. Winging one's way through the vise and expulsion of history becomes possible in creative encounters with that history. Nothing, in those encounters, is safe, or should be. Safety is the foetus of power as well as protection from it, as the uses to which masks and myths are put in Afro-American culture remind us.

"124 was spiteful. Full of a baby's venom."

Beginning *Beloved* with numerals rather than spelled out numbers, it was my intention to give the house an identity separate from the street or even the city; to name it the way "Sweet Home" was named; the way plantations were named, but not with nouns or "proper" names—with numbers instead because numbers have no adjectives, no posture of coziness or grandeur or the haughty yearning of arrivistes and estate builders for the parallel beautifications of the nation they left behind, laying claim to instant history and legend. Numbers here constitute an address, a thrilling enough prospect for slaves who had owned nothing, least of all an address. And although the numbers, unlike words, can have no modifiers, I give these an adjective—spiteful (There are three others). The address is therefore personalized, but personalized by its own activity, not the pasted on desire for personality.

Also there is something about numerals that makes them spoken, heard, in this context, because one expects words to read in a book, not numbers to say, or hear. And the sound of the novel, sometimes cacaphonous, sometimes harmonious, must be an inner ear sound or a sound just beyond hearing, infusing the text with a musical emphasis that words can do sometimes even better than music can. Thus the second sentence is not one: it is a phrase that properly, grammatically, belongs as a dependent clause with the first. Had I done that, however, (124 was spiteful, comma, full of a baby's venom, or 124 was full of a baby's venom) I could not have had the accent on *full* [/u u/u/u pause/u u u u/u].

Whatever the risks of confronting the reader with what must be immediately incomprehensible in that simple, declarative authoritative sentence, the risk of unsettling him or her, I determined to take. Because the *in medias res* opening that I am so committed to is here excessively demanding. It is abrupt, and should appear so. No native informant here. The reader is snatched, yanked, thrown into an environment completely foreign, and I want it as the first stroke of the shared experience that might be possible between the reader and the novel's population. Snatched just as the slaves were from one place to another, from any place to another, without preparation and without defense. No lobby, no door, no entrance—a gangplank, perhaps (but a very short one). And the house into which this snatching—

this kidnapping—propels one, changes from spiteful to loud to quiet, as the sounds in the body of the ship itself may have changed. A few words have to be read before it is clear that 124 refers to a house (in most of the early drafts "The women *in the house* knew it" was simply "The women knew it." "House" was not mentioned for seventeen lines), and a few more have to be read to discover why it is spiteful, or rather the source of the spite. By then it is clear, if not at once, that something is beyond control, but is not beyond understanding since it is not beyond accommodation by both the "women" and the "children." The fully realized presence of the haunting is both a major incumbent of the narrative and sleight of hand. One of its purposes is to keep the reader preoccupied with the nature of the incredible spirit world while being supplied a controlled diet of the incredible political world.

The subliminal, the underground life of a novel is the area most likely to link arms with the reader and facilitate making it one's own. Because one must, to get from the first sentence to the next, and the next and the next. The friendly observation post I was content to build and man in *Sula* (with the stranger in the midst), or the down-home journalism of *Song of Solomon* or the calculated mistrust of the point of view in *Tar Baby* would not serve here. Here I wanted the compelling confusion of being there as they (the characters) are; suddenly, without comfort or succor from the "author," with only imagination, intelligence, and necessity available for the journey. The painterly language of *Song of Solomon* was not useful to me in *Beloved*. There is practically no color whatsoever in its pages, and when there is, it is so stark and remarked upon, it is virtually raw. Color seen for the first time, without its history. No built architecture as in *Tar Baby*, no play with Western chronology as in *Sula;* no exchange between book life and "real" life discourse—with printed text units rubbing against seasonal black childtime units as in *The Bluest Eye*. No compound of houses, no neighborhood, no sculpture, no paint, no time, especially no time because memory, pre-historic memory, has no time. There is just a little music, each other and the urgency of what is at stake. Which is all they had. For that work, the work of language is to get out of the way.

I hope you understand that in this explication of how I practice language is a search for and deliberate posture of vulnerability to those aspects of Afro-American culture that can inform and position my work. I sometimes know when the work works, when *nommo* has effectively summoned, by reading and listening to those who have entered the text. I learn nothing from those who resist it, except, of course, the sometimes fascinating display of their struggle. My expectations of and my gratitude to the critics who enter, are great. To those who talk about how well as what; who identify the workings as well as the work; for whom the study of Afro-American literature is neither a crash course in neighborliness and tolerance, nor an infant to be carried, instructed or chastised or even whipped like a child, but the serious study of art forms that have much work to do, but are already legitimatized by their own cultural sources and predecessors—in or out of the canon—I owe much.

For an author, regarding canons, it is very simple: in fifty, a hundred or more years his or her work may be relished for its beauty or its insight or its power; or it may be condemned for its vacuousness and pretension—and junked. Or in fifty or a hundred years the critic (as canon builder) may be applauded for his or her intelligent scholarship and powers of critical inquiry. Or laughed at for ignorance and shabbily disguised assertions of power—and junked. It's possible that the reputations of both will thrive, or that both will decay. In any case, as far as the future is concerned, when one writes, as critic or as author, all necks are on the line.

NOTES

[1] See "Race," Writing, and Difference, ed. Henry Louis Gates, Jr. (University of Chicago Press, 1986).
[2] Among many examples, They Came Before Columbus: The African Presence in Ancient America by Ivan van Sertima (New York: Random House, 1976), pp. xvi-xvii.
[3] Tzvetan Todorov, " 'Race,' Writing, and Culture," translated by Loulou Mack, in Gates, op. cit., pp. 370–380.
[4] Terrence Rafferty, "Articles of Faith," The New Yorker, 16 May 1988, pp. 110–118.
[5] Martin Bernal, Black Athena: The Afroasiatic Roots of Classical Civilization, Volume I: The Fabrication of Ancient Greece 1785–1985 (Rutgers University Press, 1987), p. 2.
[6] Ibid., p. 310.
[7] Ibid., p. 337.
[8] Older America is not always distinguishable from its infancy. We may pardon Edgar Allan Poe in 1848 but it should have occurred to Kenneth Lynn in 1966 that some young Native American might read his Hemingway biography and see herself described as "squaw" by this respected scholar, and that some young men might shudder reading the words "buck" and "half-breed" so casually included in his scholarly speculations.
[9] See Michael Paul Rogin, Subversive Genealogy: The Politics and Art of Herman Melville (University of California Press, 1985), p. 15.
[10] Ibid., pp. 107 and 142.
[11] Ibid., p. 112.

Chronology

1931   Born Chloe Anthony Wofford on February 18 in Lorain, Ohio, the second child of Ramah (Willis) and George Wofford.

1953   Graduates with B.A. in English from Howard University. Changes her name to Toni during the years at Howard.

1955   Receives M.A. in English from Cornell University for thesis on the theme of suicide in William Faulkner and Virginia Woolf.

1955–57   Instructor in English at Texas Southern University.

1957–64   Instructor in English at Howard University.

1958   Marries Harold Morrison, a Jamaican architect.

1964   Divorces Harold Morrison and returns with her two sons to Lorain.

1965   Becomes editor for a textbook subsidiary of Random House in Syracuse, New York.

1970   Publishes her first novel, *The Bluest Eye*. Takes editorial position at Random House in New York, eventually becoming a senior editor.

1971–72   Associate Professor of English at the State University of New York at Purchase.

1974   Publishes *Sula* and an edition of Middleton Harris's *The Black Book*.

1975   *Sula* nominated for the National Book Award.

1976–77   Visiting Lecturer at Yale University.

1977   Publishes *Song of Solomon*, which receives the National Book Critics Circle Award and the American Academy and Institute of Arts and Letters Award.

1981   Publishes *Tar Baby*.

1984–89   Schweitzer Professor of the Humanities at the State University of New York at Albany.

1986   Receives the New York State Governor's Art Award.

1986–88   Visiting Lecturer at Bard College.

1987   Publishes *Beloved*, which is nominated for the National Book Award and the National Book Critics Award.

1988   Receives Pulitzer Prize in fiction and the Robert F. Kennedy Award for *Beloved*.

1989–   Robert F. Goheen Professor of the Humanities at Princeton University.

Contributors

HAROLD BLOOM is Sterling Professor of the Humanities at Yale University and Henry W. and Albert A. Berg Professor of English at the New York University Graduate School. He is a 1985 MacArthur Foundation Award recipient, served as the Charles Eliot Norton Professor of Poetry at Harvard University (1987–88), and is the author of eighteen books, the most recent being *Poetics of Influence: New and Selected Criticism* (1988). Currently he is editing the Chelsea House series Modern Critical Views and The Critical Cosmos, and other Chelsea House series in literary criticism.

CYNTHIA A. DAVIS has published articles on Stanley Kunitz and John Barth. She formerly taught in the Department of English at George Mason University.

HORTENSE J. SPILLERS is Professor of English at Haverford College. She has coedited with Majorie Pryce *Conjuring: Black Women, Fiction, and Literary Tradition* (1985).

KEITH E. BYERMAN is Associate Professor of English at Indiana State University. In addition to *Fingering the Jagged Grain: Tradition and Form in Recent Black Fiction* (1985), he has published essays on Toni Morrison and Gayl Jones in *MELUS* and *CLA Journal*.

MADONNE M. MINER is Assistant Professor of English at the University of Wyoming. She is author of *Insatiable Appetites* (1984) and has published several essays on American fiction in scholarly journals.

TERRY OTTEN is author of *The Deserted Stage: The Search for Dramatic Form in Nineteenth-Century England* (1972) and *After Innocence: Visions of the Fall in*

Modern Literature (1982), as well as numerous articles on English and American literature. He is chair of the Department of English at Wittenberg University.

MELVIN DIXON is Professor of English at Queens College, CUNY. He has contributed essays on black literature and criticism to scholarly journals and anthologies, including the collection edited by Robert B. Stepto and Michael S. Harper, *Chant of Saints: A Gathering of Afro-Amerian Literature, Art and Scholarship.*

MARGARET ATWOOD is one of Canada's most distinguished novelists, poets, and critics. Among her critical works are *Survival: A Thematic Guide to Canadian Literature* (1972) and *Second Words: Selected Critical Prose* (1982). Her latest novel is *Cat's Eye* (1989).

DEBORAH E. McDOWELL is Associate Professor of English at the University of Virginia. She has edited (with Arnold Rampersad) *Slavery and the Literary Imagination* (1989) and Nella Larsen's *Quicksand; and Passing* (1986). She is on the editorial board of *Black American Literature Forum.*

ROGER SALE is author of *Modern Heroism: Essays on D. H. Lawrence, William Empson, and J. R. R. Tolkien* (1973), *Literary Inheritance* (1984), and *Closer to Home: Writers and Places in England, 1780–1830* (1986), among other works. He teaches in the Department of English at the University of Washington in Seattle.

THEODORE O. MASON, JR. teaches in the Department of English and American Studies at Trinity College in Hartford, Connecticut. He has published essays on Toni Morrison and on Ishmael Reed for *Contemporary Literature* and *Modern Fiction Studies.*

MARILYN SANDERS MOBLEY is Assistant Professor of English at George Mason University. She has written essays on Morrison, Sarah Orne Jewett, Ann Petry, Zora Neale Hurston, and others, and is currently working on a study of narrative poetics in Morrison's five novels.

Bibliography

Baker, Houston, A., Jr. *Afro-American Poetics: Revisions of Harlem and the Black Aesthetic*. Madison: University of Wisconsin Press, 1988.

————. *Blues, Ideology, and Afro-American Literature: A Vernacular Theory*. Chicago: University of Chicago Press, 1984.

————. *The Journey Back: Issues in Black Literature and Criticism*. Chicago: University of Chicago Press, 1980.

————. *Long Black Song: Essays in Black American Literature and Culture*. Charlottesville: University Press of Virginia, 1972.

————. *Singers of Daybreak: Essays in Black American Literature*. Washington, DC: Howard University Press, 1974.

Bakerman, Jane S. "Failures of Love: Female Initiation in the Novels of Toni Morrison." *American Literature* 52 (1980): 541–63.

————. "The Seams Can't Show: An Interview with Toni Morrison." *Black American Literature Forum* 12 (1978): 56–60.

Barthold, Bonnie J. *Black Time: Fiction of Africa, the Caribbean, and the United States*. New Haven: Yale University Press, 1981.

Blake, Susan L. "Folklore and Community in *Song of Solomon*." *MELUS* 7 (1980): 77–82.

Brenner, Gerry. "*Song of Solomon:* Morrison's Rejection of Rank's Monomyth and Feminism." *Studies in American Fiction* 15 (1987): 13–24.

Bruck, Peter, and Wolfgang Karrer, ed. *The Afro-American Novel since 1960*. Amsterdam: Grüner, 1982.

Callahan, John F. *In the African-American Grain: The Pursuit of Voice in Twentieth-Century Black Fiction*. Urbana: University of Illinois Press, 1988.

Campbell, Jane. *Mythic Black Fiction: The Transformation of History*. Knoxville: University of Tennessee Press, 1986.

Christian, Barbara. *Black Feminist Criticism: Perspectives on Black Women Writers.* New York: Pergamon Press, 1985.

————. *Black Women Novelists: The Development of a Tradition 1892–1976.* Westport, CT: Greenwood Press, 1980.

Cooke, Michael G. *Afro-American Literature in the Twentieth Century: The Achievement of Intimacy.* New Haven: Yale University Press, 1984.

Davis, Arthur P. *From the Dark Tower: Afro-American Writers (1900 to 1960).* Washington, DC: Howard University Press, 1974.

Davis, Charles T. *Black Is the Color of the Cosmos: Essays on Afro-American Literature and Culture 1942–1981.* Edited by Henry Louis Gates, Jr. New York: Garland, 1982.

De Arman, Charles. "Milkman as the Archetypal Hero: 'Thursday's Child Has Far to Go.' " *Obsidian* 6 (1980): 56–59.

Dundes, Alan, ed. *Mother Wit from the Laughing Barrel: Readings in the Interpretation of Afro-American Folklore.* Englewood Cliffs, NJ: Prentice-Hall, 1973.

Edelberg, Cynthia Dubin. "Morrison's Voices: Formal Education, the Work Ethic, and the Bible." *American Literature* 58 (1986): 217–37.

Fikes, Robert J. "Echoes from Small Town Ohio: A Toni Morrison Bibliography." *Obsidian* 7 (1979): 142–48.

Gates, Henry Louis, Jr. *Figures in Black: Words, Signs, and the "Racial" Self.* New York: Oxford University Press, 1987.

————. *The Signifying Monkey: A Theory of Afro-American Literary Criticism.* New York: Oxford University Press, 1988.

————, ed. *Black Literature and Literary Theory.* New York: Methuen, 1984.

————, ed. *"Race," Writing, and Difference.* Chicago: University of Chicago Press, 1986.

Harris, A. Leslie. "Myth as Structure in Toni Morrison's *Song of Solomon.*" *MELUS* 7 (1980): 69–76.

Hedin, Raymond. "The Structuring of Emotion in Black American Fiction." *Novel* 16 (1982–83): 50–64.

Hogue, W. Lawrence. *Discourse and the Other: The Production of the Afro-American Text.* Durham, NC: Duke University Press, 1986.

Holloway, Karla F. C., and Stephane Demetrakopoulos. *New Dimensions of Spirituality: A Biracial and Bicultural Reading of the Novels of Toni Morrison.* New York: Greenwood Press, 1987.

House, Elizabeth B. "Artists and the Art of Living: Order and Disorder in Toni Morrison's Fiction." *Modern Fiction Studies* 34 (1988): 27–44.

————. "The 'Sweet Life' in Toni Morrison's Fiction." *American Literature* 56 (1984): 181–202.

Hovet, Grace Ann, and Barbara Lounsberry. "Flying as Symbol and Legend in Toni Morrison's *The Bluest Eye, Sula,* and *Song of Solomon.*" *CLA Journal* 27 (1983–84): 119–40.

———. "Principles of Perception in Toni Morrison's *Sula.*" *Black American Literature Forum* 18 (1979): 126–29.

Hull, Gloria T.; Scott, Patricia Bell; and Smith, Barbara, ed. *All the Women Are White, All the Blacks Are Men, but Some of Us Are Brave: Black Women's Studies.* Old Westbury, NY: Feminist Press, 1982.

Iannone, Carol. "Toni Morrison's Career." *Commentary* 84 (December 1987): 50–63.

Jones, Bessie W. *The World of Toni Morrison.* Dubuque, IA: Kendall/Hunt, 1985.

Kent, George E. *Blackness and the Adventure of Western Culture.* Chicago: Third World Press, 1972.

Klotman, Phyllis Rauch. "Dick and Jane and the Shirley Temple Sensibility in *The Bluest Eye.*" *Black American Literature Forum* 13 (1979): 123–25.

Lange, Bonnie Shipman. "Toni Morrison's Rainbow Code." *Critique* 24 (1983): 173–81.

Lee, A. Robert, ed. *Black Fiction: New Studies in the Afro-American Novel since 1945.* New York: Barnes & Noble, 1980.

Lee, Dorothy H. "To Ride the Air." *Black American Literature Forum* 16 (1982): 64–70.

Lepow, Lauren. "Paradise Lost and Found: Dualism and Edenic Myth in Toni Morrison's *Tar Baby.*" *Contemporary Literature* 28 (1987): 363–77.

Levine, Lawrence W. *Black Culture and Black Consciousness: Afro-American Folk Thought from Slavery to Freedom.* New York: Oxford University Press, 1977.

Lupton, Mary Jane. "Clothes and Closure in Three Novels by Black Women." *Black American Literature Forum* 20 (1986): 409–22.

McKay, Nellie Y., ed. *Critical Essays on Toni Morrison.* Boston: G. K. Hall, 1988.

Middleton, David L. *Toni Morrison: An Annotated Bibliography.* New York: Garland, 1987.

Mobley, Marilyn E. "Narrative Dilemma: Jadine as Cultural Orphan in Toni Morrison's *Tar Baby.*" *Southern Review* 23 (1987): 761–70.

Montgomery, Maxine Lavon. "A Pilgrimage to the Origins: The Apocalypse as Structure and Theme in Toni Morrison's *Sula.*" *Black American Literature Forum* 23 (1989): 127–38.

Reyes, Angelita Dianne. "Ancient Properties in the New World: The Paradox of the 'Other' in Toni Morrison's *Tar Baby*." *Black Scholar* 17 (March–April 1986): 19–25.

Rosenblatt, Roger. *Black Fiction*. Cambridge, MA: Harvard University Press, 1974.

Scruggs, Charles. "The Nature of Desire in Toni Morrison's *Song of Solomon*." *Arizona Quarterly* 38 (1982): 311–35.

Smith, Valerie. *Self-Discovery and Authority in Afro-American Narrative*. Cambridge, MA: Harvard University Press, 1987.

Stepto, Robert B. *From Behind the Veil: A Study of Afro-American Narrative*. Urbana: University of Illinois Press, 1979.

———. " 'Intimate Things in Place': A Conversation with Toni Morrison." In *Chant of Saints: A Gathering of Afro-American Literature, Art, and Scholarship,* edited by Michael S. Harper and Robert B. Stepto. Urbana: University of Illinois Press, 1979.

Story, Ralph. "An Excursion into the Black World: The 'Seven Days' in Toni Morrison's *Song of Solomon*." *Black American Literature Forum* 23 (1989): 149–58.

Thomas, H. Nigel. *From Folklore to Fiction: A Study of Folk Heroes and Rituals in the Black American Novel*. Westport, CT: Greenwood Press, 1988.

Weixlmann, Joe, and Houston A. Baker, Jr., ed. *Black Feminist Criticism and Critical Theory*. Greenwood, FL: Fenkevill, 1988.

Werner, Craig Hansen. *Paradoxical Resolutions: American Fiction since James Joyce*. Urbana: University of Illinois Press, 1982.

———. "Tell Old Pharaoh: The Afro-American Response to Faulkner." *Southern Review* 19 (1983): 711–35.

Willis, Susan. *Specifying: Black Women Writing the American Experience*. Madison: University of Wisconsin Press, 1987.

Acknowledgments

"Self, Society, and Myth in Toni Morrison's Fiction" by Cynthia A. Davis from *Contemporary Literature* 23, No. 3 (Summer 1982), © 1982 by the Board of the Regents of the University of Wisconsin System. Reprinted by permission of the University of Wisconsin Press.

"A Hateful Passion, a Lost Love" by Hortense J. Spillers from *Feminist Studies* 9, No. 2 (Summer 1983), © 1983 by *Feminist Studies,* Inc. Reprinted by permission.

"Beyond Realism: The Fictions of Toni Morrison" (originally titled "Beyond Realism: The Fictions of Gayl Jones and Toni Morrison") from *Fingering the Jagged Grain: Tradition and Form in Recent Black Fiction* by Keith E. Byerman, © 1985 by The University of Georgia Press. Reprinted by permission.

"Lady No Longer Sings the Blues: Rape, Madness, and Silence in *The Bluest Eye*" by Madonne M. Miner from *Conjuring: Black Women, Fiction, and Literary Tradition,* edited by Marjorie Pryse and Hortense J. Spillers, © 1985 by Indiana University Press. Reprinted by permission.

"The Crime of Innocence in Toni Morrison's *Tar Baby*" by Terry Otten from *Studies in American Fiction* 14, No. 2 (Autumn 1986), © 1986 by Northeastern University. Reprinted by permission.

"Like an Eagle in the Air: Toni Morrison" by Melvin Dixon from *Ride Out the Wilderness: Geography and Identity in Afro-American Literature* by Melvin Dixon, © 1987 by the Board of Trustees of the University of Illinois. Reprinted by permission of the University of Illinois Press.

"Haunted by Their Nightmares" by Margaret Atwood from *New York Times Book Review,* September 13, 1987, © 1987 by The New York Times Company. Reprinted by permission.

" 'The Self and the Other': Reading Toni Morrison's *Sula* and the Black Female Text" by Deborah E. McDowell from *Critical Essays on Toni Morrison,* edited by Nellie Y. McKay, © 1988 by Twayne Publishers, a division of G. K. Hall & Co. Reprinted by permission.

"Toni Morrison's *Beloved*" (originally titled "American Novels, 1987") by Roger Sale from *Massachusetts Review* 29, No. 1 (Spring 1988), © 1988 by *The Massachusetts Review,* Inc. Reprinted by permission.

"The Novelist as Conservator: Stories and Comprehension in Toni Morrison's *Song of Solomon*" by Theodore O. Mason, Jr., from *Contemporary Literature* 29, No. 4 (Winter 1988), © 1988 by the Board of Regents of the University of Wisconsin System. Reprinted by permission of the University of Wisconsin Press.

"A Different Remembering: Memory, History and Meaning in Toni Morrison's *Beloved*" by Marilyn Sanders Mobley, © 1988 by Marilyn Sanders Mobley. Printed by permission.

"Unspeakable Things Unspoken: The Afro-American Presence in American Literature" by Toni Morrison from *Tanner Lectures on Human Values,* Vol. 11 (1990), © 1989 by Toni Morrison. Reprinted by permission of the University of Utah Press. First published in *Michigan Quarterly Review* 28, No. 1 (Winter 1989).

Index

African-American rebellion, 36
African Americans: Du Bois on,
    54.n.15; during slavery, 54n.19
Afro-American fiction, 115
Afro-American literary criticism,
    159–61; and sexism, 150
Afro-American literature, 151–52,
    186, 201–30; and its relationship
    to American literature, 204–18;
    and Western literature, 209
Afro-American presence: 149–53; in
    American literature, 201, 217–30
Ahab (*Moby-Dick*), 1, 213–14
Ajax (*Sula*), 16, 128, 156; and Sula
    (*Sula*), 128
*All the Women Are White, All the Blacks
    Are Men, but Some of Us Are Brave*
    (ed. Hull, Scott, and Smith),
    52n.5
American Adam, The (Lewis), 102
American Jeremiad, The (Bercovitch),
    102
Amy (*Beloved*), 145
Anxiety of Influence, The (Bloom): and
    nonapplicability to black
    literature, 52n.3
As I Lay Dying (Faulkner), 4
Atwater, Lee, 2. *See* Horton, Willie
Auld, Mr. (*Narrative of the Life of
    Frederick Douglass, an American
    Slave*), 174

Autobiography of Miss Jane Pittman, The
    (Gaines), 61
Bad Faith (*Being and Nothingness*), 8–9,
    12–15
Bains, Guitar (*Song of Solomon*), 4, 13,
    17, 20, 71, 101, 103–4, 106,
    178, 181–82
Bakhtin, Mikhail, 189, 197
Baldwin, James, 29
Bambara, Toni Cade, 31
"Bear, The" (Faulkner), 74
Beauty and the Beast (film), 106
Beauvoir, Simone de, 9, 13, 22; and
    female mystery, 31; on power,
    9–10
"Behind the Making of *The Black
    Book*" (Morrison), 198n.3
Being and Nothingness (Sartre), 8–9, 12
*Being and Race: Black Writing since
    1970* (Johnson), 165
Beloved, 143–47, 165–70, 189–97;
    and the African-American oral
    tradition, 195; as antiminimalist
    prose, 146; and *The Black Book*,
    190; criticism of, 169; and the
    depiction of slavery, 145; and its
    epigraph, 147; and the "good
    white people," 145; as
    "Holocaust novel," 166; and *Mrs.
    Dalloway* (Woolf), 165; and the

241

Beloved (*continued*)
 Reconstruction, 143; and slave
 narratives, 191; and supernatural
 folklore, 144, 146
Bercovitch, Sacvan, 102
Bernal, Martin, 206–7; on ancient
 Greece, 207
Bible, the, 147
*Black Athena: The Afroasiatic Roots of
 Classical Civilization, Volume I:
 The Fabrication of Ancient Greece
 1785–1985* (Bernal), 206
Black Book, The, 189–90, 196–97;
 and Morrison, 189–90,
 198nn.2–3
black women: as artists, 12–13
Black World (magazine), 198
blacks: and the Civil War, 34; and
 their invisibility, 8
Blake, Susan L.: on Ralph Ellison, 17
Bloom, Harold, 29; and the "anxiety
 of influence," 29; and patriarchal
 tradition, 52n.3
Bluest Eye, The, 3, 7–9, 11, 15–16,
 35, 55–62, 76, 85–98, 115,
 117–22, 125–26, 218, 221
"Blueprint for Black Criticism"
 (Gayle), 150
Bojangles, 11
Breedlove, Cholly (*The Bluest Eye*),
 9–10, 13, 87–88, 220; and her
 nickname "Polly" (*The Bluest
 Eye*), 8; and Tereus, 91
Breedlove, Claudia (*The Bluest Eye*),
 13, 16, 56–57, 61–62, 117–19;
 and Pecola, 9
Breedlove, Frieda (*The Bluest Eye*), 92
Breedlove, Mrs. (*The Bluest Eye*), 8,
 10, 95
Breedlove, Pauline (*The Bluest Eye*),
 57, 119, 121, 126
Breedlove, Pecola (*The Bluest Eye*),
 13–14, 56–61, 85, 87–90, 93,
 103, 116–17, 119, 121; her
 rape, 58, 88; as victim, 13–14
Breedloves, the (*The Bluest Eye*),
 60–61, 95, 119

Brown, Innis (*Jubilee*), 34
Bundren, Darl (*As I Lay Dying*), 4
"Burnt Norton" (Eliot), 167
Bush, George, 2. *See* Horton, Willie

Chaucer Society, the, 204
Chesler, Phyllis: and the Persephone
 myth, 91–92
Christian, Barbara: on *Sula,* 163n.24
Church, Soaphead (*The Bluest Eye*), 97,
 121
Cincinnati, Ohio, 143
Circe (*Song of Solomon*), 73
Civil War, the, 32–33, 36; and
 blacks, 34
Claudia (*The Bluest Eye*), 13, 16,
 56–57, 61–62, 117–19
Cocteau, Jean, 106
Colonial literature, 212
Color Purple, The (A. Walker), 146,
 169; criticism of, 169; and its
 treatment of black men, 168–69
Conrad, Joseph, 3, 104, 208
Crisis magazine, 149–50
Crouch, Stanley, 168; on *Beloved* as
 "soap opera," 166

Daedalus, 18; and Shalimar (*Song of
 Solomon*), 18
Dalloway, Clarissa (*Mrs. Dalloway*), 4
Danville, Pennsylvania, 117
Darlene (*The Bluest Eye*), 120
Davis, Cynthia A.: and Morrison's
 existential concerns, 102
Dayton, Ohio, 129
Dead, Corinthians (*Song of Solomon*),
 21, 71, 177
Dead, Hagar (*Song of Solomon*), 12,
 20–21, 71–72
Dead, Macon (*Song of Solomon*), 8,
 18–20, 23, 70–71, 177
Dead, Magdalene (*Song of Solomon*), 71
Dead, Milkman (*Song of Solomon*), 4,
 8–9, 12, 15–21, 70–72, 106–7,
 116–17, 129–41, 174, 177–85;
 and Pilate (*Song of Solomon*), 22;
 and his sexism, 19

Dead, Pilate (*Song of Solomon*), 181,
183–84
Dead, Ruth Foster (*Song of Solomon*),
70–71, 102, 105, 176–77, 181
Deads, the (*Song of Solomon*), 70
Deal, Reverend (*Sula*), 65–66
Demeter, 90-92
Dickinson, Emily, 204
Dinesen, Isak, 208
Discourse in the Novel (Bakhtin), 189
Douglass, Frederick: 173–74, 189,
191, 197; his place in Afro-
American literary history, 173
Du Bois, W. E. B., 40, 149; and the
African-American predicament,
54n.15
Durkheim, Emile, 36

Eatonville, Florida, 39
Egypt, 206
"Egyptomania," 207
Elihue (*Tar Baby*), 116
Eliot, T. S., 167
Ellison, Ralph, 2, 17, 116, 126, 128,
138; and Morrison, 137; on
Richard Wright, 137
Eyre, Jane (*Jane Eyre*): as a black, 107

Faulkner, William, 2–5, 103, 166;
and Morrison's characters, 4; and
Morrison's fiction, 190–91; as
subject of Morrison's master
thesis, 190
Felman, Shoshana: on Afro-American
literature, 151
feminist criticism: on Afro-American
women writers, 152
Fontaine, Joan, 108
Fontenot, Chester J.: and myth in
black American fiction, 23
Foster, Dr. (*Song of Solomon*), 174, 182
Frazer, Sir James George, 91–92; and
the Persephone myth, 91
Frieda (*The Bluest Eye*), 9, 96, 117,
119
Fugitive Slave Law, the, 193

Gaines, Ernest, 61
Garner, Margaret: *Beloved* as based
upon, 193
Garner, Mrs. Paul D (*Beloved*), 144
Garner, Paul D (*Beloved*), 144–45,
169–70, 193
Gates, Henry Louis, Jr., 149, 191; on
Afro-American narratives, 11; on
slave narratives, 191
Gayle, Addison: on black literature,
150
Geraldine (*The Bluest Eye*), 9, 94; and
Pecola (*The Bluest Eye*), 94
Gilligan, Carole, 154
"Gold Bug, The" (Poe), 212
Golden Bough, The (Frazer), 91
Graham, Mary-Michael, 177
Great Aunt Jimmy (*The Bluest Eye*),
120
Greece, 206
Greek tragedy, 202
Grimes (*Jubilee*), 37
Grove, Lena (*Light in August*), 4
Gubar, Susan: on mother-daughter
"anti-myth," 24n.14

Hagar (Peace), 71–72
Hagar (*Song of Solomon*), 12, 20–21
Haley, Alex, 53n.7
Harlem Renaissance, the, 31
Helms, Jesse, 2
Hemenway, Robert, 53n.12
Hetta, Sis, 35
Hoffman, Baruch: on character in
Sula, 154
Homer, 90–92
Horton, Willie, 2
Howells, William Dean, 203
Hughes, Langston, 149–50; on
"Nordicized Negro
Intelligentsia," 149
Hurston, Zora Neale, 2, 28, 40–43,
50, 121; and Haiti, 40

Icarus: and black myth and folklore,
18; and *Song of Solomon*, 18
Incidents in the Life of a Slave Girl
(Jacobs), 189, 191

"Interview with Toni Morrison, An,"
171
Invisible Man (Ellison), 7, 116, 135;
and *Song of Solomon,* 139
Invisible Man (*Song of Solomon*), 73
Irving, John: on *Tar Baby,* 103
Ishmael (*Moby-Dick*), 214
Isle des Chevaliers, 76, 78–79 ; as
perverse Eden, 76

Jacobs, Harriet, 189, 191
Jadine (*Tar Baby*), 103, 105–11
James, Henry, 50
Jameson, Fredric: and *Beloved,* 192
Johnson, Charles, 165
Jones, Gayl: on Morrison's fiction, 55
Joyce, James, 3
Jubilee (M. Walker), 32–41; Afro-
American character in, 38; and
Roots (Haley), 53n.7; and *Sula,*
41
Judd, Whinnie Ruth (*Song of Solomon*),
72
Jude (*Sula*), 18, 44, 154–56, 160
Junior (*The Bluest Eye*), 87, 89

Kermode, Frank: on "secrecy of
narrative," 194
Killicks, Logan (*Their Eyes Were
Watching God*), 38–39
Ku Klux Klan, 115
Kundera, Milan, 205. *See also*
Morrison, Toni

Lacan, Jacques, 2
Lawrence, D. H., 1–2, 212
Leggett ("The Secret Sharer"), 104,
107
Lena, 182
Lévi-Strauss, Claude, 97–98
Lewis, R. W. B., 102
Light in August (Faulkner), 4
Little, Chicken (*Sula*), 14, 48,
123–24
Look, the (*Being and Nothingness*),
9–10, 12
Lorain, Ohio, 11

McCaslin, Ike ("The Bear"), 74
McTeer, Claudia (*The Bluest Eye*),
61–62, 117
McTeers, the (*The Bluest Eye*), 59–61
Mallioux, Steven, 193
Map of Misreading, A (Bloom), 52n.3
Mapple, Father (*Moby-Dick*), 215
Marshall, Paule, 31
Marxism, 2–3; and Morrison, 171
Medallion, Ohio, 116, 122–24
Metamorphoses (Ovid), 85–86
Miller, Karl, 207
"Mine Eyes Have Seen the Glory of
the Coming of the Lord" (M.
Walker), 37
Moby-Dick (Melville), 1, 213–17; and
race, 213–16
Morrison, Toni: as an African-
American, 3; and Afro-American
communal structures, 202; on
being black in America, 197; on
Beloved, 228–29; and black
neighborhoods, 11–16; and her
black women, 12; on canon
building, 206; and Chesler, 92;
and the development of Afro-
American culture, 116; as editor,
198n.3; on the female rites of
passage, 92; as feminine ideal,
12; as feminist, 171–72; on the
future of the novel, 172; and
gender in myth, 19; and
geography, 138; and humiliation
of the male, 13; and Gayl Jones,
55; on Kundera's view of the
novel, 205; manipulation of
characters, 38; as Marxist, 171;
on multiplicity of perspective,
137; on the myth of the Flying
Africans, 138; and her narrative
voice, 4, 175; on Ohio as her
roots, 115; and power, 7–10; and
prose, 45; on race and writing,
203; and the relationship between
rape and gender, 90; and *Roots*
(Haley), 53n.7; and Sartre, 10;
and self-ignorance, 112; and sense

of place in her novels, 85; on
slavery, 197; on *Song of Solomon,*
224–25, 229; on *Sula,* 41, 51,
221–24, 229; on *Tar Baby,*
226–29; on the superiority of
Western culture, 202; and
symbolic geography, 115; on
third world literature, 205–6;
and the use of class differences,
133; and her use of mythic
structure, 23; and her use of
names, 75; and women in
patriarchal society, 13; and
Western myth, 18

Narcissus, 91; and Pecola (*The Bluest
Eye*), 91
*Narrative of the Life of Frederick
Douglass, as American Slave*
(Douglass), 173–74, 187, 191;
and Morrison, 173–74
"Negro Art" (Du Bois), 149
"Negro Artist and the Racial
Mountain, The" (Hughes),
149–50
"Negro in Art, How Shall He Be
Portrayed?, The" (Du Bois), 149
New Republic, The: its review of
Beloved, 165
New York *Herald,* the: attack on the
Sims case, 213
New York Review of Books, The, 150
New York Times Book Review, The,
150–51
New Yorker, The, 205
Nimrod, 127

"Ogre/Bitch" complex, 31
Old Testament, 46
Olney, James: on slave narratives, 192
Ondine (*Tar Baby*), 76–80, 82, 103,
105
Orientalism (Said), 206
Other, the (*Being and Nothingness*), 8,
11–13, 15
Ovid, 85–86

Paid, Stamp (*Beloved*), 169
Paul, the Apostle, 147

Peace, Eva (*Sula*), 3–4, 15, 45, 46,
71, 157
Peace, Hanna (*Sula*), 38, 45–47, 52,
122–30
Peace, Plum (Ralph) (*Sula*) 46, 125;
and heroin addiction, 46
Peace, Reba (Rebekkah) (*Song of
Solomon*), 71
Peace, Sula Mae (*Sula*), 12, 19,
22–23, 29, 38, 44, 47–48, 52,
62–63, 101, 104, 122–30,
223–24; and Ajax (*Sula*), 128;
and her birthmark, 153; and her
community's entrapment of, 156;
and the grieving of loss, 163n.2;
and self-image, 154; and Son
Street (*Tar Baby*), 104
Pearl, BoyBoy (*Sula*), 45, 65, 130
Peel, Maureen (*The Bluest Eye*), 61
Pequod, the (*Moby-Dick*), 214; as
multiracial community, 214
Persephone (*Metamorphoses*), 85, 92;
and *The Bluest Eye,* 95
Philomela (*Metamorphoses*), 86–88, 92
Picasso, Pablo, 105
Pittman, Jane (*The Autobiography of
Miss Jane Pittman*), 61
Pluto (*The Golden Bough*), 91
Poe, Edgar Allan, 212
Porter (*Song of Solomon*), 177
Portrait of a Lady (James), 50
Prince, Dewey (*The Bluest Eye*), 60
Procne (*Metamorphoses*), 85–86
Puritan Origins of the American Self, The
(Bercovitch), 102

"*Race,*" *Writing and Difference* (ed.
Gates), 202, 230n.1
Rafferty, Terrence, 205
Rappaccini's Daughters (Shurr), 102
Raw and the Cooked, The (Lévi-Strauss),
97
Reba (*Song of Solomon*), 183
Rebecca (film), 108
"Rediscovering Black History"
(Morrison), 196
Reed, Ishmael, 2

Rich, Adrienne, 192; and "matrophobia," 22

Rogin, Michael Paul, 213, 230n.9; on slavery, 216

Roots (Haley): and *Jubilee* (M. Walker), 53n.7

Rose Tattoo, The (Williams), 124

Rosenblatt, Roger: on myth in Afro-American fiction, 17

Royal, Battle (*Song of Solomon*), 17

Said, Edward, 206

Sammy (*The Bluest Eye*), 95

Sartre, Jean-Paul, 8, 12, 14

Second Sex, The (Beauvoir), 31

"Secret Share, The" (Conrad), 104

Sethe (*Beloved*), 143–47, 165–70, 193–97

Seward, William, 213

"Sexism, Racism, and Black Women Writers" (Watkins), 150–51

Shadrock (*Sula*), 3, 48, 63, 122, 124, 153–54, 222–24

Shalimar (*Song of Solomon*), 4, 17

Shurr, William, 102

Sing (*Song of Solomon*), 23

slave narratives: Morrison's revising of, 191

slavery, 33, 145, 166, 197, 216; as paradigm, 145; in *Beloved,* 167–69; in *Moby-Dick,* 215–17

Smith, Valerie: on the relationship between Douglass and Jacobs, 192

Song of Solomon, 4, 8, 10, 12, 15, 19–20, 70–76, 103, 107, 126, 130–41, 172–86, 224–26; and Afro-American letters, 136–37; and Morrison's ancestral landscape, 131; and social classes, 133

Sound and the Fury, The (Faulkner), 3

Spiller, Robert, 102

Starks, Janie (*Their Eyes Were Watching God*), 28, 38–43, 50–52

Starks, the (*Their Eyes Were Watching God*), 28, 38–43, 50–52; and Sula (*Sula*), 50–51

Stepto, Robert: and his conversation with Morrison, 51, 98n.1

Stowe, Harriet Beecher, 145

Street, Margaret (*Tar Baby*), 103–5, 107

Street, Michael (*Tar Baby*), 104, 107–8; compared to Jadine (*Tar Baby*), 104

Street, Son (*Tar Baby*), 76–83, 104, 106–11

Street, Valerian (*Tar Baby*), 76–83, 103–11

Studies in Classic American Literature (Lawrence), 1

Suggs, Beloved (*Beloved*), 144, 146, 194–97

Suggs, Buglar (*Beloved*), 193

Suggs, Denver (*Beloved*), 143–44, 169, 193

Suggs, Howard (*Beloved*), 193

Suggs, Old Baby (*Beloved*), 143–45, 169–70, 193

Sula, 4, 8–10, 12, 15, 19, 22–23, 27, 32, 41, 44–46, 51, 62–70, 76, 103, 115, 118, 122–30, 149–63; and the Black Power Movement, 152–53; and countermythology, 52; and its lack of a "central" character, 153; and its lack of tension, 49; and the liberation of women, 52; and the subversion of women, 52; and Woolf, 45

Sula (*Sula*), 8–16, 19, 22–23, 44–45, 51, 62–70, 101, 104, 118, 122–30, 153–61, 163n.2, 222–23; and Ajax (*Sula*), 128; and conception of self, 158; and Eva Wright (*Sula*), 47; and Nel Wright (*Sula*), 44, 154–61

Sydney (*Tar Baby*), 76–80, 82, 103–5, 107, 109, 111

Tar Baby, 25n.21, 76–84, 101–12, 115

Temple, Shirley, 11, 56, 61

Tereus (*Metamorphoses*), 86, 88–89;
    and Cholly Breedlove (*The Bluest
    Eye*), 91
"That I Had the Wings" (Ellison): and
    Sula, 128
Their Eyes Were Watching God
    (Hurston), 28, 32, 38–43,
    50–52
Thérèse (*Tar Baby*), 78–80, 83, 108,
    111
*They Came Before Columbus: The African
    Presence in Ancient America* (van
    Sertima), 30n.2, 206
Tillich, Paul, 3
Toqueville, Alexis de, 211
Twain, Mark, 203
Tyler, Mrs. (*Tar Baby*), 107

Uncle Tom's Cabin (Stowe) 145, 190
University of Iowa Creative Writers'
    Workshop, The, 3

Walker, Alice, 2, 146, 168–69
Walker, Margaret, 3–4, 28, 32–41,
    50, 53
Ware, Jim (*Jubilee*), 36
Ware, Minna (*Jubilee*), 3, 36
Ware, Vyry (*Jubilee*), 28, 31, 33–34,
    36–37, 50

Watkins, Mel: on sexism in Afro-
    American literature, 150–51
Watson, Phoeby (*Jubilee*), 40
Webster, Daniel, 213
"What White Publishers Won't Print"
    (Hurston), 53n.14
Williams, Tennessee, 124
Wings of the Dove, The (James), 50;
    and *Sula*, 50
Woolf, Virginia, 2–5, 50, 190; as
    subject for Morrison's master's
    thesis, 190
World War I, 48, 63, 211
World War II, 219
Wright, Helene (*Sula*), 8, 10–12,
    102, 105, 153
Wright, Nel (*Sula*), 3–4, 8, 12, 16,
    18, 24, 44–45, 47–49, 51–52,
    126, 153–61, 22; and her
    sexuality, 155; and *Sula*, 44–45,
    154–61

Yacobowski, Mr. (*The Bluest Eye*), 87,
    93–96

Zeus, 91
*Zora Neale Hurston: A Literary
    Biography* (Hemenway), 53n.12